COPS:
CHEATING DEATH

BY THE SAME AUTHOR

NONFICTION

The Terror Fighters, Purnell (1969)

Underwater Africa, Purnell (1971)

Report on Portugal's War in Guiné-Bissau, California Institute of Technology, Pasadena, California (1973)

Underwater Seychelles, Victoria, Seychelles (1973)

Portugal's Guerrilla War, Malherbe (1973)

Under the Indian Ocean, Harraps, London (1973)

Africa at War, Devin Adair, Connecticut, USA (1974)

The Zambezi Salient, Devin Adair (1974)

Coloured: A Profile of Two Million South Africans, Human & Rousseau (1974)

Africa Today, Macmillan (1977)

The Black Leaders of Southern Africa, Siesta (1976)

Vorster's Africa, Keartlands (1977)

South African Handbook for Divers, Ashanti Publishing (1987)

Challenge: South Africa in the African Revolutionary Context, (ed) Ashanti (1988)

South Africa's Second Underwater Handbook, Ashanti (1988)

Underwater Mauritius, Ashanti (1989)

Where to Dive: In Southern Africa and Off the Islands, Ashanti (1991)

War in Angola, Concorde Publishing, Hong Kong (1992)

The Chopper Boys: Helicopter Warfare in Africa, Stackpole Books, US: Greenhill Books, UK (1994)

The Ultimate Handbook on Diving, William Waterman Publications, Rivonia (1995)

The Iraqi War Debrief: Why Saddam Hussein Was Toppled: Casemate, Philadelphia and Verulam Publishing, UK (2003)

Iran's Nuclear Option: Tehran's Quest for the Atom Bomb, Casemate, Philadelphia (2005)

War Dog: Fighting Other People's Wars, Casemate, Philadelphia (2006)

Allah's Bomb: The Islamic Quest for Nuclear Weapons (2007)

Diving with Sharks (to be published in Britain and the United States in fall 2007)

NOVELS

Soldier of Fortune: W.H. Allen, London (1980)

COPS: CHEATING DEATH

HOW ONE MAN (SO FAR) SAVED THE LIVES OF THREE THOUSAND AMERICANS

Al J. Venter

The Lyons Press
An imprint of The Globe Pequot Press
Guilford, CT 06437

The Lyons Press is an imprint of The Globe Pequot Press.

10 9 8 7 6 5 4 3 2 1

Printed in the United States of America

ISBN: 978-1-59921-107-7

Library of Congress Cataloging-in-Publication Data is available on file.

For Marilyn

So much given, so little in return.
I am deeply grateful to you, my darling.

Contents

Prologue By Jim Morris

COPS: Cheating Death is destined to become a True Crime classic. It is, of course, a story of technological innovation and invention. But from a literary standpoint, the average True Crime builds to one deadly encounter with a criminal and provides one cathartic climax—whereas this book does that every four or five pages.

Reading this book has given me a new appreciation of the daily lives of policemen and women. I've edited many stories by and about cops, but none of them had quite the effect that this one did. I remember a friend telling me what to do if I was stopped in Houston, where the cops are known to be tough.

"If you get stopped in Houston, you sit behind the wheel with your hands in plain sight," he said, "and you'll be all right."

My reaction was one of resentment. When I'm nervous, which I most certainly am while getting a speeding ticket, I like to be free to move around. My custom had been to get out of the car and talk to the officer from the same level. It never occurred to me that a cop could be afraid of big ol' friendly, easygoing me.

But, if this volume had a subtitle it could well be, "Sir, may I see your license and . . . *Blam! Blam! Blam!*" There is no reason for a policeman to assume that I am merely a solid citizen with a lead foot—and every reason to assume that I might be a crazed psychopath. Every cop knows a story of a colleague who was blown away in the course of a routine traffic stop, or a domestic call, or a simple burglary. If I'm ever stopped again, and, sad to say, I probably will be, I'll keep my hands in plain sight without resentment—and with gratitude for what these people face every day.

The odds are that a policeman will go through his entire career without being attacked by a perp with a weapon. But the stupidest thing he could do would be to assume that would always be the case. The policeman has to be on guard at all times—and it would be well for any citizen to appreciate that, and to know the cop does it on the behalf of citizens.

Another thing I had to think of when reading this volume is that I have been shot several times: three or four, depending on how you figure it, because one bullet hit me twice, and I'm not telling where. That double hit was in Vietnam and had nothing to do with crime. I wasn't wearing a vest at the time, since it was about 120 degrees and humid; but, by chance, none of those rounds would have been stopped by a vest anyway. They all hit around the periphery of my body.

Those experiences lead me to hope that Richard C. Davis will get out of the office and back in the lab. Kevlar floor plates for Humvees would be a nice thing to have. And since today's soldier faces more danger from roadside bombs than bullets, also in 130-degree heat, it would be a good thing to see Kevlar boots, chaps, and jockstraps—all, hopefully, air-conditioned. Now there's a technological challenge for you.

In the meantime, I'd like to extend my heartfelt appreciation to Richard Davis for the lives he's saved, and my equally heartfelt appreciation to the police and military who risk their lives for me and my family.

I'd also like to thank Al Venter for this splendid book.

Jim Morris served three tours in US Special Forces in Vietnam, retiring of wounds in the grade of major. He is the author of three volumes of nonfiction and four novels and also wrote the story from which the film *Operation Dumbo Drop* was made.

Introduction

Body armor is sometimes all that lies between you and a suspect's attack. It has saved officers' lives countless times. Not wearing it is [no longer] an option. As a law enforcement officer you're a walking target and like it or not, a ballistic vest is the best protection you have against the bad guys' bullets.

—from "Bullet Barriers" by Melanie Hamilton
***policemag.com*, July 2004**

Massad Ayoob is one of America's most prominent writers on lethal force, self-defense, firearms training, and police procedures in general. He has a prescient comment on body armor.

He points out that, "Richard Davis' concept of concealable, soft body armor recently passed the three thousand mark in good guys and gals saved from death or great bodily harm." Slightly more than half of that tally, he maintains, were rescued from gunfire when the aramid fiber, which he experimented on so successfully more than three decades ago, caught the bullets.

"The 'almost half' minority, he says, were largely non-ballistic events, including some officers who fell, were hurled from great heights, or were hit by cars or stabbed. But speaking as one of their number, I can tell you that we are no less grateful customers because of the 'less glamorous' manner of death that his body armor averted.

"A good thousand or so of those total saves involved Richard's own brand of vest—and remember, the numbers we have are only the ones we know about and that are documented and reported. Even so, Richard C. Davis was the man who came up with the concept and every one of those three thousand–plus 'saves' owes their life to this good man."

As is customary with this knowledgeable and well-published authority, he comes up with a lot more pointers, including the fact that many of the people whose lives were saved by Davis' invention went on to make notable successes of their professional careers. Others got married and had children, and in this regard there are more than three hundred babies born to Richard Davis' Saves over the past thirty-something years, *after* these individuals survived some of the near-death experiences related in this tome.

But it is the individuals and what happened to them that catches the eye. Take what occurred in Florida in October 1977. That event involved a youthful Florida Highway Patrol trooper by the name of Robert Wargin. He played a major role in apprehending a man who sits today in a federal penitentiary. That criminal is Eugene Garton 'Joe' Adams, convicted of abducting and sexually assaulting a twelve-year-old Miami girl. Shortly thereafter, he attempted to murder the policeman who found him with his victim.

Already on parole for child molesting, he was suspected of having raped, tortured, and killed two other young girls in the weeks before. Once he was in custody the killings stopped.

Having set up my base with my son Luke in Jacksonville, Florida, I flew south to meet Bob Wargin, who had moved on to become a district chief in charge of security at the Fort Lauderdale/Hollywood International Airport. The third largest unit in his agency, with a staff of almost a hundred and fifty, his annual budget topped sixty million dollars.

Wargin's confrontation with Adams is like something from a detective novel. The victim remains under medical supervision, and Bob has stayed in touch with the family. He calls when in the vicinity, and offers help and advice when needed. Tragically, the victim, now middle-aged, has never been able to lead a normal life, all as a result of one man's horrific obsession with little girls.

Though the jury found Adams "guilty of sexual battery with the use of threats, kidnapping, attempted murder, and possession of a firearm," and he faced a maximum penalty of life in prison plus sixty years, the man has several times applied for parole. As Chief Wargin says, "Times change and people tend to forget. So it's not impossible that this monster might be released back into society, which is one of the reasons why I personally attend each and every one of Adams' parole applications."

Bob Wargin's save is listed as #99 in the catalog of saves that Davis established at about the same time he founded his own body armor company, Second Chance Body Armor, and the story, though concise, is hot stuff. As he recounted to Richard Davis, he found himself on lonely, two-lane highway US-27 on the night of October 5, 1977. "That was the same day the little girl disappeared, something we were all aware of because it was the third abduction of a minor in a row, the other two having been murdered. The wires were buzzing . . .

"As I rounded a curve, I noticed a car on the wrong side of the roadway with its lights off. From what I could see at first glance, it was trying to back down a gravel surface road, which was when I pulled up to find out what the driver was doing.

"I spoke to him from my cruiser, and, in answer to questions, Adams said he was turning around. Which was fine, until he proceeded back onto the highway with his lights still out. Bad mistake! I followed him, turned on my overheads, and indicated that he should pull over.

"Pulling in behind him, I used my spotlight to illuminate the inside of his car. Getting out—and while still at the front of my vehicle—I saw that he had a little girl beside him on the front seat with her head in his lap. She was the missing twelve-year-old. Also, she was naked and her arms had been secured behind her back.

"Obviously, I was stunned. One isn't faced with this kind of scenario very often. But even before I could reach for my service revolver I was blinded by the muzzle flash from Adams' window. A .357 magnum hit me in the abdomen, which was quite a shock because it wasn't expected . . . sort of knocked the wind out of me and caused me to double up on my knees in the road.

"Fortunately only one shot was fired. Because I'd gone down, Adams probably thought he'd killed me. I scrambled across the highway on all fours to get out of his line of fire.

"My body armor absorbed most of the impact and I recall that it hurt. The 158-grain steel-jacketed hollow-point bullet left a weal the size of a saucer that didn't go away for months.

"With that, Adams took off. Apart from kidnapping the little girl, he'd tried to kill me and I wasn't going to let him get away. Forget the pain; my attention was focused on him. It took seconds to get back to my cruiser and give chase. At the same time I radioed in. Within minutes I had half of Florida on general alert."

With Wargin in pursuit, the two cars sometimes exceeded 120 miles an hour. Having gained a head start, the rapist lost it when he slowed down long enough to open the passenger door and, with his vehicle still in motion, he hurled his victim into the middle of the road.

"Coming upon this scene, I'm suddenly confronted by this little bundle lying there in the road. I knew precisely what he'd done; he was trying to delay me and in that he was partially successful. I knew too that I couldn't just leave her there. Also, I didn't know if she'd been hurt when he'd ditched her.

"So I pulled up, grabbed a blanket from the back, and rushed toward her. Before I picked her up, I asked her whether she was all right, not really expecting her to answer. It was then that I saw that she'd had all her teeth knocked out—he'd apparently done this with a hammer, and I don't think I need to explain why.

"Through all her pain and shame, this tiny naked creature that'd clearly been terribly abused had only two words for me: 'Get him!' she urged me through her clenched mouth.

"Which is exactly what we did at a roadblock not very long afterward."

Like many other cops whose life had been saved by concealable body armor, Bob Wargin has led a varied but eventful career. Of Polish and Irish stock, his mother was a McNally and he grew up in Newton, Massachusetts, where his father was a cop before he moved over to the Massachusetts State Police.

Having spent some time in college and not liking it, he was good enough at sports to be offered a scholarship by Colorado State. He stayed a year, and at the ripe old age of nineteen joined the US Marine Corps.

"Never did get to go to Vietnam. I went from Parris Island, South Carolina, to Camp Geiger in Jacksonville for advance infantry training. Then they sent me back to my MOS School, which is Military Occupational Specialty, and I guess they trusted me enough to be a service record clerk.

"I had to go back to Parris Island, because that was where the school was. Then I got my permanent duty station, which was the Marine Corps Air Station back in North Carolina, and that's where I spent my two years.

"With six months left, I married my high school sweetheart."

The run-in with Adams wasn't the only time Bob Wargin was faced with a critical situation. Having left the Florida Highway Patrol in May 1980, he was with another law enforcement agency when he had to shoot and kill a man shortly afterward.

"Basically, it was a domestic situation, a response to a call in the unincorporated west area of Broward County, which was not far from my earlier violent run with the child abductor three years before. First report was that a guy had battered his wife and his mother-in-law.

"I went to the trailer park and the aggrieved wife met me out front. I got her side of the story and then tried to find the husband. She'd told me he was out back in the shed, so that's where I headed. But none of us were aware that he'd crawled underneath a car parked alongside their trailer.

"I was actually walking between the two when he came out from underneath and tried to stab me with a bayonet . . . actually knocked me down. I managed to get up and kind of backed up, all the while trying to avoid him. But he just kept coming. He was a seriously troubled guy and it was obvious he wasn't going to let up. He'd beaten his family up bad, we learned later. But right then I was trying to contain a situation.

"I told him to drop the bayonet. He wouldn't listen. Eventually he cornered me next to one of the buildings and I had to shoot him."

An interesting aside to Chief Robert Wargin's save is that the original vest that spared his life was a $99 present from his wife. In those days there were almost no law enforcement agencies that provided any kind of protection for their staff. For the majority, if you wanted a "bulletproof" vest, you went out and found somebody who would sell you one. Or cops would write to Richard Davis in Romulus, Michigan. He was already acquiring a reputation with this newfangled, concealable, soft body armor thing.

"I promised my wife I'd always wear it. And I did. When the second incident took place, I had on the new vest that I got from Richard. That was after I'd sent in the old one that I'd worn in the Adams shooting. It was company policy in those days; you get shot, you send in your old vest, and you get a new one free.

"Nice touch."

The body armor vests invented by Richard Davis could not have saved so many lives without that magic space-age material known as Kevlar. This product was originally developed in the 1960s by an unusually gifted scientist, Stephanie Kwolek, of the giant DuPont conglomerate. Originally it was to be used to make stronger and more durable motor vehicle tires. When Middle East passions put that project on hold, Richard got hold of a roll of the stuff in 1973 and used it to make the first "bullet resistant" vests. (It should be noted that the term *aramid* is a generic for this life-saving space-age material and is derived from the technical term *aramidic polyamides.*)

Initially, the term used both by the media and by Congress was *bulletproof.* But this is a misnomer because there never was and never will be anything that is totally impervious to the kinetic energy of every possible kind of projectile; up the velocity and size, and you're eventually able to penetrate just about anything.

Then one must ask the obvious: what happens when a vest stops a bullet? Richard Davis explains that when one is caught in the mesh of soft, pliable, specially woven Kevlar or Twaron fibers—anything from twenty to thirty layers of five-times-stronger-than-steel material—they absorb and dissipate that incredibly violent impact. The vest not only halts the progress of a bullet in full flight, but it can also cause it to deform or mushroom. All of this takes place barely a fraction of an inch from the body surface of its intended victim. Talk about a close shave . . .

In terms of energy, that impact—which for a nanosecond can sometimes top 1,000° Fahrenheit—generates a pressure of several hundred pounds per square inch. Which is why some police officers end up with blunt trauma bruises that are saucer-sized. Also they hurt, as some officers like to add, "like hell!"

In a release put out on the fortieth anniversary of the discovery of Kevlar, DuPont went to unusual lengths to tell the world what Kevlar was all about.

The company explained that the rigid molecular structure of the product had not only saved the lives of thousands of people worldwide, but had been used in both the aeronautical and space industries.

The new Airbus A380, for instance—the world's largest-ever commercial passenger liner, which seats nearly eight hundred passengers—relies on the unique light weight and high performance of Kevlar "to reduce weight versus traditional materials in its three-hundred ton frame." DuPont is also working with the Massachusetts Institute of Technology and the US Department of Defense to develop from Kevlar new protective materials for what it terms "the soldier of the future."

But let's go back a little and trace the history of modern body armor. Commercial nylon was first invented by Wallace Carruthers at the DuPont experimental station in Wilmington, Delaware, in 1937. It was the first fiber created from petrochemicals, and like the Kevlar that followed a generation later, it changed a lot—including giving us parachutes, women's "silk" stockings, and, with ballistic nylon (which is twice as strong as ordinary nylon), the first flak jackets in the Korean and Vietnam wars.

The most important property of a fiber is its tenacity or, more fundamentally, its break-strength. This is expressed in techno-geek terminology as *grams per denier.*

Wool fibers, for instance, have a break-strength of about seven-tenths of one gram per denier. Cotton is up to about 1.4. Then we get into rayons and acetates that have strengths fairly near to that of cotton. Steel, on the same basis, is about 4 grams per denier. Ballistic nylon, used in the very first flak jackets, more than doubled that to roughly 10.

Then, with Kevlar, the figure leapfrogged to 23 grams per denier. That was followed in 1978 by the first generation of the contemporary flak jacket, when the US Army adopted Kevlar as the principal material. The United States military, in the mid-1980s, adopted what it termed the PAASGT Jacket, which in typically convoluted US technical jargon stands for Personal Armor Assistant Ground Troops. In fact, this was the first iteration of the fragmentation-resistant jacket and helmet that has saved—and is still saving, in places like Iraq and Afghanistan—the lives of an awful lot of our youngsters.

It is worth mentioning that by then Richard Davis' invention of concealable body armor had already notched up its first fifty saves.

One astonishing revelation from researching this book was the extraordinary number of cops whose vests prevented them from being impaled by fractured steering columns.

Case in point is youthful Deputy Sheriff Jason Alexander of Crawford County, Michigan. He took an almighty hit in February 2003 on Michigan's Interstate-75 during a blizzard. This highway, running north–south through this remote countryside, is notorious for winter crashes—usually during or after snowstorms.

That accident was so serious that his rescuers had to use the Jaws of Life to get him out of his cruiser. A picture of what was left of Jason Alexander's squad is in the photo section of this book. The crash was horrific, but judge for yourself.

Officers at the site thought it would be impossible for anyone to emerge alive from that heap of twisted metal, but Jason Alexander did. He was finally stretchered to the hospital with multiple bruises, including a damaged liver. He had no broken bones, though.

What saved his life was a 1.5mm-thick hardened titanium steel plate insert in the front of his body armor. The impact was so violent that it actually bent this piece of metal, considered by the manufacturers as "unbendable." Titanium is not supposed to yield to pressure under impact, which is why it is the metal of choice in the arms industry.

The cockpits of both American and Russian helicopter gunships are encased in *titanium bathtubs*, to deflect ground fire. I was to see this for myself in the summer of 2000, when I flew combat in Sierra Leone for five weeks in a former Soviet Mi-24, which has its entire cockpit encased in a titanium bath. That protection was pretty effective against most types of ground fire.[1]

Deputy Alexander tells us that he'd been called to check two vehicles that had slid off the road into a ditch.

"It was the mother of all blizzards," he recalls, "a complete white-out. Getting to the accident, I dared not exceed twenty-five miles an hour. Having checked the cars, I was preparing an accident report on the side of the road, my overheads flashing, when a semi-hauler, doing something like sixty, crashed into me. It had been called out for another accident involving a big truck.

"I knew nothing until I found myself completely surrounded by crushed steel . . . couldn't get out . . . couldn't radio. Nothing!

"The driver responsible for the accident was apparently desperate to get home. Well, weren't we all? Only I could have been killed. He was in such a hurry that the subsequent investigation caused him to be charged with 'failure to yield' and to be fired. Could have been worse, I suppose, but it was bad enough."

The incident didn't prevent young Alexander from continuing his service with the Michigan National Guard. Based at the Maneuver Training Center at Camp Grayling; he was on standby and waiting to ship out for Iraq when we conducted our interview.

The morning we spoke, he'd made an attempt to serve a Fugitive Warrant at the home of a suspect with whom he'd had a run-in a while back. The man went on the run before they could get to him and this wasn't Alexander's first time he'd had dealing with him. A few months before, having chased down a car that was being erratically driven, he was attacked by its two intoxicated occupants when he eventually forced them to stop. He pepper sprayed, subdued, and had them both cuffed by the time back-up arrived.

Why does this recently married twenty-seven-year-old who joined the force straight from school do this kind of work? In the private sector, he could probably do quite well.

"I've had quite a few years of police work involving accident investigation. I've also turned down several offers from insurance companies to come and do the same thing for them . . . could probably command upwards of a hundred grand a year in that line of work. But it's not for me."

It is worthy of note that a very similar kind of accident involved another of Richard Davis' Saves. The subject there was Jamie Longolucco of Norwich, Connecticut, and that save is listed as #885. This police officer was on his way to answer an alarm call when a truck rounded a sharp curve, crossed over the centerline, and slammed headlong into Longolucco's cruiser. As these things sometimes go, another car a short while later also crossed the centerline and drove into the police wreck at speed.

Having been knocked unconscious by the impact, Longolucco's legs were pinned to the dashboard. Worse, his driver's side door was pushed in so far that it ended up on the passenger side of the patrol car. This cop eventually had to be extricated by the Jaws of Life and, because of the condition of the vehicle, that maneuver could only be achieved by hauling him out through the roof.

Critically hurt, Jamie Longolucco survived. Had he not been wearing body armor, his physician disclosed afterward, he would almost certainly have been killed. His vest had apparently absorbed much of the impact.

In this book, readers will meet a lot more cops like Jason Alexander—many of them young, enthusiastic, and full of spunk. Almost all conceded—almost as a single voice—that they were in police work because of the service they were (and are) able to render their communities.

Police Officer Michael Francis of North Carolina—who is alive and shouldn't be—empathizes: also youthful and ambitious and well educated, he can't really see himself in any other kind of job, though he'll admit that the variety of everyday experiences might be part of the appeal. A great guy and an exemplary law enforcer, Michael's save is dealt with in chapter 19.

It is something indeed that among the young officers whom I spoke with in the thirty or so months that it took to put together this material, quite a few tended to put ideals before financial gain. In these difficult and troubled times, that was quite revelatory to this cynical old hack.

It also says much about America's younger generation.

Deputy Jason Alexander's wreck, though horrific, was neither unique nor isolated. Cops are regularly hit by cars. The bottom line is that accidents happen all the time and sometimes to the most well-intentioned people.

For a police car to be involved in a wreck not of its own making is an almost hourly occurrence in America. Michigan State Troopers lose a car a week while patrolling a single road, the Detroit Expressway. They are very often rammed by a second drunk while investigating the first DUI, irrespective of warning signs and flashing lights. Some authorities are of the opinion that there are drivers—usually under the weather—who are attracted to flashing lights like moths might be to a headlight.

When Richard Davis first invented concealable soft body armor, he initially only considered their application to stopping bullets. It didn't take long for him to realize that his vests were equally useful in knife attacks, or in car accidents, which kill or maim as many cops as bullets do.

The latest statistics show that because of concealable body armor, and better training—both interdepartmental and by the American Society of Law Enforcement Trainers (ASLET) and the International Association of Law Enforcement Trainers (IALEFI) instructors—there are these days more officers dying in road accidents while on duty than by felonious assault.

Richard Davis' personal list of a thousand or so saves achieved by the company he originally founded shows that while a good deal of attention is given to spectacular magnum and shotgun shootings, there are also more deaths and casualties from road wrecks and officers hit by passing cars. He also makes the point that for every single car accident listed as a save, there are two or more "semi-saves" that form a category of their own and are consequently unlisted: the majority did not fall within the category of "life-threatening" circumstances.

Instead, as Davis likes to explain, the body armor normally worn by officers prevented them from being more seriously injured.

Over the years there have been quite a few saves that verged on the miraculous. Not all ended happily. Some officers emerged alive but incapacitated. Others were partly crippled as a result of being shot.

I deal with one such incident in great detail this book, though the outcome wasn't nearly as dramatic. John Aguiar of Hoboken, New Jersey, was shot twice by a criminal with a .45 ACP pistol. John later became a poster save for the Second Chance Body Armor company, but as a consequence of trauma that he suffered, he left the force. John was Richard Davis' Save #900, which, as you will see in chapter 7, was memorable.

Others did better. Take Steve Gazdik of Chardon, Ohio. Having entered a bar he was attacked by somebody who was looking for trouble. The result was that he took a butt in the side of his head with a cue stick. That knocked him senseless long enough for the felon to remove Gazdik's own revolver, a .357 magnum, and shoot him four times. Gazdik was hit twice in the chest—his vest doing the necessary—with the third round going into his arm and a fourth gazing his hip.

Talking about it afterward with Richard Davis, Steve recalls seeing no flashes as the gun was fired. He maintains that he also felt no impact. The felon used the officer's firearm to commit suicide shortly afterward.

Some years later, Sheriff's Deputy Ronald Page of McHenry County, Illinois, survived three blasts from a 12-gauge shotgun which is listed as Save #375. It's a gripping and unusual story. Likely as not, this is something that he'll tell his grandchildren about one day.

Having arrived at the scene of a "suspicious noises" call, Page apparently frightened away two suspects who were in the process of stripping a car. Believing that the situation was clear, Page was checking the car when he took two shots in rapid succession, both of them into his back. As he lay on the ground the felons shot him again. While his body armor absorbed the bulk of it, the blast spray outside his armor caused serious injury to his neck and shoulder, including a two-and-a-half inch tear alongside a major artery that might have been fatal had he not been given prompt medical attention.

Page was able to tell Richard Davis afterward that because he survived, he had the evidence that resulted in the arrest of his attackers.

Save #899 was more recent and involved another sheriff's deputy, John Channell of Elkins, West Virginia. He and his partner were attempting to serve a warrant for domestic battery at a residence when, in the approach to the house, both officers were hit by bullets fired from an SKS 7.62mm rifle—something for which soft body armor is simply not geared for.

Channell was hit in the right lower back and his partner in the arm. Both men were able to make it to cover but were pinned down for another forty-five minutes after which they were able to make good their escape. The stand-off that followed lasted thirteen hours, with four officers wounded in the fray. The warrant was eventually served and the suspect taken into custody.

Another fortunate cop was Steve Snyder of Lima, Ohio. He was hit five times by a felon wielding a .38 Special and wounded in the right leg, right arm, left hand, and took a bullet in his forearms, which was deflected into his vest. Had it penetrated his body armor, it would have gone straight into his heart. In retaliation, his attacker was shot four times.

There are saves in this compendium of survival that are startling, and to which I sometimes devote several pages. One of these involves Keith LaFazia of Providence, Rhode Island. He tangled with juvenile gangs and almost got himself killed, not once, but several times. Some of his colleagues weren't so lucky. Chapter 14 gives the reader a disturbing insight to the kind of urban violence that has come to beset so many American conurbations. The same with Tom Huerbin, whose epic tale is also featured in a forthcoming volume.

Danny Rieg's almost fatal clash in Pittsburgh with a nutty professor who ended up shooting him is another forceful drama that could have gone either way. Turn to chapter 13 and you'd be surprised at the antics of some so-called respected academics. Rieg is one more cop who ended up leaving the force as a result of a tangle that was both gripping and momentous.

And if you want to know about a man who had everything stacked up against him and eventually came out on top, I suggest you turn to chapter 6 and see what Reggie Sutton has done—not only with his life but with those of a host of youngsters whom he has taken in hand over the years and molded into classic sportspeople. Born on the proverbial wrong side of the track, this African-American policeman, who today works as a detective in New Haven, Connecticut, emulates much of the American dream.

That African safari that we're both going on is still very much on the agenda, Reggie . . .

Then come overseas saves—and there are many. In Germany alone there are said to be dozens. Numerous British and Canadian saves are listed, including one that involved Detective Elamine Soufi of Winnipeg, Manitoba, and which is listed as #842.

Detective Soufi was involved in a drug search warrant that took place one evening on the outskirts of his city. As it went down, a suspect ran out of the house toward a wooded area. Soufi took off after him and at full pace, both men toppled over a riverbank they couldn't see in the dark and dropped thirty feet onto frozen ground. Soufi said afterward that it was "like hitting concrete." According to Dr Clement Lang, Elamine's vest protected this cop's torso from serious injuries. He doesn't say what happened to the other guy . . .

Canada's very first recorded save was #344 and involved Officer Rob McRea of Vancouver, British Columbia, who admitted afterward that the reason there weren't more Canadian saves wasn't due to the lack of officers wearing their vests; it was because there were fewer shootings. That might have been the case then, but as we have seen in spates of recent violence north of the border, the Canuks are catching up fast.

In Rob McRea's case, he was wearing body armor when he was flagged down by a bank employee who told him that they'd just been robbed. He pointed toward a man fleeing down the street. The Canadian cop set off in pursuit and being in good shape, he was able to make up a lot of ground, to the point where the robber, seeing he was being outdistanced, turned and fired a sawed-off shotgun at his pursuer.

Officer McRea dropped to the ground. That was when the robber calmly walked up to him as he lay there and pumped another round into his back. This Canadian cop took wounds to his face, neck, head, arms, and legs. His torso, in contrast, was relatively untouched by the double blast of his attacker's shotgun pellets.

One of Richard Davis' most notable saves involved Paul Lee Gardner of Kingston, Jamaica, a member of the Special Anti-Crime Task Force that responded to an intelligence report that there were criminals with high-powered rifles in the city's Content Avenue Gulley area. As Gardner, together with a bunch of his colleagues, searched the district, he came face-to-face with a suspect who shot several rounds at him with a semi-auto 9mm pistol.

The first round hit Gardner in his shooting hand, crippling it. As he fell backward, another round hit his chest, which was protected by his vest. Rolling right around on the ground he took another bullet in his back and was also saved by his body armor. In response, left-handed, Gardner managed to fire fifteen rounds from his M-16, mortally wounding the man who tried to kill him. That made for Save #740.

Since then there have been quite a few more Jamaican police involved in shoot-outs, several of whom have avoided being killed by wearing body armor. The authorities are loath to go into detail because of the exceptionally high level of crime on this Caribbean island.

Farther west in Maracaibo, Venezuela, Officer César Colmenares had his own personal brush with fate when he was notified that there was a suspect with a firearm in his area. He and a partner started a search based on information that had come in from a confidential source: the perp was apparently wanted on multiple charges.

While searching the ground of an abandoned house, Colmenares was accosted by man who emerged from behind a clump of bushes and shot him five times with a Rossi .38 Special. His body armor and its K-30 plate absorbed all the hits.

Nobody is saying what happened to the attacker.

Canada features prominently in the saves category. One save that involved concealable body armor, but not Richard Davis' brand, is among the most gripping stories in the book. It involved a trio of youthful armed bandits on a month-long run, two of them having escaped from prison in Calgary, Alberta. They stole cars and robbed businesses along a trail that led halfway across Canada, some two thousand miles. It all ended rather dramatically in Northern Ontario in some of the most rugged lake and bush country on the continent.

There, two native Canadians and a white girl kept a pretty substantial police contingent at bay for days, irrespective of the fact that their pursuers were backed by all the resources that the government could muster, including helicopters. That outcome, curiously, also involved a dog.

The denouement ultimately resulted in the attempted murder of Ontario Provincial Constable Jan Nickle who operates the Canine Unit out of Sault Ste. Marie. Shot at close range with a 12-gauge shotgun, two of his attackers committed suicide not long afterward in a panoply of drama and intrigue that would almost certainly have quickened the pulse of the late Truman Capote.

What is also astonishing is that some enterprising young writer hasn't yet latched onto this theme. It would almost certainly be grabbed by one of Hollywood's production houses. The trial records of *Regina v. Alfred Bradley Cardinal* total almost a thousand pages and some of the photos that appear in this book are there as well—as are a huge number of depositions of all the major players, victims as well as the families of those involved. The incident is detailed in chapter 12.

Of significant interest is a letter written from prison by Alfred (Freddie) Cardinal, the one surviving member of the gang. Seized by the police and admitted to record, it was addressed to his brother, Clifford. Since it sets the tone, I quote:

> Well me and Gordon sure had a lot of fun while we (were) together. We drank, smoked a lot of drugs, me and Donna fixed a lot of blow fuck . . . the cops

chased us (afterward) for about 20 miles . . . and then after we went into a ditch we ran into the bush so they couldn't follow us . . . Gordon really enjoyed it and the danger itself was a big rush for him. Near the end he lived for danger.

We got chased by that copper with his dog who was right behind us. There was also the (helicopter) above with more snipers all around . . .

Anyways we had to stop . . . and that our first shoot-out [sic] and Gordon got shot in the head (which was) more or less a flesh wound. So Gordon shot him and he said 'he got me Bro, but we got away' and we all had a good laugh . . . and that night we broke into a shack and found four bottles of rye and got drunk.

We thought the cop was dead because he flew about 3–4 feet plus all the cops all over the place . . . then I (stole) a .22 semi-automatic and sawed off the end to make it into a handgun. It also had a scope (and) looked pretty cool . . . like we called our shotgun 'Johnny' we named this (gun) CK which stood for Cop Killer . . .

In fact, Jan Nickle, the police officer involved in this confrontation in dense bush country to the west of Timmins, wasn't dead. As the photos show, he took a mighty thump to his chest from a shotgun and was indeed knocked down. But he remained conscious throughout, still with his dog Magnum's leash in hand. Shortly afterward he radioed in that he'd been shot. Against orders (because the area hadn't yet been cleared) the pilot of the helicopter landed nearby and airlifted him to safety from where he was rushed to St. Mary's Hospital in Timmins.

"After I'd been hit I lay on the ground for a minute or two, all the while checking the bush around me. Having been dropped, I was aware that the three of them could come back and finish me off. That's why I watched the reactions of Magnum very carefully: he would have alerted me if they were still around.

"But they weren't. One of their members who we now know as Gordon had taken a hit in his forehead. Unfortunately the 9mm bullet didn't penetrate his skull and he and his group ended up in another high-speed chase that included a furious fire-fight with our guys along the highway . . . about forty shots fired over a distance of about twenty miles. Which is why I carry a .40 caliber pistol today."

It is worth mentioning that Officer Nickle fired eight rounds at his attacker immediately after he'd been hit. He remembers none of it: either emptying a magazine in the firefight or actually reloading his pistol while still lying on the ground.

"I have no memory of any of that . . . it was all instinct which I suppose is what good training is about."

* * *

Very little is made of military saves by the media, which is a pity because there have been bucketsful.

Apart from the normal body armor or battle jacket worn by troops in active duty, quite a number of servicemen and women prefer also to wear something concealable for that "extra something" protection. Kevlar-based vests have saved lives there as well.

One of these belongs to James Kuiken, about whom little is known except that he was in Al Wafra in Kuwait when his vest prevented him from becoming shrapnel-porous in a booby trap explosion.

Perhaps the most striking military save that we know about involved a remarkable Special Forces operator who is not only a doctor but also a scientific mind of note with several medical discoveries to his credit. I interviewed Colonel Charles (Chuck) Fisher when my son Luke and I visited him at his home in Indianapolis. Apart from sharing a couple of bottles of vintage Chateau Lafite Rothschild, at several hundred dollars a pop, he offered me the very unusual events that surrounded his own escape.

The good Colonel was at the Al Rasheed Hotel in Baghdad early in the second Coalition invasion of Iraq when the ninth floor—where he and other senior US Army personnel had their rooms—took a rocket hit, probably from one or more 122mm Katyushas. The explosions ripped parts of the building apart and there were people killed and wounded. Had Chuck Fisher not been wearing his vest, he would also have become a statistic because though the blast threw him violently to the floor, his body armor prevented several large pieces of steel from penetrating his torso.

As the attack continued, he, though wounded, and others had to crawl between collapsed walls and engulfing fires into some pretty tight spots to rescue the wounded. The one man brought to safety, also a US Army Colonel and Fisher's boss, was physically hauled down nine flights of stairs by Fisher and some guys who appeared out of nowhere. That action saved his boss's life because they were able to get him out there in double-quick time and rush him to the local hospital. Some had already given him up for dead by the time he emerged from the stricken building. Chuck Fisher thought otherwise . . .

I got part of the story from a bunch of South African private military contractors who were on the scene and rushed in to help, some of whom I'd spent time with in a few African wars. All were former Special Forces personnel themselves and they saved a few American lives that day.

This is the gist of the e-mail that arrived when I inquired about the event. The men referred to are all South Africans who, at the time, were the bodyguard team for Andy Bearpark, the British ambassador. They included Lawrence Jacobs (Colonel ex–Task Force), Garth Eloff (ex-SA Special Forces), Arthur Norval (ex–101 Battalion), and Jim Maguire (a former member of the British Parachute Regiment who went on to fight for the South Africans):

> Jim, Andrew and Arthur were on the ninth floor of the Al Rasheed when they had a rocket attack. Garth took one injured American down the stairs to the ground floor. Meantime, through thick smoke and a succession of localized fires caused by the blast the others were checking rooms. In one of them they found US Army Colonel (Chuck Taylor) busy digging a colleague (also a Colonel) of his out of the rubble that had collapsed onto his bed. Between them they placed this critically injured man on a bed sheet and carried him down, with Garth and Jakes clearing the way. Later the same guys went back up and checked room for room for more survivors . . .

In researching and writing this book—which meant that I was obliged to travel in both America and Canada, from one coast to the other, and in the process covered about thirty thousand miles (or more than the circumference of the world)—I got to know some very out-of-the-ordinary people, all of whom shared the distinction of having had their lives saved by wearing concealable body armor. Many have become firm friends and we still communicate when the mood takes us.

Among the more motivating "characters" is David Miles of Port St. Lucie, Florida, a bald-headed Kojak look-alike who made Richard Davis' Save #456. Apart from being a former cop, David has the same insouciant demeanor and smile of the late Telly Savalas, which could have been assimilated from having worked undercover in Japan while still in the U.S. military.

I drove up from Miami to see him and he told me in his usual straight-in-the-eye businesslike manner that he had been married for more than thirty years. He met his wife while still working in the Far East and though there were difficulties when she first came to America, this little lady has acclimatized well. It helps that they visit Japan regularly and that he has made a relatively accomplished golfer of her. This, I might add, is a passion shared by her husband.

David was working just south of Fort Lauderdale for the Hallandale Police Department when his shooting happened. He'd responded to a silent alarm at a local bank and though he didn't know it yet, one of the robbers was dressed as a security guard. Having pulled up in front of the building in his cruiser, he entered the bank to be faced by this crook wielding a .38 Special revolver.

A struggle ensued and David Miles took a slug in his stomach. It was fired at almost point-blank range and while it dropped him, his vest stopped the bullet from penetrating. Thinking that he'd killed the cop, the shooter turned his attention elsewhere, which was when Miles pulled his own gun and an exchange of gunfire followed. One of the robbers was shot dead, another surrendered, and the third member of the team escaped capture.

This contradictory little story is symptomatic of what happens—body armor or not—when things go wrong. What else can you do when you react to a situation and on arrival you are greeted by an armed and uniformed man. Ostensibly, he is the guardian of the peace; but instead, at gunpoint, he takes you hostage, as he'd already done to everybody else in the bank.

Quite a few chapters in this work deal with drugs and those involved with spreading this noxious menace, particularly among America's youth.

Greg Lovett—who today works security in Iraq—spent most of his time as a cop fighting drugs, usually in an undercover mode. At the end of it he was shot four times by a twelve-year-old with a shotgun, which in itself is a compelling event. All these issues are dealt with in chapter 4.

What we do know about drugs, and methamphetamines especially, is that this is a scourge that has become rampant throughout America. It is not only restricted to the lower or criminal classes. As Greg points out there is no sector of society not affected by meth: it includes gang members as well as professional people, teachers, law enforcers, legal authorities, administrators, as well as housewives who use it to limit weight gain together with the rest.

Something of an insight here is a report carried in the March 2006 issue of *American Police Beat*. The report involved a survey of two hundred hospitals in thirty-nine states as well as Washington, D.C.

Almost half the respondents disclosed that methamphetamine addiction is, as I write, the top illicit drug involved in emergency room visits. Tom Goodman, a spokesman, said that this was a national problem. He added, "The costs of methamphetamine are placing a great strain on county governments." He disclosed that three-quarters of the hospitals surveyed said that ER cases involving the drug had increased markedly in the past five years and, as a consequence, hospital costs had risen exponentially.

More disturbing is the revelation that twelve million people in the United States are estimated to have used meth at least once. Who knows, the figure could be twice that. Across the board, as stated in the magazine, prison officials report huge increases in the costs of medical and dental care for inmates who have long histories of meth abuse.

• • •

For all that, the situation with regard to crime in the United States is not hopeless. It is bad. But at the same time, a measure of security is being maintained, even if the price sometimes paid includes the lives of those who protect us. They do their job so citizens might sleep securely at night.

As Jim Morris said when he was done editing this book, and his sentiments are reflected in part in the Prologue that precedes this section, "My thinking on the role of the average cop has undergone a pretty dramatic change. I was cynical about law enforcement before. And though nothing is perfect, these folks are doing one hell of a job."

Since so much of this book relates to the use—legal or otherwise—of firearms, it is perhaps apposite that the final word should come from somebody who visits many of us quite regularly in our living rooms roughly once a week.

In a CBS *60 Minutes* program that was broadcast in the spring of 2006, Andy Rooney offered a few observations of his own about life in America. One of these concerned the use (or misuse) of firearms, and I quote: "Guns do not make you a killer. I think killing makes you a killer. You can kill someone with a baseball bat or a car, but no one is trying to ban you from driving to the ball game."

Al J. Venter
Sault Ste. Marie, Canada
March 2007

[i] Al Venter flew combat in the Sierra Leone war for five weeks in "a rickety old Mi-24 helicopter gunship that leaked when it rained" in 2000. That adventure is detailed in his book *War Dog*, published in 2006 by Casemate Publishers, Philadelphia.

CHAPTER 1

Heart of Starkness: A Woman's Survival Epic

> An Ohio State Highway Patrol officer shot and killed a hitchhiker Sunday during a gunfight on Interstate-70 in Preble County in which the the officer was also shot. Trooper Angela Watson, 26, was listed in fair condition in the intensive care unit at Miami Valley Hospital in Dayton.
>
> —*Dayton Daily News*, Sunday, April 5, 1998

A slip of a girl at five feet two inches and a hundred and fifteen pounds, Ohio State Trooper Angela Watson recalls both the impact and a sharp shock of pain when she was hit just below the left breast by a .44 magnum bullet. It was fired from a little more than arm's length away, so close that the muzzle flash momentarily blinded her.

As she recalls, "The initial impact didn't knock me down, but I do remember thinking to myself, 'Shit, this is for real; this guy is trying to kill me.'"

She drew her own pistol and fired, hitting her attacker, thirty-year-old itinerant George Snyder from Akron, with three of the eight .40-caliber shots she fired. Then her weapon jammed.

"When the slide locked back I thought I was out of rounds. Only when I reloaded did I realize I had a jam." She threw herself sideways behind her patrol car and set about clearing the obstruction. The felon fired again in her direction.

The attempt on her life would have succeeded had she not worn concealable body armor. The 240-grain Federal Hydra Shok bullet from a six-inch Model 29 Smith & Wesson revolver should have gone straight through her. Had she taken a hit from the side, it would almost certainly have ripped both her lungs apart. As it was, the hollow-point finally came to rest halfway into the twenty-four layers of her Kevlar protective vest.

Eight years later she showed me where the projectile hit. Not immodestly, she lifted the shirt of her parade-ground-smart trooper's gray uniform to expose the lower part of her chest; she didn't need to point to a slightly raised dust-colored welt more than two inches across.

"It hasn't lost much of its original color," she said, adding that the wound remained sensitive to touch.

Angela's ribs were clearly visible. The Level II ballistic vest, not officially rated to stop .44 magnums, had absorbed most of the impact—but not enough to stop some damage to her ribs and lungs, which caused a breathing problem immediately after she was shot. The subsequent trauma resulted in four days in an intensive care ward.

The prognosis on her admittance card indicated that she might have two cracked ribs and a punctured lung. That was one smart medic because he was right.

Angela Watson's story, as well as that of the man who tried to murder her, and who died in the encounter, is classic cops-and-robber stuff.

The coroner's report indicated George Snyder was high on a combination of amphetamines, methamphetamines, and cannabinoids. His father, Theodore Snyder, a prosperous real estate broker from Akron, Ohio, said afterward that his son had been taking ketamine, an animal anesthetic (known on the streets as Special K), and that he had seriously considered having him committed two weeks before the shooting.

Found in Snyder's car, parked a couple of miles down the road, was a note. Written in Snyder's spidery script, it said his actions had divine sanction. Addressed to God, it read, "I give this Holy Instant to You. Be in charge. For I would follow You. Certain that Your direction gives me peace."

A subsequent intelligence report circulated to law enforcement agencies across the United States, indicated that ketamine affects the part of the brain that controls a person's emotions and sense of identity. "Depending on one's state of mind, ketamine's rush of energy and mental confusion can, in rare instances, nudge a depressed person toward suicide. It can also push an agitated individual to be violent."

Working the late Saturday night/Sunday morning shift from an hour before midnight to dawn in patrol car 536, Angela Watson—since married to Captain Mike Spitler of the Preble County Sheriff's Department—was assigned to patrol roads in the area. Another female officer, June Clark, handled traffic in nearby Darke County. As is customary in Ohio, the two women worked alone, as do many of the roughly two hundred females among the thirteen hundred or so uniformed officers in the Ohio State Highway Patrol.

Apart from writing a number of speeding tickets, the night was uneventful for them both, except that at about one in the morning first reports came in of a man spotted walking along one of the highways. He was sighted at various locations, though no one pinpointed his exact position. On radio dispatches he was called "our phantom pedestrian."

"I went to where the walker was last seen and reported back to Beverly Ruxer, our dispatcher. 'Negative,' I told her. 'Nobody there, either on the highway or alongside it.'

"By about five that morning, it still being dark, I stopped briefly at the local police department at Lewisburg. I was getting tired and starting to feel that I needed my sleep." With the sun barely visible on the horizon, the day was already warm and she turned on her air-conditioning.

Dispatcher Ruxer called again. "Angela, I've had a cell call from Bill Donoghue of Brookville. Says there's a pedestrian walking on the freeway with a dog on a leash." She provided coordinates, west-bound on Interstate-70 from US Highway 127. "Can you check it out?"

Trooper Watson drove west on US 40 and then south. About two miles out of Eaton on the road to the Indiana state line she spotted a white male of average height, perhaps a little overweight.

"As I got closer, and saw his dirty black shirt, and big baggy khaki shorts, I recall thinking, what a vile man. He was grimly sleazy—Zolaesque almost."

She hit her red lights, pulled up, and saw the dog. Under other circumstances, he might have been taking the mutt for a walk. But not on the Interstate.

"I thought it odd that while he had seen my cruiser—and I'd already activated my lights—he just kept walking. When I pulled up and got out, he stopped and turned toward me. For a few moments, as he approached, I was able to observe him from up close."

George Snyder, sweaty and unkempt, wore rumpled baggy clothes, and had on a black canvas backpack. He looked unbathed, she recalled. A two-day stubble framed his round, swarthy face and his sneakers were filthy. The lenses on his steel-rimmed glasses were also smudged.

In one hand he held a piece of cardboard that read, in hastily scrawled letters, Colorado or Bust.

"'Morning,' I called when he was about twenty feet away, but he didn't reply.

"You know it's illegal to walk on the highway, never mind that you've got your pet with you," she told him. Still there was no reaction.

"What are you doing here?" she asked.

"I'm trying to find a wrecker for my car. Broken down," he said, pointing behind him. At that point no one knew he'd left his car in perfect working order at a nearby truck stop. Keys were found in his pockets later.

"I knew that something was wrong because his answers didn't tally. I hadn't seen any abandoned cars that night, and I'd covered the area three, perhaps four times in the past eight hours. Also, the sign in his hand told me he was trying to get to Colorado. Something was out of kilter, but I couldn't decide what."

Angela Watson should have been concerned. But, as she said afterward, she was not. She had to have been aware that in the previous three years there had been seven major shooting incidents involving highway patrol officers, including, six months before, the killing of Trooper James R. Gross. He was murdered during a traffic stop along Interstate-70 in Ashland County.

But Angela was tired and not her usual alert self.

"Think you can give me a lift?" he asked, his face tightening into a squint against the early-morning light.

"To where?"

"To the nearest exit, like a gas station or a truck stop," he replied. Without thinking, she said okay.

Explaining her decision afterward, she said she had often given lifts to stranded motorists, probably hundreds of times. There was no reason not to do so, except when things looked suspicious. On the face of it, Snyder, though slovenly and not the friendliest soul on earth, did seem at ease with himself, which was always a good sign. Also, a man with a dog on an open road with a fair amount of traffic seemed ordinary, though what he'd told her earlier indicated something else.

She noticed that he'd shifted the dog leash from his right hand to his left.

"Normally I'd ask whoever wanted a lift whether they were carrying guns or knives. It's a formality, and until then, just about everybody would admit to a pocket knife or something and give them to me. So I quizzed him, 'You carrying any guns or knives?'"

With that George Snyder reached into his right-hand pocket and hauled out the gun. Pointing it at the trooper, he said "Yes!" and with that he pulled the trigger.

Watson: "My first reaction was that it was a fake. Nobody had ever pulled a gun on me, and, I suppose, I had no reason to think they ever would. But then, that's the story of so many incidents in which cops get shot. What I did recall, once I was in the hospital, was that he'd changed his dog's leash from his right hand to his left. That should have been a warning of sorts.

"I also remember his eyes, real serious, but with that vacant distant stare . . . kinda spaced out . . . an indefinable nothingness." Someone else once described Snyder as the master of the tranquil gaze into the middle distance.

The entire episode, the encounter on the road, the exchange of fire, Snyder's death, all took place within barely thirty seconds.

Not long before this ordeal, something similar happened to Illinois State Trooper Sergeant James Pinney, of Logan County. He'd stopped to offer a bearded pedestrian a ride to the next town. When the subject came to the driver's side, he reached in and sliced the policeman across the forehead with a knife.

Before the trooper could react, the stranger pulled out a .32 auto, shoved it hard against the policeman's chest, and pulled the trigger. He quickly fled by climbing the highway fence to escape.

While this attack was Richard Davis' Save #619, Pinney's Second Chance body armor had saved his life in another attack fourteen years earlier. On that occasion he also took a slug in his vest while out on the road and survived with little more to show for his ordeal than a large bruise.

Angela Watson's experience was very different. She didn't go down, though she should have.

She felt the blow, which was more of a sting than a wallop. In a flash, she added, any kind of objectivity had evaporated. "It was my life on the line; it was me or him!"

She had seen many movies where heavy caliber handgun bullets hit people, and they would topple over, or their legs would buckle under them. "But that didn't happen. I was still on my feet, but by then my reflexes had kicked in and I knew I had to do something, *like right now*!"

Before Snyder could fire again, she turned, ran, and ducked behind her patrol car. She also drew and fired her .40 caliber Beretta service pistol, which then jammed. What astonished her was that she was able to get behind the cruiser without taking another hit. One moment she'd been standing before Snyder just ahead of her cruiser, the next she was twelve yards away and wounded.

"I was not yet aware that I'd hit him, though I'm pleased I spent so much time on the range as I did the previous year: paid off handsomely. Also, my training kicked in because I was able to retaliate without thinking, even though the shot to the side of my chest began to affect my ability to breathe."

Though she was struggling to get air, the more immediate threat quickly focused her attention: "A man was trying to kill me, and in my hand was a weapon that had malfunctioned."

With the slide locked back, Trooper Watson managed to drop her magazine. With a single, fluid movement of her right hand, she extricated another from her belt and clipped it hard and fast into her pistol. All the while she was expecting Snyder to suddenly loom over her with his magnum.

"I looked for him, but couldn't see him from behind the car. Also, he'd stopped shooting at me. Everything went quiet. I kept raising my head from side to side to try, to pick up any movement. At the same time I felt where I'd been hurt to see how bad it was. I didn't know if I was bleeding; I felt a warm a trickle down my left side, and that worried me . . . didn't even think about the vest until the medics arrived and took it off."

By now, identifying herself by her coded signal—officer in trouble—normally used to verify to base that it was her talking and not an imposter, she called for back-up. She also gave the dispatcher a short version of events on the portable mike attached to her lapel.

"I need a squad (ambulance)," she radioed. "One down, and I've been shot! He's down, to the side of my vehicle . . ." The answer from Dispatcher Ruxer was affirmative. Cars were headed her way. Because of the pain, she was unable to reply immediately.

Senses acute, Watson suddenly spotted movement.

"I was alerted by a tall shadow against the grass on the side of the road and knew immediately it was him. His gun was pointed at me but was motionless. I couldn't tell from where I crouched whether he'd been wounded. All I saw was a gun and Snyder.

"I didn't know 'til afterward that, apart from having struck his gun hand with my first volley, I'd also hit him in the groin, and, as I was told later, he would probably have bled to death eventually. But that would have taken time, and, frankly, I didn't have any."

What happened next was instinct. It was also, she recalled afterward, totally atavistic and survival-orientated, exactly as she had been trained.

"I didn't wait for him to move any closer. I fired several more shots and Snyder went down again though I didn't actually see him drop. By now my breathing had become even more labored. Also, the pain in my chest was worse, and I could barely answer questions over the radio." These kept coming. "How many attackers are there? How bad are you hit Angela? Are you okay?"

"For a while I kept trying to reply, but couldn't maintain a discussion. I could barely breathe. My condition was deteriorating; I tried hard to concentrate. I knew that if anything, I simply had to regain my equanimity. But that's difficult when your lungs don't function right. It was like someone had crunched the side of my mid-section and was standing on my chest."

Unobserved at first by either adversary, a van had stopped about fifty feet behind and a man approached, gingerly at first and then with more determination. By now Trooper Watson was sitting on the ground trying to remain conscious with waves of pain almost overwhelming her. The policewoman had no idea how much of the shoot-out the newcomer had seen, except that when he eventually got alongside her—after first being waved off by her gun, twice—he asked her for her weapon.

"It was crazy. Right there in the middle of it all a guy comes up and asks me for my auto. It's the last thing I'm going to give anybody, and certainly not to somebody I don't know. He could have been the shooter's accomplice.

"So I said no, but did ask him to stay with me until back-up arrived." At a national police convention two years later she got a few laughs when she said the only way he was going to get that pistol off her was to pry it from her dead hands.

The Good Samaritan was later identified as US Army Reservist Bobby Jones of Richmond, Indiana. Jones later said to Wendy Hundley of the *Dayton Daily News* that he'd spotted the trooper getting out of her patrol car and approach a civilian on the other side of the highway. He'd heard the "pops" of gunfire after he'd passed. It was then that he decided to turn around and investigate.

"I was pretty close . . . when I heard a couple of pops that sounded like gunshots," he later told investigators. By the time he reached Angela, she was leaning on her squad car pointing her gun at Snyder, lying on the ground in front of her car.

Still crouched behind her cruiser, Jones was distressed by Watson's condition. This time his offer of help wasn't spurned, and moments later the dispatcher heard a new voice on the radio, "This is a civilian, stopped to help the officer . . . she's down. Also the suspect is down. I need to know when back-up is going to arrive, and the officer needs an ambulance."

The pain seemed to increase, with Angela in shock from her wound. There was no noise from her attacker. She had been able to hear him breathing heavily earlier; now there was only silence. She leaned across and for the first time had a clear view of George Snyder. He was lying on the grass at the side of the road, perhaps a dozen feet away.

The first back-up car arrived shortly afterward; it had taken only four minutes to reach her but it felt like an hour. A minute later June Clark also pulled up. The newcomers were tentative, wary of the strange man alongside the downed officer. The National Guardsman, Bobby Jones, had been trying to help her, Angela explained breathlessly.

When she left the hospital four days later, she learned that more than a hundred law enforcement and emergency rescue personnel had followed her drama on the radio.

Along with two cracked ribs, Angela Watson received a blunt-trauma wound about half an inch deep, a bruised left lung, together with burn marks on her skin from where vest fibers had cauterized the point of impact. There were blunt trauma bruises on her left arm all the way down to her knee. Her body absorbed all of what the body armor didn't. A large caliber magnum bullet traveling at roughly 1,400 feet per second does that.

George Snyder took five bullets from Angela's gun, all of them non-lethal. Five of her eight shots hit the target—more than triple the national average when reacting to life-threatening circumstances. Police case histories on the national database indicate that only 10 to 20 percent of shots fired by police under attack hit where intended.

When back-up finally approached Snyder's lifeless body, lying as he was on the grass alongside the cement berm, they found him dead. He had shot himself in the head. But the way he had done it, with his thumb almost severed from his hand, raised questions later.

A Lewisburg officer found Snyder's .44 magnum under his body. On arriving at the scene, back-up police were puzzled when they found no firearm, and actually spent a while searching the grassy knoll near the body. Only when they moved Snyder did they discover the weapon lodged near his midriff, probably when he fell forward after committing suicide.

Dispatcher Ruxer confirmed later that there were bullet holes from a .44 magnum revolver lodged in the front left headlight, as well as in the right passenger side of the trunk of the patrol car.

As for his story about his vehicle being immobile, Snyder's VW Jetta was found a short while after the shooting at the BP Station at Exit 10. It was fully operational, its gas tank full. The engine started when its key was turned. His letter to God was on the front seat. A newspaper report the next day said that his mother stated that he had been acting weird and talking to spirits.

George Snyder was not a well man.

Something similar had happened a short while before to Deputy Sheriff Dale England of Chelan County, Washington, when he noticed a lone hitchhiker off to the side of a lonely road between two towns. After passing him, England made a U-turn and headed back to check him out.

As England explained afterward, "The man was kind of strung-out," with his hands stuck down deep into his pockets. Having pulled up, with the subject illuminated by his headlights, the officer asked him to show his hands. When they emerged, one of his hands had a revolver in it; the hitchhiker shot England twice, hitting him both times in his vest.

Deputy England was able to react, disarm his attacker, and haul him off to custody and a subsequent trial.

• • •

Angela Watson had a premonition that something like this would happen. She'd joined the force years before, but quit after a year. She decided to rejoin the Ohio State Highway Patrol when she accepted that she could do the job: until then, she'd lacked confidence. The Snyder incident happened almost exactly twelve months later.

"I was actually scared that something like this would take place, or that someone was going to get hurt or killed because of me. It was something that bugged me for a long time, kept me awake at night, which was probably why I took my weapons training so seriously.

"We were always warned that we might face a 'them or us' situation and, I suppose, that's the way it eventually came about. It was my life or George Snyder's."

George Snyder had acquired the gun only the day before. He'd been at a rave at Ohio's nearby Miami Valley. As someone told the cops, he'd started a coffee bar that had folded, and because he needed money to survive, he tried to call in a loan. The man who owed him couldn't pay, but suggested that he take his Smith & Wesson .44 instead. It came with a bunch of ammunition.

Among the first civilians to call the Ohio State Highway Patrol, after he'd heard news of the shooting, was Richard Davis. Though he'd never met Trooper Watson at any of his functions, he had been responsible for supplying the concealable vest she wore during the normal course of her duties. Because he was told by the hospital staff that the policewoman had suffered serious trauma and was obviously concerned to know how the vest had held up, Davis kept calling until he was able to talk to her personally—but that only came after her release.

Apart from a genuine interest in her progress, he also wanted to know the extent of her injuries. He needed this information so that he could possibly compensate in future versions of his body armor for small-framed individuals.

The big news, he divulged—beaming at the other end of the line—was that not only was she a milestone in his career, but hers was also the seven-hundredth life that had cheated death by wearing his body armor.

Chief Coroner Dr. Lee Lehman of the Preble County Coroner's Office greeted me when I stepped into his office as if I were infected with a tropical virus. It had taken a while to see him. It didn't matter that I was writing a book: I was a scribe and I was poking about on his turf.

Things went a little better once we started talking about George Snyder and the circumstances of his death, but only marginally.

On the positive side, he let me see the coroner's video of the autopsy. It was a grim, revolting experience. Though I'd encountered death often in my four-decade journalistic career, seeing the video of Snyder, laid out as he was on a gurney with the camera in close on bullet damage, was unsettling. I was glad when it was done.

"As you can see," he said, "it was a contact gunshot wound to the right side of the head, with the wound entrance just above the right ear. And it has soot deposits on the entrance wound, soot deposits on the periostium and the durra, the layers of the skin."

"Which means?"

"Contact wound, right up against his head."

"And if it hadn't been that close?" I asked.

"Some distance away, say a foot or two, and you would have a clean entry hole about the size of the bullet itself," he said, explaining that the muzzle gases would have been dissipated by distance.

I pointed to where a portion of Snyder's brains had been forced out. Dr. Lehman explained that a blast so close always creates a very big hole.

"The gases from the cartridge firing," he explained, "blow everything back . . . and that's what you see there on his right shoulder."

In Snyder's case it would seem that a chaotic childhood, and apparent parental indulgence—as well as that of his two older siblings—of just about his every whim, including dropping out of school, were all significant contributing factors to his dysfunction. One can only speculate as to how they came to terms with the drug use that ultimately made him unemployable. His last real job had been as night watchman on one his mother's properties.

Having spent time with Angela Watson, followed by a morning with the Preble County coroner, I headed northeast to Akron to talk to the family. I did so unannounced, aware that, with the controversial publicity the Snyder case had generated over the years, they might regard my visit as an intrusion. I was wrong.

Instead of hostility, Barbara Snyder, George's elder sister, greeted me with enthusiasm once I had stated my aims. I walked into her office in a nondescript part of downtown Akron, at 36 South Maple Street, and told her what I had done so far, and whom I'd seen. My mention of Angela Watson prompted a flicker of hostility, though she didn't hesitate to offer me a seat. She intimated that perhaps the truth would come out this time.

A slim, attractive, and enthusiastic woman of about fifty, she seemed to relish the cut-and-thrust of the family realty business that she had taken over when her father retired. By all accounts, business was good. Judging by the catalog of achievement awards on the walls of her office, Barbara Snyder ABRM, CRS, knew exactly what she was doing.

Elsie Snyder, her late mother—and her brother George's eternal protector—had died a few years before. Barbara was guarded as to how her parents had viewed the actions of their errant son.

Meanwhile, Barbara called Tom, the surviving brother, on his cell phone. As it was late in the day and he was home from his job as a carpenter, he was there within minutes.

The Angela Watson diatribe began in earnest. What emerged in that discussion, which I recorded on tape, was that the family vigorously disputes most aspects of the case, including the fact that George Snyder had actually shot himself. Rather, the sister suggested, Watson had killed him without good reason. It was plain as day, she suggested.

Barbara Snyder: "Our theory is that, yes, he had a gun, and it was in his backpack . . . When he was walking down the road he had a sign in his hand. He had a leash as well because his dog was with him.

"So what we're conjecturing is that she asked him for identification, and George carried a big black wallet on a chain. And it was in his back pocket. We're thinking that perhaps he reached for his wallet, and she mistook it for a weapon and fired on him. And then, once he'd gone down, that's when he was somehow able to get his gun out of his knapsack, which was on his back."

Let's think this one through. Watson shot him, because he pulled his wallet, and then stood there with a drawn weapon, while he took off his backpack, unzipped it, took out a .44 magnum, and shot her. Then she dived behind her unit and shot him four more times while he blazed away, hitting her squad car twice. Hmmm?

Barbara sat back for a moment, looking to her brother for agreement, before going on. Tom Snyder nodded enthusiastically.

"He did *not* have the gun in his pockets, or in a holster, or anything like that. It was in the backpack. He was able to free that out, and return fire because she was shooting at him," she declared, eyes hostile and her face aggressive.

Tom, younger than his sister, concurred throughout. A small man of perhaps five feet three or four, with a goatee and a tattoo on the back of his hand, he seemed the antithesis of his dynamo sister. He added a few observations of his own but wasn't prepared to explain how Angela had taken a bullet, or that Bobby Jones had been a witness to most of it. Nor, for that matter, was she.

Further, the drama had played out to the side of a busy highway where a police car with its lights flashing was pulled up, and where there was obviously a confrontation between two people, one of them in uniform. Such things tend to attract public interest.

Nonetheless, immediately after the shootings, Barbara Snyder sparked a growing controversy surrounding the death of her brother George. She was among the first to contact the coroner's office with questions about motive, timing, the trajectory of bullets, as well as the nature of the wound itself.

She kept calling for a year or more. Nor was she shy about sharing her sentiments with the press, which almost immediately took the line that the shooting was something that somehow should not have been allowed to happen.

Leading the pack was reporter Wendy Hundley. She wrote stories under headlines that read, "Doubts Still Surround I-70 Shooting," coupled to a subhead, "The case is closed and the injured trooper has returned to work, but nagging questions remain." The first of her reports was slugged "Hitchhiker Slain in Shootout."

Another subhead section declared, "I asked him if he had any gun or knives on him, and he stated, 'Yeah,' and pulled a weapon out of his right front pocket and pointed it at me," which, on the face of it, is dishonest reporting. George Snyder pulled his gun and *instantly* shot Trooper Watson, which made Hundley's story misleading.

Angela Watson subsequently became something of a recluse. Because of biased press reports in local newspapers and on television, she preferred not to speak to the media. Explaining her decision afterward, she declared she had done nothing wrong; it was the one-sided, partisan approach of the media that dismayed her. Also, she'd been told by her superiors not to talk to the media.

She and her colleagues were furious about many of the negative reports that had appeared about the case, but as public servants, they could do nothing. At one point George Snyder was even portrayed as the "victim" of a brutal police act.

Staying noncommittal, as she did in the months that followed—as Trooper Watson was to observe—had the effect of fostering, rather than nullifying, suspicion. "Because I wouldn't talk to them, it was implied that there must be something suspicious about the circumstances of the case." Which could be one of the reasons Dr. Lehman was not altogether pleased to see me.

The surviving Snyder siblings were convinced that Angela Watson's injuries were faked, and that she was not wounded at the scene of the crime. They concocted a convoluted theory that she had been hurt in some other way, and that much of what had taken place was staged.

Also, the fact that George Snyder had all but lost his right thumb was proof enough—as far as they were concerned—that he had put his hands up in surrender and had then been shot.

As to the final bullet to the head, the inference was, as Barbara Snyder stated, on tape with some vehemence, "Somebody helped do that with his gun . . ."

Both older Snyders were a little more forthcoming about their brother's addictions, with Barbara adding that, "They made him sound like he was the most freaked-out drug addict in the world, so they could play it down like he was a crazy lunatic. In truth, he was the brightest and most wonderful person in the world."

To which Tom Snyder added, "He wouldn't have hurt anybody."

"No," chirped Barbara. "He never would have hurt a soul . . . he'd never shoot a person unprovoked. *Never! Ever!* He didn't have a mean bone in his body." She said nothing about the drugs the coroner found in his system during the postmortem.

Since the incident on Interstate-70, the Snyder family has presented what they considered a meaningful argument. It centered almost solely on the implausibility of the suicide, particularly because George Snyder's gun was found under his body and not alongside it. Yet law enforcement case histories—in the United States and many countries abroad, some dating back a century—cite instances of guns used in suicide falling aside, under, behind, and sometimes twenty feet from the body.

In that final convulsive moment, there is no telling how a man's reflexes will react when he pulls the trigger. At the same time, as Davis suggests, it is axiomatic that had it been "murder by police": the sensible thing would have been to place the gun conspicuously next to the body, not *under* it.

It is notable that among the first messages State Trooper Watson received while still in the hospital was a get-well card from Theodore and Elsie Snyder, the shooter's parents. They regretted that their son had tried to kill her.

The gesture was unsolicited and by all accounts, a genuine act of contrition.

While in Akron, I also asked about the dead man's background. Barbara Snyder admitted that brother George had little in the way of education, and her comments are illuminating, though not necessarily as intended.

"He was too brilliant for school. He couldn't sit through school. He was hyperactive and very intelligent . . . traditional schools didn't work for him. He'd remember stuff."

Barbara: "He had an amazing mind, with a photographic memory. He was just so intelligent . . . yeah, he was just—I mean, he was out there a lot of times, because he would think about stuff that you and I wouldn't even think about thinking."

In conclusion, I asked them why hadn't they taken the matter further?

It was Tom who answered that his parents were too old to spend their last years in court. He added that they didn't want to drag their son "through the mud of a trial."

"Basically we let her off the hook," were his last words before I headed back to Dayton.

Still on the job along Ohio's highways, State Trooper Angela Spitler (neé Watson) says that if she were to accost George Snyder today, he would face a very different procedure. She has become something of a hand fetishist.

"Hands are big with me now, because when Snyder reached for his gun I didn't see them. So I don't care if it is grandpa or grandma, if I make a traffic stop, I want to see your hands. And if there is a gun—and there have been quite a few times, depending on the situation, where there have been firearms—I ask the driver or passenger to tell me where it is. Then I physically remove the weapon from the vehicle. I do it, not them. I'll click out the magazine, clear the chamber, check documentation, and finally, when I'm totally done, I'll hand it back.

"We recently passed a law in Ohio making it legal for people to carry concealed weapons. That makes our task even more difficult, which is why I often start by asking people that I've stopped whether they have weapons in the car."

Following her save in 1997, Watson has been invited many times to describe the circumstances of her shooting. Of particular interest was her ability—within a second of being shot—to return fire, take cover, swiftly clear a jammed pistol, and shoot back at someone singlemindedly intent on ending her life.

That happened at the International Association of Law Enforcement Firearms Instructors (IALEFI) Convention at the Black Canyon Range, just north of Phoenix, Arizona, where Richard Davis sponsored her address to the gathering. Her speech centered on the need to wear body armor on the job, and, "the wonderful training that I got from my firearms instructor." Among the guests was Mike Spitler, the second person to respond to Angela Watson's call, and, by then, her fiancé.

Prior to her address to all five hundred delegates, every one of them senior in rank to her, and the majority many years older, Richard kidded her about Mike, saying, "You'd better be good or I'll tell your Daddy that you've got your boyfriend out here." Her reply was a flat, matter of fact aside, "Richard, I don't have a father."

Stunned, Davis tried to apologize, but Watson laughed it off. However, he was even more surprised when Trooper Watson came to him about an hour later with a proposal of her own. "Richard," she said, "I've been thinking. Since it was your vest that gave me a 'second chance' at life, and because I don't have a father of my own, would you consider coming to Ohio when I get married? I'd like it to be you that gives me away to Mike."

The couple was married in West Alexandria, Ohio, on December 7, 2002. Proudly, Richard Davis walked her down the aisle.

CHAPTER 2

Three Thousand American Lives Saved, and Counting

In 1971 Richard Davis created the first prototype of soft concealable body armor, the same "bulletproof" vests that law enforcement agencies all over the world wear today. The first of four patents was granted two years later. Since then, Second Chance Body Armor, the Michigan company that Davis formed, and then lost, has saved the lives of a thousand people who had been shot, stabbed, crushed, impacted, run over, wrecked, or, in several instances, either fell from great heights or were hurled a long way.

The event that would ultimately change the way Americans kill each other took place on July 18, 1969, the night after Apollo 11 took off for the moon.

Davis jokes that though he defeated two men in a gunfight, he was fighting three of them at the time, which is why he ended up in the hospital. He fired six shots into three criminals who tried to rob him. That came after he had been lured to an abandoned property to deliver pizzas. Then, as he was turning to leave, one of the attackers whom he'd floored seconds earlier shot Davis twice.

Ten minutes later, the future inventor of concealable body armor was being treated in an emergency room with the man who tried to murder him alongside on a gurney, under police guard.

Richard Davis didn't suffer unduly from his bullet wounds, but the attempted mugging had an altogether different outcome from what might have been expected. It set the twenty-six-year-old Davis on a search for protection for those subject to bullet damage. That included the roughly a million law enforcement officers in the United States. There was another three-quarters-of-a-million needing similar protection, either guarding the nation's civilian infrastructure or prisons.

The consequences of that June 1969 event would alter the security face not only of America, but of every civilized country in the world, as well as some not so civilized.

Richard Davis' invention of concealable body armor not only saved the lives of more than three thousand law enforcement and security officers over the next three decades, but this burly former Marine—who can still, at the age of sixty-three, do a dozen standing presses with 125 pounds—would become something of a cult figure among cops.

"The man who bulletproofed America's police," was what they called him, though few would be aware that the soft, concealable "bulletproof" vests so many of them wear on their duty shifts had their beginning not in a police gun battle, but in an armed citizen's shoot-out with criminals.

He also formed the Second Chance Body Armor Saves Club, which lists every known "Save," and a brief description of the event—which to those involved is cathartic. A forty-eight-page booklet celebrates most of them; but because of federal or other constraints, as well as some involving clandestine operations, there are some that receive only vague, passing mention.

Only a handful of military saves are detailed—including a bloody episode in Baghdad that involved a Special Forces doctor and operator Colonel Charles 'Chuck' Fisher (Save #921). There have been hundreds more during the course of the half-dozen or so conflicts in which America has found itself since Vietnam.

There are also two journalists that Davis knows of (though he has been told there are more), including a French scribe who is so emotionally anti-American that he wouldn't recognize a US attribute if his life depended on it (if the reader will excuse the pun).

Jonathan Thornton of Reuters (Save #595) was a news photographer assigned to cover the war in Bosnia. In July 1993, Muslims broke through the Croatian lines in a pre-dawn attack on the village of Buna, which Thornton was covering from the Croatian side. As he approached the Croatian command post, two soldiers intercepted him and demanded his ID. As he was searching his Second Chance vest, equipped with a K47 chest plate, one of the soldiers peeled off an armor-piercing incendiary AK round from about fifty feet, striking Thornton.

"The bullet hit my chest with a shove. Feeling no pain, I swung around and ducked back up the path . . ."

Thornton was hit again in the arm and left thumb. He spent three days in the ICU, eight more on a recovery ward, and another fourteen as an outpatient, before returning to America. As Davis recalled afterward, "The K47 had a perfect round hole through it. The tungsten steel core stopped in the Kevlar-Twaron soft armor pad. What's more, the K47 was specifically designed to just barely stop the extra-powerful Soviet-type 7.62 x 39mm API (Kalashnikov) bullet at that range."

Thornton's letter he wrote to Richard Davis afterward said it all: "Your vest and a bit of luck made the difference between life and death."

So too with international news photographer Jim Craig, who was hit by a high-powered sniper's bullet in his Command Jacket while working on a photo project for the humanitarian aid effort in Bosnia and Herzegovina and made Save #596. Craig was aware that snipers knew most media people were wearing plated body armor, which, he commented afterward, was probably why the shot landed on his left-hand side panel, close to his heart.

"The impact knocked the wind out of me . . . the sound of the bullet hitting the plate was extremely loud and at first I didn't know what had happened. I was up on my feet in a couple of minutes . . . a little sore but mostly shaken up. Only afterward did I realize that it was mostly the surprise of being hit and not the actual impact that caused me to fall down."

A German doctor who examined Craig afterward said that without the vest, the chances of surviving a shot so close to a critical part of his anatomy (he was struck only half an inch from his aorta) wouldn't rate comment.

Six Helsinki SWAT team members were saved in a hostage situation that ended when a bank robber blew himself and one of his hostages up. It caught the attention of the entire Finnish nation in August 1986. Having been cornered during the robbery, the man took eleven hostages and demanded a car, which, after a long parley, was provided. He warned the cops that he had twenty pounds of explosives and would detonate the charge if they approached.

They didn't believe him. Six specially trained police officers moved in. The robber triggered the device, resulting in a huge explosion. He and the remaining hostage were killed. The six SWAT members survived metal and glass fragments because their body armor offered good protection. For security reasons, their names were never released.

There are new Richard Davis developments in this field, including lightweight, specially hardened, three-sixteenth-of-an-inch-thick steel inserts that can take the full impact of either a Kalashnikov bullet or that of the more powerful 7.62 x 51mm NATO rifle. His new company, Central Lake Armor Express, supplied 80,000 of these plates to the newly reconstituted Iraqi police and army units in 2004–05.

Davis is astonished that it took so long for someone to develop the concept. History has shown, he says, that man has always made an effort to protect himself. First he used skins, and later skins together with hardened shells. The Zulus so perfected cattle-hide shields that in the nineteenth century they were able to take on Britain's redcoat best.

Millennia before there was malleable bronze armor, initially worn by the Ancient Greeks, and then by Roman legions. The Vikings arrived in the Western Isles with chain mail, which the Crusaders copied and took to Palestine.

In Napoleonic times, their innovation was to lay thirty to sixty layers of silk under thin iron plates to create protection that only the richest of the rich could afford. Silk was expensive and had to be brought overland from China, since a sea route to the East had not yet been navigated. While such protection might have halted the large-diameter, relatively slow and softer lead bullets fired from blunderbusses, it wouldn't stop the high velocity "smokeless" powder rifles introduced in the 1890s.

Weight plus tensile strength were the dominant factors—very much as they are today. The extra ten or so pounds was an unwelcome encumbrance to anybody having to march halfway across Spain in the Napoleonic Peninsula Wars—or for that matter, all the way to Moscow.

The first modern flak jackets, as we know them today (which are vaguely similar to those being worn by our troops in Iraq and Afghanistan), were primitively effective. In the 1930s they were manufactured of nylon and subsequently used in World War II by aircrews.

According to Sir Arthur Conan Doyle, the British had experimented with body armor in the Kaiser's War but rejected the idea in the belief that it was cowardly—which on the face of it, Davis commented, was absurd.

"Anybody who has protection and doesn't use it," says Davis today, "isn't thinking right. And because there were many experienced policemen in the early days who regarded body armor as 'sissy stuff,' there were also many more deaths in the line of duty in the old days than were necessary."

Even today, he states, there are cops who go on duty without protection, although most police departments supply the stuff free of charge. "Consequently, when they get shot, more often than not they die."

In the months following his ventilation by three young men in a Detroit alley, Davis began to take a serious look at what he could do to protect himself if he came under fire again. He checked on the equipment then being issued to US forces in Vietnam, and before that, in Korea, where experiments were conducted on the first nylon ballistic plates for infantrymen. He also spoke to manufacturers about synthetic fibers, DuPont included.

By now, because his uninsured pizza shop in northeast Detroit had burned down, he'd taken a job as a security guard, and that involved a lot of night work. Also, he had recently married and his wife, Karen, was pregnant.

"I was so broke that if a trip around the world cost two dollars, I wouldn't have been able to get out of sight," he laughs today.

He knew how vulnerable the average security man was, especially in isolated industrial areas. That set him to experimenting with steel plates for cover. His own encounter with shooters gave him motivation. To paraphrase Boswell, that experience marvelously focused the mind.

Davis enclosed two plates, weighing a hefty five pounds each, in a cotton carrier Karen had sewn together for him. He slung this rig over his shoulders and hoped for the best. Weight didn't allow for the plates to be more than eight by ten inches: one in the front and the other covering his back.

"It was a strange feeling," he recalled. "Suddenly I had a secret protection. I wasn't Superman, but I felt a lot more secure than before."

Two months later Davis had worked out the basics of unobtrusive soft body armor that could be worn under a shirt or a jacket. Vests became so discreet that when cops wear them under a uniform shirt, they are difficult to spot.

It took him another six months to mass-produce the world's first concealable vests that would absorb the full impact of a medium caliber handgun fired at close range. Made of soft nylon, the cloth was cut to shape on Karen's kitchen table with nineteen layers stitched together by hand—front and back—with a three-dollar awl.

His first official United States patent #3,783,449 was granted in January 1973. Several months before that, Richard Davis registered his first save. The vest was worn by Gary Boiger, a member of a Detroit Police Department (DPD) undercover decoy group named STRESS, an acronym for Stop the Robbers and Enjoy Safe Streets.

Boiger survived a murder attempt a couple of months after he got his vest. In civilian clothes, he was assigned to carry an empty gasoline can in a notoriously volatile area. He'd been at it about fifteen minutes when half a dozen thugs tried to jump him. One of them rammed an eight-inch combat blade into his chest. It didn't penetrate the protective layers and Boiger suffered only bruises. However, his colleagues shot two of the criminals.

A month later, on the night of May 17, 1973, Officer Ronald Jagielski, a uniformed narcotics officer, also of the DPD, together with several other agents carried out a bust. As he was about to enter a suspect residence, a shot rang out. It hit him square in the chest. A .38 caliber slug was taken out of his chest afterward.

On May 21, only four days later, Bob Simmons of the East St. Louis Police Department was in a shoot-out in which he took the blast of a 12-gauge shotgun. Loaded with 00 buckshot, it hit him from a distance of about thirty feet and, as he says, certainly took the wind out of his sails. But Simmons was unhurt. His commanding officer wrote to Davis afterward, commending his vest and saying that the officer would have been dead without it.

In police circles, whether in Britain, Australia, or America, the word gets around—and it certainly did thirty-five years ago. Suddenly there was talk in police departments everywhere about "bulletproof" vests.

Davis says that no product is actually *bulletproof.* The term is a misnomer. "What is made by man can be destroyed by man," posits Davis. Survival is a function of the caliber of the gun and the thickness and resilience of the body armor.

"Obviously, what we were producing then wouldn't stop a rifle bullet. We've got effective body armor today that will achieve that objective, but it took years of research to get there.

"Also, nothing that a man can strap onto his body will halt the impact of a .50 caliber round designed specifically to go through World War I tank armor. Fortunately when we started in the early 1970s, we were faced with lesser calibers, up to .357 magnum.

"What was important then," he suggested, "is that those first vests that came off Karen's kitchen table were doing an exemplary job of saving lives."

And with that, a brand new industry was created. Adding a 20 percent margin for profit, Richard and Karen Davis sold their first primitive concealable nylon body armor for fifty dollars each. As many of the survivors of those early hits will recall today, it was the best fifty bucks ever spent by American policemen and women.

Only two months later, Officer Jerry Blair of Louisville, Kentucky, responded to a "shots fired" call. A man had shot his father, and when ordered to put down his gun, he shot Blair in the chest at short range. Though winded, this policeman was able to shoot back and bring down his assailant. In his after-action report he said that his vest had absorbed three-dozen shotgun pellets.

From a few dozen vests a month, production soon became a hand-over-fist scramble of receiving orders, making, and dispatching them. Within a short time, the Davis family was hard-pressed to cope. A year later, they were selling that many sets a day to police units across America. That culminated two decades later in orders in the tens of thousands from police departments in Los Angeles, New York, Chicago, and elsewhere.

Davis' sales pitch in his first brochures was simple, and, as it turned out, astonishingly effective: "We've got the answer, but not to everything. Nothing can make you immortal. But Second Chance can prevent about seventy-five percent of all police killings and critical woundings."

At the same time, said Davis, even body armor would not stop all police deaths. About one in four cops, vest or no vest, still faced death from a multitude of threats. "They get into terrible car accidents, are crushed or burned to death in fires. Some of them fall off buildings, which can be equally traumatic." Delmar Rhodes of Danville, Illinois, had the impressions of his body armor tattooed on his body after he survived a fifty-four-foot drop. Whatever takes place in the line of duty, Davis adds with grim satisfaction, "is the nature of the job, and if it's the vest that saves you, chalk one up for the good guys."

By now Second Chance was also selling abroad with large orders for a range of body armor from countries such as Germany, the Philippines, and even some Islamic states such as Saudi Arabia, Abu Dhabi, and Dubai. Soon Davis was visiting these countries himself, usually performing his trademark demonstration, shooting himself in the stomach at point-blank range with a .44 magnum revolver.

When he turned the gun inward toward his own chest in Dubai—in the presence of the ruling Crown Prince and in the company of members of his armed forces—he was presented with a gold Rolex watch. As Davis recalls, he followed bits of the discussion after the event and it seemed that the Crown Prince had won a bet with one of his skeptical generals.

If Richard Davis was the innovative whiz kid of American law enforcement in the 1970s and 1980s, it was the country's motor industry a decade before that produced Kevlar, a remarkably versatile space-age material that eventually became the standard for concealable body armor.

This was 1965, and Elvis, the Beatles, Carnaby Street, and free love were in. Lyndon B. Johnson had stopped bombing North Vietnam and wanted to talk, while Frank Borman and James Lovell made their 206 orbits in Gemini 7.

The year 1965 was a time when you could live well in modest circumstances. The median price of a family home was $21,500 while the Dow Jones touched a magnificent high of 969. It cost five cents to post a letter. Most important, gasoline was twenty-five cents a gallon.

It was also the era of fine-tuning and building bigger, better, and faster motor vehicles. There were powerful lobbies, inside government and out, to build new roads on which cars could travel 150 miles an hour.

Ford, General Motors, and Chrysler loved the idea; they wanted to build 500-horsepower cars that could run on those roads. The idea was cherished by concrete makers, engineering concerns, realty firms, labor unions, and Washington lobbyists and lawyers—all of whom visualized an industrial boom like no other.

But then, oops, there was a hitch.

While it might be a wonderful idea to have cars going almost a quarter the speed of sound for eight- or ten-hour stretches at a time, Firestone and the others had yet to produce a tire that could take that kind of stress. Heat and centrifugal forces at that speed would melt nylon and rip the tires apart. Neither natural nor synthetic rubber could do the job.

So, the DuPont corporation produced a remarkably tough, strong, and heat-resistant aramid called Kevlar. Richard Davis considers this invention as significant to the body armor industry as the jet engine was to aviation.

"It was what the publicity folk would call super-strong . . . ideal for the kind of tires these people had in mind, envisioning speeds of two hundred miles an hour or more." Also, he added, "Stephanie Kwolek, a lovely, unassuming little lady—she was a chemist at DuPont—provided both the inspiration and the perspicacity that went into its development.

"In fact, she put a yellow-colored material which they first called Fiber B, and only later Kevlar, on the map. Years later, my wife and I were invited to a new DuPont factory in Virginia. We had our photo taken with Stephanie, which I still have in my office."

A Dutch company developed a similar invention called Twaron, which some international body armor manufacturers like to use as an alternative when DuPont's prices become exploitative.

Then, to spoil everything, along comes the 1973 Arab-Israeli Yom Kippur War, which puts the kibosh on all these elaborate plans. Not only that, but OPEC, the Organization of Petroleum Exporting Countries, instituted an oil embargo—with the result that gas prices doubled, if you could find any. Months later, still more of the unthinkable happened when Congress enacted its fifty-five-miles-an-hour speed limit on all American roads.

These events and their consequences brought all Kevlar development to a halt. Overnight, the DuPont management—having poured umpteen millions of dollars into aramid research—was left holding a yellow "white elephant" for which there appeared to be no large-volume practical use.

Enter Richard Davis. Aware that Kevlar had passed the experimental stage and that quite a lot of the thread had been run off and woven into fabric, he asked for and was given half a roll to do with as he pleased. Someone at DuPont must have been hoping for a miracle because certainly, there was nobody else interested. The chemical giant was contemplating cutting its losses and closing the Kevlar line.

Davis: "Big companies are like that. They will spend millions and if they don't achieve the desired result, they'll close up shop in that department and move on.

"So I made some Kevlar pads and started testing them with live-fire rounds. The results were fantastic. The stuff was more than twice as strong as nylon. In fact, it had almost two-and-a-half times the strength, which meant that it had more than twice the stopping power. Here we're not talking light stuff; I was using the full gamut, 9mm, .45 ACP, and magnum calibers like .357s and .44s."

Meanwhile, the saves were beginning to add up. Among those who survived shootings while wearing Davis' body armor was San Francisco motorcycle cop Bob Hooper, who'd spotted a vehicle with a noisy muffler. He stopped the car. Approaching the driver's side, as he had a thousand times before, he took a .38 bullet an inch below the center of his heart. Shaken, but alive and with no injuries to speak of, Hooper radioed in, and the shooter was arrested later by fellow officers. Hooper was Davis' thirteenth save: thirteen was no longer his unlucky number.

Two near-stabbings followed. Zac Hartman of Santa Rosa, California, took a broken beer bottle in his back with no result, and Jim Indoranto of Chicago survived the downward thrust of a four-inch blade into his chest.

William Fisher of St. Joseph, Missouri, has an even better story for his grandchildren. He was stabbed in the chest with a heavy metal Afro comb, his vest taking the thrust.

There was also Jim Krakowiecki who made an unusual Save #7 by stopping a seventy-five-pound windowpane with his body armor. It hit him square in the chest. Without his vest, this sheet of plate glass, which had fallen some distance, would probably have cut him in half.

For his save, Chicago Officer John Faris was making door-to-door inquiries. In one tenement block a woman answered the door, and in answer to his questions, she grabbed a pitchfork and slammed it into his chest. Shaken, but otherwise unhurt because the sharp tines didn't penetrate, Faris grabbed the pitchfork from his attacker and arrested her.

Strangely, his first thought was, "Where the hell did she find a pitchfork in downtown Chicago?"

It's rare for somebody to get up in the morning and say, "Right. Today I'm going to kill Officer Jones." Most times the shooting of a cop is a split-second decision. The criminal is taken by surprise and tries to use a firearm to get out of a situation that would otherwise land him in jail.

Theophilus (Theo) Mixon of Highland Park, Michigan, had that kind of run-in when he became Davis' Save #158 in the late 1970s. It is worth mentioning that in a near-fatal car accident a quarter century later, it was again his vest that prevented him from becoming a statistic. Mixon came out of that one barely alive, his chest having taken the full impact of the steering wheel in a head-on.

In the earlier incident, Mixon was on a one-man patrol in Detroit's Highland Park when he spotted a prostitute's john driving a large, white-walled Cadillac making a pickup. As the girl jumped into the car, he pulled in front of the vehicle and asked the driver for ID.

Presumed to be reaching for his wallet, the man pulled out a .357 magnum and shot Mixon in the midriff. Fortunately, his five-year-old vest wasn't penetrated by the 158gr hollow-point bullet.

Mixon retaliated instinctively, getting off six rounds, four of which hit the target. Two went into the would-be-cop-killer's chest, mortally wounding him.

As the criminal slumped back in his seat, his last act was to put the car into gear and slam his foot down on the gas pedal. Then he died, with the vehicle heading down the street out of control. It banged into three parked cars before stopping. Mixon had iced one of America's most dangerous professional narcotics hit men. At the time he was wanted by the police and the FBI for eleven known murders.

In a re-enactment of the crime in one of the films that Richard Davis made on Second Chance Saves, Mixon played himself. When Davis said something about the killer still causing trouble even after he'd been shot dead, Mixon, in a deep reverberating voice, growled the perfect retort: "Well, he won't be causin' no mo'."

Clarence Jones of Hays, Virginia, was fortunate. Police were called to a domestic disturbance. A "shots fired" situation quickly turned into what is known as a *barricaded gunman*. Negotiation produced no results, so tear gas was used. The gunman came out with a loaded, sawed-off 12-gauge shotgun and the first man in was Jones, who took a full on hit in the chest.

It was a powerful blast, enough to blow pockets and buttons off his shirt. The shooter ducked back and moved from room to room firing from just about every window in the building.

The gunfight went on for five minutes, which, by shoot-out standards, is long. Undeterred, Jones tried again, and once more the crazed gunman unloaded on him. A short while later a police sniper fired a single shot and killed him.

Jones emerged from the event with shotgun pellets in every part of his body that hadn't been protected by body armor. He took stray pellet hits in his face, head, groin, back, arms, and legs. But, as he told Davis a year later, "I'm alive!"

Sometimes there are unusual scrapes with death. Save #828 took place in Buffalo County, Nebraska. Deputy Sheriff Chad Hunt had pulled over a vehicle in Kearney. His chief, Sheriff Neil Miller, told Richard Davis that as Hunt approached the vehicle, a male suspect stepped out and fired a .357 magnum, hitting the officer between his nipples. Knocked back by the impact, Hunt was able to struggle with the shooter as he approached for the kill. He forced the gun out of his assailant's hands and killed him with his own weapon.

The shock from being hit at close range with a .357 magnum broke Hunt's skin and flesh, but the bullet never penetrated. It was later found lodged in his vest.

There was also the New Jersey man who was angry with his wife for undercooking their Christmas ham. Neighbors called police after a domestic dispute became ugly. The first officer to respond was Dana Saxton of the Collingwood, New Jersey, police.

Entering the house, he was hit by a blast from a .44 Special handgun square in the chest, causing him to back outside. Again, concealable body armor saved the officer. A three-hour standoff followed, after which the shooter was arrested.

Saxton, who is Save #438, would joke afterward about the two promises that he made his wife when he married her.

"I told her that I would always call if I wasn't going to be home by five. And, I'll always, *always* wear your bulletproof vest." Body armor was her idea. She'd bought it for him when they were still engaged.

Officer Bryan Power of LaFeria, Texas, also answered a domestic call for a lunatic fielding a 12-gauge shotgun. He had no police record—not even a traffic ticket in sixty years; but he was very clearly deranged. Apparently he'd flipped because his common-law wife had washed their teenager's clothes before doing his.

When Power arrived at the home, alone in his cruiser, the man's wife and daughter had taken refuge behind the family car. "He's trying to kill us, officer; he wants to murder us," she shouted. "Terrified as hell," the policeman recalls.

Trying to calm the wife, telling her to stay down and take it easy, the next thing Power hears is *Blam!* A solid 12-gauge slug slammed into his upper left shoulder. While his vest did stop the slug from killing him, there was some blunt trauma when it forced fibers into his skin. He was also knocked down by the blast. As he told the story later, he was saved by a raggedy old Second Chance Model Y he'd bought from a fellow officer. Though ten years old, it did the trick.

In the meantime, Power was cut off from his car and had no way to call for back-up. Instead, he sought cover, crawling on hands and knees toward the vehicle behind which the hysterical woman and her daughter cowered. Doing so, he took a grazing shot in his buttocks, from which the slug tore a strip off his hip.

Having reached the two women who, by now, were terrified beyond reason, he tried to calm them. Somehow, he realized, he had to end this confrontation as he was worried about a numbness spreading down his left arm. It affected his shooting hand.

As Power told Richard Davis afterward, the two females could barely be controlled. "Though they were standing behind the car, they were exposed and the man was shooting," he explained.

"I ordered them down, to which the mother complied; but her daughter remained on her feet. When she wouldn't listen, I whacked her across the back of her knees, which caused her legs to collapse out from under her. That happened one-tenth of a second before the stepfather took another shot. He hit her, but the 12-gauge slug struck her on her way down, skimming across the top of her skull and taking a clump of hair and a small piece of her scalp with it."

Had the daughter been standing where she'd been an instant before, her head would almost certainly have been split open by the solid, one-ounce chunk of lead.

Power fired more than a dozen rounds with his police .357 magnum, two of which, it was found later, hit the shooter in the torso. Quite suddenly everything went quiet. Then they spotted smoke coming out of the garage.

The shooter had made his way there, where he kept a lawnmower and gasoline. He poured half a tank over his head and set himself on fire. One left-leaning Texas rag later ran the headline: "Police stand by while man burns to death."

Noted American gun writer and active part-time police captain Massad Ayoob has done a series of studies on body armor saves. His research reveals that not all such incidents are related either to shootings or to stabbings. Many policemen have been saved when their body armor absorbed the full brunt of an impact during a car crash.

He stresses that some 40 percent of saves came from vehicle wrecks, which was an estimate he made after talking to almost a thousand cops. "Others fell from great heights, or were hurled considerable distances. It was their vests that saved them," he told me.

"Sergeant David Morganthal, an officer in my PD at Hooksett, New Hampshire, was making a car stop when a drunk driver hit him as he stood alongside his patrol car. He was thrown some thirty feet and was in the hospital for a while, though he suffered virtually no trauma to the torso." Ayoob, having spoken to the doctors on the case, says they were in agreement that Morganthal would have been crushed to death had he not been wearing Kevlar. Notably, that save is not even listed in Richard Davis' Saves Club.

"So," says Ayoob, "I got into the habit of wearing it all the time, and I still do so religiously while I'm working for the police department. In chilly weather (of which we have a lot in the Northeast) I got to putting it on anyway; it just became a convenience, which is a good idea in sometimes-icy New England, where some visitors are not familiar with the dynamics of driving on ice and snow.

"I'd feel awfully stupid in my last seconds on earth, realizing that I had left my steering wheel–proof vest at home if I did end up in such an accident."

* * *

Possibly the most unusual save of all took place in Mexico. It involved a still-unnamed American DEA officer who was working undercover with two *Federales* in a drug sting in a remote northern part of the country.

The bust was about to go down when the two men turned to the Gringo and said they now had to kill him, adding that they were very sorry because he was actually quite a nice guy. They had their orders "from the other side," they told him: they were apparently in the pay of a major drug lord.

One of the Mexicans shot the DEA agent twice in the chest with a .38 Super auto, which some cognoscenti like to think of as a kind of 9mm magnum. The shock and surprise knocked him down but didn't incapacitate him because, dutifully, he wore concealable body armor. The American promptly pulled out his own gun, killed the shooter, and wounded and arrested the other Hispanic who later expressed great surprise at the officer's instant resurrection.

Another Mexican Save, #600, involved DEA agent Kent Alexander at the airport in Apatzingan, Michoacan. The American and several CENDRO agents were passing the airstrip when Alexander noticed an airplane with ID numbers that matched those on an aircraft raided in Campus, Sonora, a year before.

The group stopped, approached the plane, and Alexander's K9 made a positive alert for the presence of narcotics. When its door was forced open, a quarter-ton of cocaine was discovered, at which point they spotted a small van speeding off the field and gave chase.

When the vehicle eventually stopped, the driver and his passenger ran from the van. As Alexander left his vehicle, thinking the situation was under control, the back door of the van was suddenly thrown open and two automatic weapons—an AK-47 and a MiniMac—opened fire at the DEA operator and his friends.

Approximately eighty rounds were fired by the criminals before Alexander and compadres were able to neutralize their attackers, killing all four of them. The American took six hits, all of them from the AK. Three went into his right leg and three lodged in his soft body armor.

The fact that the bullets first hit his vehicle door before striking him made all the difference.

On a more confidential basis, Richard Davis was told not long ago of a US Marine who had been working in what was then still Noriega's Panama. His job was undercover and he was lured to a nighttime meeting with two contacts at a remote spot in the interior along the canal. Having done what he came for, he turned to return to his car when one of the men shot him twice in the back. Totally unfazed and possibly anticipating the unexpected, the Marine turned around and killed both men with his .45 ACP. Then, instead of returning to base to report two bodies, he quietly dumped them both into the canal and by doing so avoided the rigmarole of an official inquiry.

More recently, Davis was accosted at the Las Vegas Shot Show by somebody who saw his name on his lapel badge. When the man had established that he was talking to *the* Richard Davis, he furiously pumped his hand and thanked him for saving his life. When our inventor asked him where it had all taken place, the man, embarrassed, backed off.

Davis bumped into him a couple of days later and the guy apologized—which was when he told Davis that the incident had taken place when he'd been entrusted with a huge parcel of diamonds "in some foreign country." A couple of the man's so-called colleagues tried to rob him, shooting him in the chest.

As he explained, the eyes of the two attackers became as wide as saucers when, by some miracle, he didn't drop into the dirt after taking two serious hits in the chest. Instead, he hauled out the pistol he'd been carrying in his belt and killed them both. The diamond courier was out of the country, with his $15 million worth of precious stones, a few hours later.

Though Richard pressured him, he never did say where the shooting had taken place. He suspects that it might have been in Africa somewhere.

There was also The Massacre that Never Happened. Save #377 was police officer Jim Martin of Mena, Arkansas, perhaps a half hour drive from the Oklahoma state line.

In a routine stop of a weaving pickup that was headed for a shopping center in Fayetteville, Arkansas, Martin ordered the driver out of his vehicle. Somebody who was not only big but tall as well, and who must have weighed about four hundred pounds, confronted him. As Martin recalled, he had arms like cords, and he was very drunk.

The drunk was terminally ill and having come all the way from Texas, he was dead set on going out—as it was phrased in a document found afterward in his cab—"in a blaze of glory." Also discovered in his vehicle was a semi-automatic "tommy gun" type .45 carbine together with enough ammunition to kill hundreds of people. Afterward, the police recovered more than five hundred rounds of ammo in thirty-shot magazines from his truck.

The authorities concluded that had the man, named Howard K. Massey, not been pulled over by Officer Martin, he would probably have made it to Fayetteville, loaded all his guns, ammo, and spare magazines in a duffle bag, walked into the shopping mall, and slaughtered as many people as he could.

It would have taken a while for a SWAT team to reach the area. Thus what should have been the largest massacre of innocents by a lone gunman in American history never happened.

Another drunk, this time in Missoula, Montana, caused local cop Chris Schultz to almost lose his life.

Having just cleared the station from a DUI arrest, the policeman got a call to respond to a domestic. Not the most cherished of callouts, domestic disturbances have led to the shooting of hundreds of American officers over the years.

Most times, those involved are drunk, and the offender is violent—sometimes uncontrollably so. A few might have had run-ins with the cops; others might be on parole. They frequently turn on the investigating officer, and quite often with deadly vehemence.

In this case, as Schultz approached the area, he spotted a man and woman on a street corner. They were in the middle of a loud, nasty argument and the man was slapping the woman around. The officer had neither stopped nor activated his lights when the man abruptly turned toward the police cruiser and fired several rounds with his .357 magnum handgun. Five rounds were later found to have hit the vehicle—one of which entered through the windshield and hit the policeman's vest.

Quickly improvising, Schultz put his car in gear, gunned the engine, and drove right over his attacker. Having satisfied himself that the woman was okay, he pulled the offender out from underneath his vehicle and cuffed him. What emerged afterward was that the man was trying to kill a cop as an "entrance exam" into an outlaw motorcycle gang—and thus was recorded Save #382.

Similarly, but with more serious consequences, Jack Mendendorp of Kent County, Michigan, became Richard Davis' Save #186. He answered a domestic squabble that involved a long gun and that almost ended his career as state trooper.

Having dismounted in the driveway, he was confronted by an irate husband with a .30-06 rifle. Outgunned, he turned toward his car to radio for help when a shot rang out and slammed into the front fender, just below the driver's doorpost. The fragmented bullet ricocheted to where Mendendorp stood and knocked him back into his cruiser. Jagged pieces of metal tore into his body, destroying police equipment inside the car.

The largest piece of the bullet was stopped by his vest from entering the policeman's chest, alongside his right nipple.

Then, occasionally, miracles happen. Gary Laird of the Corpus Christi, Texas, PD found himself on the ground with a fifteen-year-old prowler standing over him saying, "You're a dead pig!" Laird was about to be shot for the fifth time with his own gun that he'd somehow lost in the altercation, which underscores unofficial Police Premise Number One: *never, ever* underestimate your adversary.

Fired at very close range, three .38 caliber bullets had already crashed into Officer Laird's chest and been stopped by his vest. The fourth hit his unprotected right thigh, causing a serious wound.

Aware that death was imminent, Laird lunged desperately toward his assailant's legs and had almost managed to scramble through when the fifth and last bullet cut through his arm and went to his chest. That was also stopped by his body armor. Photos released afterward show deep brownish-yellow bruises on Laird's chest where there might otherwise have been holes.

Laird was released after four days in Spohn Hospital and the four saves were counted as one, #194. Laird's single comment afterward was, "The vest is what it's all about."

Within a year, as reports of these and other saves began to come in, it was clear to Richard Davis that he had created a winner.

To ensure that he was made aware of lives saved, he let it be known that anybody who had taken a hit on his Second Chance vest would be issued a new one free of charge. This policy was not because the vest was unable to take future possible hits but because after the shooting, the armor remained evidence, which might be used against dead criminals' families in wrongful death lawsuits.

As has since been observed in dozens of legal actions, if the would-be cop-killer went to trial, the bullet in the vest would become the prosecutor's best friend.

Even years later, when the criminal comes up for parole, the bullet-laden vest can counter his lawyer's no-harm-done argument. As the company began to grow, Davis was also able to invite many of his saves to Northern Michigan for a celebratory visit, usually with their wives and kids along. Photos would be taken, new vests presented, often within an hour or two of the officer's arrival.

More important, friendships were cemented—some of which have grown to become close enough to have persevered over time. When the burley black cop Theo Mixon was almost killed in the fall of 2004, one of the first people he called from the hospital was old buddy Richard Davis.

Davis was also aware that in the wrong hands, concealable body armor could cause harm. Consequently, it was company policy, from the beginning, to sell vests only to recognized law enforcement agencies. For the first ten years he was able to keep knowledge of concealable body armor from the general public.

While Second Chance under Davis continued that policy, several firms making concealable body armor had no qualms about selling their products to anyone who had the money to buy.

One immediate consequence was that, with time—and as body armor demonstrated its potential many times over—professional criminals began to acquire "bulletproof" vests for themselves. Cops these days will deliver a head shot where indicated, aware that the suspect might be wearing protection. We also have the example of two hardened criminals wearing body armor and taking on a large number of Los Angeles cops in one of the most celebrated bank robberies of all time. It has since become known in police lore as The North Hollywood Shoot-Out.

Not very long before this development, Save #54 was registered. It belonged to Steve Gazdik of Chardon, Ohio, who was hit twice in the chest and once in the arm with a .357 magnum. The shooting might have been terminal had Gazdik not worn his vest. More seriously, he was shot with his own service revolver.

While attempting to arrest a "docile" dope-head, a so-called old customer who had never before given any resistance, Gazdik's gun was wrestled away by the man who suddenly unleashed an incredible surge of strength. This sometimes happens when a person's mind is fueled by peculiar substances.

The first bullet stopped by his vest was fired with the barrel only an inch away from his chest. For the second, the distance was about four inches.

As Richard Davis points out, of all the individual guns in the world, the gun with which a cop is mostly likely to be shot will be his own, and second, his or her partner's firearm. Official records show that about a fifth of all on-duty shootings involve the officer's own gun.

Case in point: Not long after Davis had established his company at Central Lake, which lies four or five hours north of Detroit, a Michigan cop told his buddies that he didn't need body armor. He was pretty verbose during a roll call, telling everybody, "I got my trusty M-29 nickel-plated .44 magnum, with its beautiful four-inch barrel, and fast-draw holster. I've got *this* baby to protect me."

The man was murdered the following week, shot in the back with his own weapon after a felon had crept up from behind and hit him over the head. He would almost certainly have survived the onslaught had he been wearing a vest because criminals rarely hang about to admire their handiwork after shooting a cop.

Michigan State Police Sergeant Bill Stenbeck, one of Richard Davis' old friends from Detroit, told him a couple of years after he had been producing body armor in quantity—and still at the low rate of fifty dollars a vest—that a Michigan State

Trooper had been shot dead by a .380 bullet in the heart. Sadly, he'd been intending for some time to buy body armor but never got around to it.

"Felt that it couldn't happen to him," Stenbeck recalled.

Not so with former officer Melvin Johnson, one of the original "brothers" who was entrusted to secretly transport two million dollars worth of diamonds from Dayton, Ohio, to Chicago. Once inside the Chicago loop, Johnson was attacked by three big-time pros, also African-American. Shot in the stomach part of his vest with a .357 magnum, the courier was able to return fire, wounding the man who'd shot him.

He didn't go down and the attackers watched in disbelief as Johnson continued to fire back. They had clearly seen him take a hit and he remembers the incredulity on their faces. After that, all parties involved decided to go their separate ways. That was Richard Davis' Save #55.

From the beginning, marketing had been a priority on Davis' list of essentials in getting the "save" message out.

While he was the first to produce a brochure on his life-enhancing product, Davis was also ahead of everybody else in getting out a range of videos that described—sometimes in very graphic detail—how actual saves had taken place. Instruction was part of staying alive on the job.

His first video was a rather unglamorous production titled *Second Chance versus the UAPs*. An unbridled satire on the Symbionese Liberation Army, or SLA, the initials referred to Unorganized Asshole Punks.

Davis: "At the time the SLA seemed a pretty formidable crowd to some cops. They'd been labeled terrorists and that had a somewhat debilitating effect on the minds of some of the younger officers. We made the point in the film that it wasn't the SLA you had to be wary of, but rather the sixteen-year-old psycho on the street corner with his Saturday Night Special." Filmed in 1975, it depicted the experiences of five cops who had been shot and survived.

Second Chance versus Magnum Force followed in 1988. A two-hour film, it covered ten officers who had all been shot with magnums, and each one of them ended up participating in the actual film shoot.

The final, classic film, *Second Chance versus the Cop Killers*, included most of the first two videos, plus twenty new attempted murders. It was to become a seven-hour, forty-five-minute marathon and bears the distinction of being the first of its kind. The film showed not only how cops were almost killed, but it included interviews about what had gone wrong—or could have been done better. It became a critical learning experience for most viewers.

That the film achieved cult status is an indication of what Davis has done to orientate the American law enforcement community to the use of body armor. One of the results is that there are few police or prison guards who don't wear vests today.

Davis always gave his films away for free. He'd do so at the annual American Society of Law Enforcement Training (ASLET) or International Association of Law Enforcement Firearms Instructors (IALEFI) shows in Las Vegas and other venues where he was a guest speaker.

"We worked out that to produce a quality brochure would cost us about two dollars and fifty cents a copy, if color was used. An ordinary tape—even the one that was hours long—cost us about three dollars apiece . . . Eighty percent of brochures don't make it back to the office, while people like to hold onto videos, especially if they're entertaining. Mine was about saving lives: about a thousand saves to date."

Richard Davis estimates that roughly forty thousand of his films went out, and that even today there are few police departments without at least one copy somewhere in the office.

CHAPTER 3

Two Hits for History

Richard Davis was shot twice by felons while delivering a pizza. He took a hit in the leg and a bullet lodged next to his skull. But he gave as good as he got; two of his attackers wound up in the hospital with gunshot wounds. Afterward, Davis lay there, pondering how to improve the odds of cheating death.

There was nothing random about Richard Davis being shot twice on July 18, 1969, the day after Neil Armstrong and Apollo 11 blasted off for the moon.

The stick-up of this pizza store owner who was also its deliveryman—which usually netted between twenty and thirty dollars per heist—had been planned. Further, it resembled a robbery from eight months before. In the previous mugging, the same bunch had robbed Davis' fiancée, Karen Troskey, together with one of her girlfriends, who was driving.

As before, the incident happened late on a Friday. The robbers had phoned in an identical order: two large pepperoni and ham. They asked that the pizzas be delivered.

"I'll never forget the address," said Davis. "It was 19379 Pennington Road. Not too bright, to do it the same way. And in the same area."

There were two significant differences. The first time the women offered no resistance and there were no shots fired. While only about thirty dollars was taken, one of the attackers grabbed Karen by her wrists. She struggled free before he could drag her into the darkness. The incident was chilling and lingered in Davis' mind.

Karen Troskey was specific about the men who had robbed her and her friend. "One was a tall and skinny black male, perhaps seventeen or eighteen years old with a nickel-plated automatic pistol," she still remembers three decades later.

Since pizza store robberies were increasing, and because firearms had been used in the hold-up, Richard Davis considered his options. As he recalled, the police had been unable to do much about this kind of crime in northwest Detroit, "and, let's face it, Detroit can be tense late at night, especially if you're delivering things and have cash for change in your pocket."

A few months before, the night manager at Farmer Jack's Supermarket—not far from Davis' location at 15724 West Seven Mile—had opened six cash registers and a couple of safes at gunpoint and handed robbers more than $12,000. He thought that by offering no resistance and yielding to them, they'd take the loot and run. But the robbers killed him anyway, with a single shot behind the head.

"It was a callous killing, and it worried me, which is why I took to reading gun magazines. So I spent thirty bucks and bought myself a cut-rate .22 caliber, six-shot Harrington & Richardson Model 622 revolver with a six-inch barrel. I sawed it down to five inches, because the front sight was too big. A Colt .45 ACP, or one of the 9mm autos, would have been better, but cash was tight; the rimfire was all I could afford," Davis told me.

Once he'd bought the gun, he spent as much free time as he could at a range or in the woods or in a basement with .22 shorts, usually firing close and fast from the hip at one, two, or three targets at a time.

To further ease his own mind, and those of Karen and his parents, Davis kept a back-up gun in his store. This was a 16-gauge sawed-off shotgun with the stock cut away behind the pistol grip. Loaded with buckshot, it was like having a pair of jacks in a poker game. "Very good for openers, but don't count on winning a big hand with it . . ."

Fondly dubbed "Magic Pizza" by Davis, the shotgun would be illegal today. He was able to register it under a federal amnesty on Class III weapons due to the Gun Control Act of 1968, a measure aimed principally at legalizing weapons brought home by troops returning from World War II, Korea, and Vietnam.

The shotgun was concealed in a pizza box behind the counter, but when he took it along to deliver pizzas, it was stashed in a separate box at the bottom of the pile, within easy reach.

"So come July 18, it's a warm evening and I get a call for two pepperoni and ham pizzas and I scratch my head. Same order, same area, I told myself. These guys must be plain stupid if they think they can get away with it twice in a row, even eight months after the first attack."

The address wasn't in the best part of town, but it was active commercially. When he arrived, the building was dark.

"So, leaving the Ford Falcon, I slip the .22 I'd been carrying cross-draw in my belt so that it rests in my palm alongside my other hand, right under the pizza boxes."

When he rang the doorbell, no answer. A moment later he heard a rustle behind some bushes that lined the perimeter fence.

"Did you guys order a pizza?" Davis asked.

"Yeah. Bring it 'round the back," said one of the men who emerged into the half-light.

"My mind works quickly, and I suppose I could have dropped the boxes right there and made a dash for it. But I'd have to go past more bushes, and there could be someone waiting there. Also, Karen had counted four of them. Then what? I'd already decided it would be better for me to take my chances when I was ready for them [rather] than later, when I might not be.

"The first man turns and heads down the side of the house, and, with a wave of his arm indicates that I should follow. That I do and I find two more guys waiting for me in a kind of V formation, one of them a tall and skinny black man with a nickel-plated auto in his gun hand pointed directly at my face.

"Intentional or not, he makes sure I see his gun, obviously thinking he could stun me into inaction. But the immediate effect was that I knew I couldn't back out. *There is going to be shooting*, I told myself.

"The gang couldn't have been more than ten feet away, all of them standing on a knoll that was about a foot higher than where I was.

"Strangely, I wasn't stunned. I recall quite clearly that I suddenly went cold all over, accepting with an almost predetermined fatalism that I was on my own. Though my heart had been pounding like a jackhammer to begin with, it suddenly went normal, as if I had just awakened from sleep."

Davis recollected afterward that he felt no fear, just a calculated sense of anticipation. By now the man who was more than six feet tall and who was holding the gun had moved closer, to about five feet from him. His firearm glinted very clearly in the half-light and Davis could see that it was still aimed right between his eyes.

"He's surly and he's cocky at the same time, and by his attitude, I know he's going to use it if he gets any resistance from me."

Davis can remember the exact exchange of words. The tall skinny man said, "Step in the backyard; don't make any noise." Another in the group steps forward and makes a gesture that I should hand over everything.

"This was the kind of scenario I'd anticipated. It had already gone through my mind many times during months past, because Karen had been graphic about what happened to her when she faced these felons. She'd detailed how they came out from behind some bushes, and the almost total lack of streetlights.

"In my mind, I'd even reenacted what I'd do and I actually did so quite a few times. I determined from the start that I'd first fire two shots, one at the head and the other at the body of the person holding the weapon. Then I'd turn my attention to the others.

"But, the problem was that the Harrington & Richardson .22 held only six rounds and there were three of them. What if I missed? I asked myself whether there wasn't any other way out of this." At which point the gunman grew impatient with Davis' five-second delay. Watching only his hand, he saw the man's fingers tighten on the gun."

In less than two seconds Richard Davis had fired five shots, first at the gunman to his left, hitting him in the head, with another to the torso. He didn't even think about turning the .22 on the others; it was pure reflex. The pizza boxes went flying over his left shoulder.

"My first shot was beautiful. The bullet hit him on the side of his chin, going straight through his jaw. It emerged from his ear with some blood, just like you see in the movies. *Bam!*

"My second shot," as the police reconstructed it afterward, "hit him slap bang in the center of his chest. It turns out later it skidded off the edge of his sternum and missed his heart by about an inch. He fell backward with his arms flying, and I thought, shit! I've wasted a shot.

"Looking back, I realize now how your mind works when you face real danger . . . everything goes into overdrive, almost like slow motion."

Davis reacted a little too quickly for his third. It went wide, ending up between the two perps nearest him, missing them both.

"Number Two guy grabbed his stomach. To this day I don't know why, because he wasn't hit. I surmised he might have a weapon in his belt and was going for it. I didn't hesitate. My fourth shot hit him in the shoulder, which spun him round away from me. I fired again, and he took the .22 bullet square into the spine. If it hadn't hit bone, the bullet would have gone into his heart.

"That's two down. The third guy, bigger, with an Afro, takes off running and I've still got one shot left. So I turn toward him and aim for his head. I didn't know it then, because it came out in the police report afterward, but the bullet went right through his Afro. No damage, though."

The entire exchange went down so fast that the men responsible for the robbery complained afterward, when writing their confessions, that they had been shot at by a man firing a small machine-gun.

"That's a joke," exclaimed Davis. "They try to kill me and they *complain* when I defend myself with too much force!"

What happened next isn't altogether clear in Davis' mind. Satisfied that he'd neutralized an otherwise dangerous situation, and with his cylinder empty, he didn't need to linger. So he stepped back a pace or two. But as he turned to leave, a shot rang out and something hit his glasses and the side of his face.

The man with the nickel-plated auto lying prone on the ground had fired the gun. A split second later he hit Davis with another bullet in the back of his left thigh.

Partly blinded by blood streaming down his face, and helpless without his specs, Davis staggered back to the road, aware that wearing his nice though badly-stained white uniform, displayed under the neon light blinking on the Ford Falcon, placed him in a bad tactical situation. There was nothing to stop his attackers from coming for him. But they didn't.

"I imagine they didn't follow me because they hadn't been counting my shots. Very few shooters do when there are bullets flying. *But, I did!*

"I counted for good reason. With a small caliber weapon, I was at a disadvantage. I had to know at all times what my options were.

"If I was out of ammo, I'd have to take the gap, which is what I did that night, but perhaps a little too late."

One of America's top gun writers, Massad Ayoob, wrote a while back in his *Ayoob Files*, that in almost a thousand cases of high-volume fire that he'd examined carefully, he'd found only two cases in which the individual involved accurately counted his shots. Richard Davis, he tells us, is one of them.

Meantime Davis had been shot twice. He had no idea how bad his injuries were. He was aware that his thigh shot might have punctured an artery. Also, he was bleeding heavily from his head wound. He needed an ER. Back in his car, he cleared Pennington and headed straight for Mount Carmel, three miles way. He sped. He ran red lights.

"As I got to the area where I thought the hospital entrance was, I was confused by side streets, and wasn't sure which road led directly to Mount Carmel's ER. So I rolled up alongside a guy in a red Mustang, revving my engine, and he thinks I'm challenging him to a race. 'I've been shot,' I told him. 'Where's the hospital?'" With blood everywhere on his otherwise lily-white uniform, it was clear Davis wasn't lying.

Mister Red Mustang didn't hesitate. He shouted, "Follow me!"

At the ER entrance, a security guard put his hand up, palm out. He thought Davis was making a delivery. Then he too saw the blood.

"Go right in . . . Leave your car . . . Just get yourself inside. But give me the keys, so I can park for you," was his reaction, which worried Davis. Did he look *that* bad?

One of the first things Davis told the police when they got to the hospital a short while later was that he'd thrown the .22 under the front seat. They recovered it, and already squad cars had been dispatched to Pennington to find the criminals.

Initially they found only the dropped pizzas and blood stains.

• • •

The police did an extraordinarily good job that night. Davis told the cops he had shot two of his attackers and they picked them both up shortly afterward.

The robbers left, but they came back a short while later to fetch their eighteen-year-old buddy with a bullet in his back, still on the ground at the scene of the crime. They dragged him the few blocks to his mother's house, tossed him on the front steps, and rang the doorbell. Then they ran. His mother came to the door, saw her son, and started screaming.

When she calmed down, he told her he'd been driving around with his buddies when a car drove by with three white guys who shot him.

"Lordy!" she replied. "I'm calling the police."

"No, don't do that, Mama," he begged. But she did.

By the time the law arrived, the wounded man was already in an ambulance. Wounded or not, he was arrested and taken to hospital under armed guard. Partially crippled for the rest of his life, he lay on a gurney in the ER next to Davis.

Davis' injuries were superficial. The bullet under the skin in his head was cut out by the senior surgeon, and it was only as an afterthought that he told the doc he might also be wounded in the leg. Sure enough, when they turned him over, he was. An intern then spent a good half hour, with Davis under local anesthetic, probing his thigh for the second bullet.

The intern, as Davis remembers, was a nice little guy from Thailand who looked about fourteen. First he probed the bullet entrance hole—no luck. Then a portable X-ray machine was brought over and they took pictures.

Brilliant, thought Davis, here's solid geometry in action . . . They'll have it out in no time.

"We could all see the .25 bullet: it hadn't mushroomed or cut any major arteries but was lodged about three-and-a-half inches into my leg. So while the senior surgeon worked on the two stick-up men, the junior intern began to measure and cut in order to remove my non-critical .25 chunk of metal.

"This went on a while with him cutting and probing deeper and deeper, well past the area deadened by the local anesthetic they'd administered earlier. Obviously now I'm in big pain, and I'm almost biting the mattress as I lay there on my stomach.

"Finally the intern had a quick confab with his surgeon boss and I heard the older man say, 'Inches darn it. Not centimeters! This is America . . .'

"Having measured again, it was a case of slash and grab and the bullet emerged. The little guy was proud enough of his handiwork to show it to me and several other nurses and doctors in the ER, though they weren't particularly interested since for them it happened every night."

It is worth mentioning that something vaguely similar happened more than thirty years later when NASA realized that a Mars probe had been lost because of an error in English to metric conversion . . .

While Davis' leg wound caused him to limp for a couple of weeks, and he had to return to the hospital to change dressings, there were no after-effects. He was back on the range within a week.

In the following weeks, Davis became something of a semi-celebrity with area law enforcers.

Once it was established that four of his six shots had hit robbers, *in the dark*, he ended up with a sore right hand from shaking the hand of every Detroit policeman who came within greeting distance. They stopped him on the street to tell him what he'd done was fantastic. "We need more citizens like you," they'd say.

"Great shooting!" "You the man!" "Fantastic shot!" It was heartfelt. Everyone agreed that taking on armed robbers in an isolated area and in the dark, with a .22, was lunacy. He shouldn't be alive to talk about it.

As he admits even today, it wasn't all that surprising that he was being greeted like a hero, because the average policeman then was lucky to get one hit out of six. According to Massad Ayoob, the national police average with double-action revolvers is *less* than 25 percent.

Karen, Davis' future wife, wasn't told of the shooting until the following morning.

"I'd been asleep when he called in the middle of the night. He wasn't too specific, said that something had happened and that I shouldn't worry. He'd tell me in the morning. Of course, I went back to sleep.

"So in the morning, my mother's making breakfast, and the radio is on, and I hear that a pizza deliveryman has been shot. I thought, Oh my gosh! I knew immediately that it was Richard.

"A little while later the phone rings and it's Richard. He tells me everything, so much so that I'm late for work."

Three years later, running the fledgling company Second Chance Body Armor, Davis sold vests to two Detroit policemen. They remarked casually that they were the first responding officers to his crime scene back in '69, and that his pizzas tasted real good.

"Wait a minute!" Davis responded. "You talking about the two pizzas I was *supposed* to deliver?"

"Yeah," one of them answered matter-of-factly. "You'd taped them shut. Jumbled up a bit from being dropped, but still clean. We took them back to the precinct and ran them through the toaster oven. They were great!"

"You gotta love cops," ventured Davis. "If it's free they'll eat anything . . ."

CHAPTER 4

Serious Drug Business

Greg Lovett, an Arkansas policeman and undercover drug cop "with hair down to my butt," survived years on the force without being shot. Rotated to School Resource Officer, he took five hits from a 20-gauge pump shotgun in the hands of a hostile twelve-year-old intent on settling a grudge.

Gregory Lovett—his friends call him Greg—is the original camera-shy policeman. He doesn't like the media and he's not afraid to tell you so . . . if you can find him.

I'd gone from Michigan all the way to Prairie Grove, a small town in northwest Arkansas to interview him. Though I'd made contact with the local chief of police—his former boss—as well as half-a-dozen others who knew where he hung out, the same message came back each time: "He don't like to talk to journalists."

Still, I'd come that far and I persisted. Eventually I managed to track down a phone number, but by then I was in New Orleans. When we eventually did speak, this tough, wary fighter—with years of police and, more recently, war work in Iraq behind him—agreed to fly to Louisiana where we were able to spend a bit of time together.

In former Police Officer Lovett, I discovered a man whose mind could best be described as a series of locked cupboards, guarded by the cherubs of self-discipline. Someone in Arkansas suggested that he was the original no-nonsense cop.

His reticence, he told me, was because he'd just arrived back home from Baghdad, where he'd worked first with a K-9 Squad, and then in VIP protection against suicide bombers and like-minded religious zealots. He was due to ship out again in a week. Before that, he had been in Kosovo, operating with about 150 others out of Ferzi, a small town just beyond Pristina.

We were able to exchange more "no bullshit" notes on the Internet once he'd reached the Iraqi capital. Since he's a minimalist, he is rarely effusive about anything, either in the Middle East or chasing drug barons back home.

There were other reasons for Greg Lovett's reluctance to talk about what he regarded as little more than a series of historical recollections. He had spent much of his professional life in law enforcement, working undercover. Based in a remote part of the country—even though Prairie Grove is only twenty miles or so from Bentonville, the global headquarters of Wal-Mart—he'd had his dust-ups while working with a variety of Federal agencies, including the FBI and DEA, as well as some multi-jurisdictional task forces involved with serious crimes. Some of these ended with shootings.

He'd also made his share of collars and commented that there were people out there who didn't forget. Consequently, he liked to walk a pretty thin line. But he had done what was necessary, and to his mind the world was a better place for it. On the other hand, Lovett believes he's lucky to be alive.

He was shot in the face by a twelve-year-old named Michael Nicholls, who picked Lovett for target practice with his 20-gauge pump shotgun. Before it was over, Lovett was hit four more times. The youngster had been playing hooky. When Lovett went out to look for him, young Nicholls laid an ambush.

That happened on May 11, 2000, making him Richard Davis' Save #812.

Greg Lovett was twenty-two years old when he joined the force. Until then he'd worked mainly for his brother-in-law in a fabrication company; he'd slogged through school as a shop student.

Looking back, he calls his upbringing "the school of knocks." Even though his father was a car salesman and they enjoyed their small-town existence in rural Arkansas, money was tight.

A friend from childhood first interested Lovett in the law. Pat Scaggs had joined the force a few years before and though he was a bit older, Lovett followed him as an example. Also, the film *Serpico* had left its imprint.

It was the first cop movie that he felt told it like it really was. "They left out none of the things that mattered . . . the language . . . the police work, the lies, deceit, and the way those cops went about doing their thing. Also, it was real life, since Serpico had been betrayed while actually working for the NYPD." He recalls a pretty clear message, and looking back, he says, "It affected me in a peculiar way, so much so that I felt I could identify with those cops.

"Then, in my first month in uniform something happened that seems to be fated. In a sense, it sealed my choice of career.

"We'd been called out for a burglary. One of the deputies reported that he'd spotted movement inside a restaurant, and—as we discovered afterward—somebody had gotten into the building and rifled the money box. Moments later a guy runs out. He's got a pair of pliers in his hand, and the deputy thinks he's got a gun. So he shoots at the man and misses."

What happened next was a flurry of confusion, with gun-in-hand police yelling at the man to stop, the suspect deciding otherwise, taking off. Several officers hotfooted it after him down a dark and dusty back road.

"I was younger than the rest so I quickly gained on the runaway, at the same time shouting at him to stop. We got to the top of an incline, at which point the suspect must have decided he wasn't going to escape. So he stopped. Just like that, and in the dark I ran slap bang into him.

"The force of impact resulted in him kinda tumbling down the hill, with me rolling down after him. Once we reached the bottom, I found myself on top of the suspect. In the most official voice I could muster, I told him he was under arrest. It just happened kind of lucky."

After Benton County, Lovett moved to the Decatur Police for about eighteen months and in October 1984, went on to do undercover work for Arkansas' Lincoln Police Department, about six miles west of Prairie Grove. Most of these duties were drug related.

"It was strange, even in that small community we had a substance problem, though, to be fair, things were exacerbated about then after a ten-year-old girl overdosed on drugs. It wasn't intentional, as we discovered later . . . she'd been given something by an older child on the school bus ride home and almost died. Overnight it became a very big thing in such a small town, which often happens in places where everyone knows, or is related to, everybody else. Parts of Arkansas are like that," he explained.

"So my chief puts me up in a real sleazy, roach-ridden apartment in town and tells me that my job is to hang out and see who's doing what. Since Decatur is some distance north of Lincoln, I wasn't afraid that I'd be fingered. But you're always cautious.

"Because the locals didn't know I'd been working elsewhere as a cop, I managed to clean things up a bit, all within about six months. It was mostly low-level stuff and we were able to prosecute everybody we targeted. There were about fifteen of them in all."

In April 1985, Lovett started as a uniformed patrol officer with the Prairie Grove Police Department. He stayed seventeen years, though moving to drug control again—and once more undercover—four years on. He made sergeant in the interim and, as he says, a good deal of his activity was multi-jurisdictional, or federal, sometimes taking him into other counties and occasionally across state lines.

Several major cases involved the Organized Crime Drug Enforcement Task Force (OCDETF), some of which were linked to suppliers as far afield as Mexico and Florida. A lot of dope-runners as a result wound up either dead or behind bars, as well as some cops.

These activities didn't go unnoticed. The Mob became especially interested in Lovett. As he exclaimed tartly, "Doing this kind of work eventually gets to be like preparing your own cross for your crucifixion." He had his share of scrapes, including two white gangsters coming to his home and trying to strong-arm him into their car. Lovett shot one of them in the arm and the other ran off.

"My wife was really upset, not only because of what they might have done to me—they certainly weren't taking me on vacation—but also what they could have done to her and my stepson. She felt very strongly that these were desperate people. She argued that they could have taken hostages, though the boy was at his father's house when it all went down."

The two felons were apprehended, one getting thirty-six years and the other—claiming to be an innocent passenger in the car—was sentenced to a year.

This was also a time when crack cocaine started to appear in the Arkansas backwoods underworld—and it soon made an impact even on small communities, as it does today throughout the United States.

Lovett: "It was really a progression from the bigger cities. Local people go there, get addicted, and then they come back home and pass it on to their pothead friends. There was no racial pattern—everybody was doing it: Whites, Hispanics, Blacks. Then, not very long afterward, we began to see methamphetamines. It very soon began to overwhelm the system as it spread."

Greg Lovett today rates meth the biggest single problem facing contemporary America. It touches almost everyone. His eyes flashing anger, he stated that drug use in the United States "is a process of what some might term 'progressive desiccation of both the mind and body.' You can legislate 'til the cows come home, but if these substances are not your prime focus, then this work is like writing a novel without using the letter 'a.'"

In Portland Oregon, he told me, life expectancy on the street for a kid using the stuff was about two years. "Twenty-four months, perhaps thirty max, and they're either off it or they're in a box," he said.

It was marginally better in the rural areas because families in trouble tend to rally. Obviously that helps, he said. "But, somebody who's into meth is in one God-awful devil's grip of self-abuse. All of us on the other side have seen what it does to people and that it is almost impossible to break if the addict doesn't recognize that he or she needs help. You simply can't *force* salvation on them."

Meth is deadly in other respects, he reckoned, because so far there were a hundred and thirty-five different recipes for making the stuff. That brew sometimes includes drain cleaner and even strychnine and arsenic. "There are specific components, but in poor areas, if the guy that manufactures it doesn't have one ingredient, he'll substitute another."

The sad thing about it, he added, was that while all that was going on, the department that started out with ten officers handling drugs was whittled down to five.

"Instead of being doubled, the legislators started cutting back on budgets, and things began to go the other way. The consequences we see today, with more drugs than ever before, stem from that period—even though the feds got involved not long afterward."

Call it overfamiliarity, a face seen once too often, but Officer Greg Lovett finally had to rotate out of the drug unit. He was taking too many risks, his superiors felt. One of their best officers had become too well known to remain successful in their most dangerous assignment.

"Unfortunately, that's the way it is on drug jobs. Perform too well and people start coming at you, most times because you're doing them harm, or there are too many of their friends or associates in prison." In 1997, he was appointed Prairie Grove School Resource Officer, with duties that included teaching classes in alcohol and drug abuse.

Occasionally the department would call him in for an investigation, or a raid, or perhaps as back-up. But the thrust of his work was to get the kids at school on his side in an anti-drug abuse program. Though he followed a canned lesson plan, he was able to add his own experiences—and that made things both real and interesting for the youngsters.

Looking back, Lovett says that with more than twelve hundred kids it wasn't an easy job. He was not teaching a popular subject. Though things weren't as bad at the Prairie Grove School as in other districts, sometimes youngsters brought drugs to school. A lot of times when this happened, some of his students would tip him off.

"I could never go directly to one of them and say, 'Hey, tell me what you know.' It didn't work like that, even though the school had an honor system. But when, during the course of an investigation, I asked, especially if there was something serious going on, they would sometimes be more forthcoming than a grown-up.

"Generally we maintained a very good discipline, which tells you that rural schools may be better than city schools. Sometimes."

Then came Teacher Appreciation Day. As Lovett explained, in Arkansas, the seniors and some juniors brought different dishes to school for a staff lunch. It was to give special thanks for work accomplished during the year and was much appreciated.

"Since I was part of the teaching staff, I was going to get some of this good chow. It was something that we actually looked forward to.

"At about ten that morning, while working in the library ordering educational videos for the next year, I got a call from the police department, asking whether I was in uniform. Yeah, I told them uneasily, I was. I always wear my uniform to school because it's part of the system. You're visible, which is the way it works.

"So they tell me they had a call from someone who said there was a kid wandering around Viney Grove Road, acting kind of strange. I asked for more info, but that was all they had. And since the road goes right by the school, I got in my car, a marked police Jeep Cherokee, and set out looking."

Lovett hadn't gone far when he spotted Tom Louks, the school superintendent, walking down Viney Grove with Pete Bennett, an elementary school teacher. They'd received the same call from somebody else.

"Our consensus was that it was a student who'd skipped school and was trying to sneak back . . . When I stopped to talk, it was Louks who said, pointing, 'Hey, we think we just saw him. He's in the field right there.'"

Since that was his job, Lovett said he'd go and look. He turned his car around, pulled into a gate just ahead of a hay field fenced with barbed wire, and stopped. Because of heavy mud, Lovett decided to walk the rest of the way rather than drive, in case his vehicle got stuck.

"I had to go a couple of hundred yards through knee- to waist-high grass. As I got to the far end of the pasture a head pops up, and then ducks back again. I called his name, but he didn't answer, so I kept on walking. When I got to the fence I spotted him very briefly again, by now on the other side of where I was. I shouted, looking for some kind of a reaction."

The twelve-year-old, by now identified as Michael Nicholls, was the usual Prairie Grove middle school student. Of average height, about five feet, he was on the chubby side and wore glasses. His narrow, suspicious-looking eyes and unfriendly demeanor immediately caught Lovett's attention when his head popped up again.

Then he saw why. The boy had a canvas bag in his hands which fell away the moment he stood erect. He held a 20-gauge pump shotgun comfortably in a shooter's stance, one foot ahead of the other. For Lovett the same sort of thing had happened before, though under these circumstances, considering that he was dealing with a juvenile, he didn't consider the situation an immediate threat.

"Silent, aggressive, pensive, I couldn't help thinking that Nicholls was actually going to use it. But this was a child, my God. It was impossible that he would."

In a single swift and fluid motion the student raised the gun, took aim, and fired. The blast of birdshot hit Lovett full on the left side of his face.

Instinctively the cop raised his hands. Then he turned his body away from his attacker as two more shots followed, both on target and also on his left side. Like a professional the youngster had cycled three cartridges through the shotgun chamber in a second or two and let rip. As Lovett said afterward, "He was a country boy and a pretty good shot."

Michael Nicholls was thoroughly familiar with his weapon, having hunted frequently with his father. Among the guns in the family arsenal was a powerful 30-30 hunting rifle that he could just as easily have used. But the 20-gauge did a lot of damage, being a bit less powerful than the traditional 12-gauge.

Lovett reacted the only way he could, and that was with utter incredulity. For a second or two, he tried to tell himself, this wasn't happening. As he remembers those moments, he recalls that slow Novocain of shock from a glimpse of death, which prompted his next action.

He drew his Smith & Wesson .40 caliber, and though partially blinded, pulled the trigger. His gun jammed. With that, Michael Nicholls shot the policeman twice more, his soft body armor absorbing most of it.

Undeterred and expecting more any moment, Lovett worked blind, and dropped his magazine. This time the auto cycled properly and he fired a single shot. The shooter went down, though with his vision clouded by blood streaming down his face, he wasn't sure whether he'd actually hit the boy. He hadn't.

"We had a six-foot-high fence between us, my only cover. So I went down behind it to consider my next move. I was hurting, but I knew I didn't need to kill the youngster. There had to be a reason for his actions.

"I contemplated going over to where he lay, because I knew that the confrontation couldn't end with him having shot me and getting away.

"Then he made up my mind for me by popping up once more, and firing two more shots in quick succession. This time he was in my sights and when I pulled the trigger again I heard him squeal as I hit him square in the stomach.

Teachers Louks and Bennett had meanwhile crept up from behind. They took up positions on either side and with Nicholls hit, rushed forward to help the policeman. By now he had blood everywhere down his face and neck. His hands and arms were also covered in blood. Remarkably, his vision was spared: not a single pellet had touched his eyes.

A later count in the ER indicated that Greg Lovett had taken more than a hundred shotgun pellets, with sixty-four still in his flesh. All were removed later under surgery. As he ruminates, if the gun had been 12-gauge, or loaded with buckshot, "I'd probably have been killed." It is also significant that with a dozen or so shots fired by the two adversaries, the drama played out in less than ten seconds.

It was Bennett, the elementary school teacher, who now rushed forward to attend to one of his students lying on the ground.

"Michael, my God, what were you doing?" he asked the boy after he'd climbed over the fence. Nicholls was holding his stomach and crying. His exact words, uttered without emotion above the sobs, since he thought he was dying and had nothing to lose, were: "I was going to kill that son-of-bitch Dalmut."

Then it emerged: the Junior High School principal, Dalmut, had been Michael Nicholls' original target.

The previous day he had received a roasting for pushing a girl on the bus. As he declared under interrogation, he had decided to "get even." By the time the case got to court months later, Nicholls had renounced the murder threat and claimed that he intended to make the school principal "listen to me."

After a lengthy, high-profile, and politically sensitive trial at which the prosecutor Terry Jones was constantly at loggerheads with Judge Stacey Zimmerman, Michael Nicholls was sentenced to and served eighteen months in juvenile detention.

As the case went on, it became clear that the judge and the prosecutor had personal issues with each other. Prosecutor Jones had previously fired Zimmerman, who, as a junior prosecutor, had run for the position of juvenile judge. She'd put forward a strong case for probation as opposed to detention.

"We in the police had to fight hard to put this matter to rights. There were moments when it became extremely nasty between the two, but it worked out in the end," said Lovett.

The boy's parents apparently had very little to say during the court process, even though they attended the trial from start to finish. Both were respected local people.

The person who had originally phoned the police and advised them of a boy walking around outside the school grounds was on his way to see his probation officer from a drug case that Lovett had made. First thoughts were that he had phoned in without mentioning the gun to get even.

Afterward, he visited Lovett and swore he hadn't seen any gun. Neither had teachers Louks and Bennett. Nicholls later admitted that he'd laid the weapon down each time he saw someone approach.

Later, in juvenile prison, Michael Nicholls and another boy were overheard discussing the event by a junior probation officer who happened to be passing at the time. They were sharing stories about how they had been arrested.

The other kid said he'd gotten into trouble after shooting some road signs. Nicholls answer was, "Well, all I did was shoot a pig."

In a situation very much like Lovett's, Officer Michael Crawford of Anchorage, Alaska, was shot from a distance of three feet by a sixteen-year-old using souped-up Super-Vel .38 Special ammunition. That was in April 1975 and is listed as Richard Davis' first juvenile shooting (Save #29).

Crawford's vest absorbed the impact of the first bullet, but the second, in the hip, almost killed him.

Using shotguns in trying to kill cops is almost an American tradition in some quarters. Just about every household in rural areas has one, so they are invariably the first weapon at hand when there is a confrontation. Shotguns are also used in many robberies.

One of the early saves listed by Richard Davis in the Second Chance Body Armor Saves Club was Officer Herman Joiner of Gainesville, Florida. Joiner was working a stakeout on a grocery store. During a robbery he was struck on the head by a 12-gauge shotgun. Then the robber fired a load of 00 buck into his chest as he lay on the floor. Joyner's vest took the brunt of it, but he was left with a bruise five inches across. That was Save #71.

In another shooting (Save #340), Steve Draper of East Hempfield, Pennsylvania, was caught up with a dozen officers in a "barricaded gunman" situation. Plans were to use tear gas and a fire hose to disable and possibly dislodge the criminal. Draper's job was to man the hose, but things went awry when water pressure failed. Draper was left standing face-to-face with a shooter about to discharge a 16-gauge slug.

Hit in the chest, he was dragged to safety while his fellow officers nailed his assailant with a multiple gunshots.

More serious was a confrontation in Texarkana, Texas (a modest place that boasts several other soft body armor saves), by Officer W.P. McElhiney. A suspect in a house opened fire on him with a 12-gauge. McElhiney dismounted and approached the house from an alley but the assailant was waiting for him. He stepped out from behind some brush, firing.

Wounded, McElhiney shot back, downing his attacker. But, as he approached, the man got up again and shot him in the right upper arm and chest. His vest—equipped with side panels—absorbed most of it. That made Save #273.

• • •

Working as an undercover cop for almost a decade, Gregory Lovett didn't know when he joined the force that aspects of his career would strongly resemble that of Serpico, his childhood hero.

Operating in small-town Middle America did give him an unusual insight into the way criminals go about their business—if only because they were right there, sort of in your face, as he puts it. He got to know his "neighbors" much better than might be the case in places like Jacksonville or Seattle. The majority of crimes, he found, were similar to those in big cities, though perhaps not quite as mindless and, the Michael Nicholls incident aside, not nearly as violent.

"Also, people didn't slaughter each other quite as readily in Washington County as gangs might in Chicago or Atlantic City. The drugs are the same though, as are most drug-related crimes."

The methamphetamine range of drugs—regarded by law enforcement agencies the world over as a scourge—was less commonplace in Prairie Grove than it might be in downtown Boston or Portland, Oregon. But it was there, Lovett told me, and it would sometimes arrive in quantity. Furthermore, if those who thought they needed it couldn't afford to buy their meth on the street, they'd make their own.

He observed that while cocaine and heroin had crept almost silently across America, the methamphetamine plague had descended on all these communities with a roar.

Lovett: "My first real experience in the world of methamphetamines was in the 1980s. I'd been in law enforcement since 1982 when I received a new assignment. My department—it was still Prairie Grove—received a government grant for the so-called War on Drugs.

"We, [along with] some other small towns in that part of Arkansas, banded together and formed a rural drug unit. The larger cities, like Fayetteville and Springdale, were big enough to field their own narcotics units and detective divisions. The result was that they worked only the drug cases they encountered in their jurisdiction . . . rural drug issues weren't their concern, though looking back, they should have been.

"So, there was little or no cooperation between departments, even though we were only a short distance away.

"If you received any information from a detective in another jurisdiction, it was usually on a personal basis, perhaps a payback for a favor. Everyone protected their personal piece of the pie and there was almost no trust outside their own units."

As Lovett explained, this was caused by extremely generous federal drug grants to police departments across the country, the idea being to fight a nationwide drug war. "And when a department is fighting city administrators almost every day, sometimes for basic essentials, this was a windfall to be protected at all costs."

The problem for small communities like Prairie Grove was that they had neither the manpower nor the resources to dedicate staff specifically to fighting narcotics. But, with government money flowing in, these same towns could suddenly add personnel, buy equipment, and most important, get their hands on cash, which could be used for drug "buy money."

"In December 1989, I was the only detective assigned to the task force representing the smaller cities. I worked by myself for the better part of the next year, but because Washington County had three separate Drug Grant Programs for 1989/1990, state authorities decided there should only be one grant for the entire county.

"So, starting early 1991, there would be one Drug Task Force in Washington County. Thus Prairie Grove and several other local towns joined with the larger cities to create the task force. From the start, being rural, I was the odd man out, since some of my new partners couldn't accept that, because I was from a small department, I might know much about the problem. Fortunately that bias didn't last forever.

"We must have done a pretty good job because the region's Drug Task Force didn't take long to develop into one of the best and most respected law enforcement agencies in the state." The last time he was home in 2006, the accolades were still coming, "And what's more, they've actually maintained standards that we originally established."

As Lovett explains, none of this happened easily. There were multiple problems that sometimes delayed implementation.

"When drug task forces began to take shape across the nation, in the late 1980s and early 1990s, we had to feel our way around, because there were simply no rules. There were also no guidelines about spending grant money.

"Lots of task forces fell victim to corruption. Illegal searches generated huge numbers of lawsuits." There were even some homicides that followed, he stated. Not many, but enough to taint the process. The result was that many careers were ruined. They ranged from prosecutors and sheriffs to police chiefs.

"But Washington was determined to counter what it regarded as a powerful, debilitating drug menace, and the cash kept on coming. Any agency that could justify a grant—even vaguely—got one. Some departments went so far as to take informants, junkies, and thugs with arm-long rap sheets straight off the streets and make 'cops' of them.

"It didn't matter that they had no training, no certification, and no experience in police work; they had the connections and, I suppose, that was what counted in the minds of some of these desk-bound administrators. Everybody wanted to enlarge their budgets, which was easy when the government was picking up the tab.

"When you've got hundreds of thousands of dollars to spend during your fiscal year, and obscure guidelines on how the money could be circulated, things can go squirrelly. People went wild. One police department sponsored a training class for narcotics officers, which in itself wasn't unusual, but the class was held aboard a cruise ship in Cancun, Mexico.

"So the effects of the drug war had victims on both sides of the law."

Gregory Lovett worked narcotics until February 1997, seven years undercover, which in some departments is still a record.

"When I rotated out, I had hair down to my butt. I also had a different attitude about what Washington called 'The War on Drugs,' as well as about the dealers themselves. Obviously, I'd sent my share of bad guys to prison, but I was no longer convinced that everyone who sold dope belonged there."

As Lovett points out, his first few years of the task force were largely marijuana-oriented. It was the drug of choice in his area. As more information came in and he was able to spread his workload across a wider area and made more arrests, he discovered that things were rather different from what he'd expected.

"What we found was that while there was a lot of talk about pot or marijuana, that was only the visible tip of an extremely large and complex iceberg of controlled substances. Undercover, we encountered people every single working day who were part of every possible sector of society.

"On the surface and on the books, these were all 'drug dealers' and worse. But what I soon learned was that the majority of these people were everyday folks, good people who had simply made some bad choices."

Clearly, there are what he terms "the bad guys, real drug dealers" out there, like the ones we see every day on television.

"Those are the criminals. They're easy to send to prison. They are also easy to forget. But I know that they're a relatively small minority. In contrast, the majority of what we call *dealers* are actually people who want to cover their own costs as users.

"For whatever reason, they might be addicted to methamphetamines. They get up on Monday morning, they send the kids to school, and then they go to work—just like you and me. They celebrate their holidays, anniversaries, and their kids' birthdays like we all do, and there are those among them who are involved with things like Little League games and amateur theatrics.

"I was buying from this one guy who would only meet with me after his son's practice was over, or if it was a game . . . when they came home from the local pizza place. He had his sense of responsibilities. He was the coach. He was also on meth.

"People generally believe that drug addicts almost always fall into categories, that they are a certain class of people. Ask Joe Average, and he's likely to tell you that druggies come mainly from the bottom rung of society. Trouble is, it's a trade-stamped stereotype and it's wrong."

Anyone can be addicted, insists Lovett, and many people are. "These include students, mothers, fathers, coaches, teachers, cops, you name it," he said. "Nobody is immune from it, or its all-encompassing, sometimes terrible effects."

This is the astonishing conclusion of a man who made combating drugs the focal point of his career.

He indicated that studies had showed that the meth trade was having a domino effect across American society, and "the most ominous part of all is that it is getting worse."

Then, and probably now, methamphetamine is the Arkansas drug of choice, with more arrests made in the state among its cookers, users, and dealers than for any other drug, including marijuana. It is the same in Oregon, Minnesota, Connecticut, the Carolinas, Texas, California, and the rest, Alaska and Hawaii included.

Once called "the poor man's cocaine," methamphetamine has become very popular with what Lovett refers to as ordinary working class people. He believes truckers originally helped make popular what is known as *cross tops*, the tablet form of meth. Take a couple of these and you can work for days without sleep.

Most people enter this spiral by buying small amounts . . . a quarter to a gram at a time. The average cost is about $100 per gram, or about $500 an ounce for small buys, though with larger amounts the price improves substantially, which, in keeping with the capitalist system, is why distributors encourage their dealers to sell in quantity.

Experience taught Lovett that just about everyone starts by getting their drugs from someone they know, though why was anyone's guess. Peer pressure, unhappy family life, or sheer boredom perhaps. But the chain reaction resulting from using is *always* self-destructive.

"So your average citizen buys small amounts of meth. Every payday they will take a couple of hundred dollars, go down the street to their local connection, and get a couple of grams for the next week. It doesn't take long to get behind on bills. Or child support or the mortgage.

"Many times the user will do what everyone before him did, and is still doing. He'll buy a gram or two and cut it with anything, baby powder, B-12, even rat poison. The guy who did that told me that the customers liked that extra kick.

"Eventually, they'll go from a couple of grams to three or four grams a week and again, they'll do what the person ahead of them did. They mix stuff in to bulk it up and resell it to the next guy in line. So the original investment of, say, $200 is now recovered and they still have their meth. But it's not as pure as it was before, which means they have to increase the amount to get that same high.

"As with everything else, if they don't have a job, they use other ways to get the stuff. They steal, they rob, they forge checks or whatever it takes to get the extra dough to get high." At one point, Lovett reckoned that thefts related to the drug trade were somewhere around 75 percent in his area. It might have increased since then, he believed. It was worse in the cities.

The physical and mental effects linked to this drug can last a lifetime, starting with chronic memory loss that becomes more severe with time. Methamphetamine affects anyone and sometimes involves innocent victims, especially family members who are robbed blind by their relatives to support the habit.

There are two types of addiction: physical and psychological.

Methamphetamine creates a physical addiction in the body. The system has to have the meth in order to function, much like that of an alcoholic. In contrast, other drugs like cocaine create a psychological addiction. The brain tells the body that it requires it to function. Consequently, the effects of meth addiction are far worse than those experienced by a user with either cocaine or heroin, which, he warns, are serious enough.

Lovett was graphic when he described the consequences. As he said, "When a person starts using meth, they get a high that makes them feel like they're ready to take on the world. They have energy, lots of it. They want to paint the house, mow the yard, and polish the car . . . all at once. The effects can last anywhere from several hours to days, depending on the individual and, of course, the dose.

"At first your user may only get high once a week or so. But it's not long before that can increase up to several times a day. Usually after several months of snorting meth, a person will switch to smoking the stuff and then needles, all of which gets more of the drug into the system faster."

Depending on the user's personal hygiene, he or she may elect to inject the body in places that are not easily visible, which could be anywhere, behind the knees, between the toes, or in the groin area. Most addicts remain traditional and use the arm. If needle marks are a problem, they use Preparation H to shrink the swelling.

For that too, there is a price. After months of this kind of abuse, the lesions become visible. They also don't heal easily because meth slows the body's natural healing process. After years of use, the teeth begin to blacken, rot, and fall out. This is known as *meth mouth.*

Somewhere along the way, paranoia can set in. After prolonged use, the user becomes fearful of everyone and everything. In a sense, observed one policeman, the addict ends up being persecuted by his own scrambled mind.

Lovett: "We've arrested people and during the interview they would say to us, 'I knew this was coming. You people have been following me for weeks.' Maybe we'd only had the guy's name a few hours before arresting him. But in his mind . . . we were right there, after him all the way, all the time.

"Of course," he added, "there's the additional downside of sharing needles, which brings hepatitis and AIDS into the equation. Throw in the cost of health care for those people and we all end up paying a price."

Then there are times when things can go badly wrong for drug users, like they did in Detroit in late May 2006 when almost fifty people overdosed during the course of a ten-day spell. Health officials said they believed the deaths to have been caused by a dangerous combination of heroin or cocaine and the painkiller fentanyl.

The numbers have always fluctuated, declared a Wayne County spokeswoman. Some days, the source declared, there were three or four deaths. On others there might be one. The surge in fatalities came to the public's attention because a dozen people had died in twenty-four hours.

From September through April 2006, more than a hundred drug overdose deaths were recorded in metro Detroit. Again, most were believed to have been caused by the deadly heroin/fentanyl combination.

What was noteworthy about this report is that in the majority of cases, it was buried deep inside most national newspapers: fifty deaths and barely an eyebrow raised. Yet great prominence was given to three American troops KIA—which, right or wrong, possibly underscores the premise that the life of one American soldier who dies serving his or her country is worth more than the countless useless and unproductive lives that are wasted on drugs.

During his years on a police drug squad, Lovett consistently encountered resistance on issues to which police departments refused to take a broader view. This was that the drug problem was escalating. There were people in charge who wouldn't accept anything but the obvious, but how can you prove this contention apart from annual sets of statistics, and that's only once or twice a year.

"When you arrest a thief . . . the money from the theft, or the item itself, more often than not, is used to buy or trade for dope. And it's here that the issue gets fuzzy. Each month, every police department in the country completes a Uniformed Crime Report, a UCR. This document is sent to the FBI and is used to compile national crime statistics.

"But, as I've seen myself, there is much leeway for creative thinking in putting together these reports, which ultimately centers on the money a department will get the following year. It is interpreted in terms of staff, communications equipment, vehicles, monitoring devices . . . the list goes on.

"Then you have a situation where a department can make the stats look any way they like. Several years ago Baltimore and some other larger cities got caught being remarkably creative with the numbers they submitted. When tens of millions of dollars of federal grant money is on the line, people try to justify the cash they're getting, and let's face it, it looks bad when, in spite of taking good federal money, the problem just continues to escalate.

"It works something like this. In numerous little boxes that are checked off in the UCR, nowhere is there anything that might link the current crime (theft) to a related misdemeanor or felony (for example, drug dealing). So no accurate figures exist for this, and 75 percent of such crimes are drug-related, as I mentioned earlier."

It is also worth noting, he added, that when federal grants for drug enforcement were initiated in the 1980s, there were some unexpected consequences. For one, the increase of nationwide enforcement meant a flood of drug-related arrests and jail overcrowdings in just about every state in the Union. Then came the "hot topic" for state and federal politicians: the inevitable catchphrase *War on Drugs* was always a popular campaign-slogan, from the president on down.

Soon there were more prisoners in the system than society had the means with which to cope. With few or no alternative measures in place for drug offenders, and everyone wanting to appear tough on drug dealers, the state prisons—if not already filled to overcapacity—were soon making plans to expand. The era of outsourcing had arrived and we had something that had never been tried before: the privatization of the prison system. Like we have today in Iraq and Afghanistan, the privatization of war[1].

Lovett was emphatic that history played a significant role in what is taking place in the United States right now. In the early 1970s and 1980s, he said, the meth plague wasn't anything like it is today.

Most of your large meth dealers were either Mexican or had connections with cartels south of the border, or out west in California and Arizona. These were your hardcore bad guys and included outlaw bikers, the one-percenters, and rogue chemists who between them dominated the trade.

Also, those were days when the methodology was complicated and meth formulae were secret and closely guarded. To get a decent batch, one needed a good twenty-four hours of work, a certain level of skill, lots of glassware—and, of course, a smidgen of luck.

At the same time, if the technologies were secret, the ingredients weren't. Not yet, anyway, because the Internet hadn't come into play. But once it did, it was inevitable that the IT revolution would change the industry—forever. Any eight-year-old with a computer can find a hundred ways to cook meth on the Web, and can do so in less than an hour. Throw in a trip to Wal-Mart and you're in business.

Most meth cooks today started as users. Then, after a while, they begin cooking, if only to underwrite their habit. "Most meth cooks," he declared, "only make enough money to stay high and keep cooking. I haven't seen many wealthy meth cooks.

"These days there are revolutionary methods of making the stuff, involving very little technology or skill. Instead of complicated glassware and formulae, you can use a plastic Coke bottle and about twenty dollars worth of over-the-counter ingredients.

"If one of the ingredients isn't available, or is too expensive, then these chemical-age chefs will use something else in its place," says Lovett.

As Greg Lovett likes to point out, anyone doing meth production can go to a neighborhood Wal-Mart, 7-Eleven, or hardware store and buy a shopping cart of ephedrine-based products, the main ingredient in today's recipe. Though some states have banned sales of these medications, most have not. So in Oregon you go across the state line and get what you and a dozen of your user-neighbors need. You buy in bulk; it's cheaper.

In this regard, Wal-Mart was singled out for several reasons, even though the company has always been exemplary in its cooperation with law enforcement agencies. First, in much of the country, there's a Wal-Mart in just about every town. Second, Wal-Mart prices are often cheaper. A person could make a variety of purchases of the same item without anyone taking notice. All they had to do was go to a different checkout line each time.

Recently, things have changed. Now the stores have federal watch lists, with a number of over-the-counter ingredients detailed. When a person buys more than one—in combination with other items on the list—the store is supposed to call the local police department.

Lovett listed some of the ingredients. These include any large amount (more than three packages) of any ephedrine-based medicines, Red Devil Lye, Coleman fuel, coffee filters, salt, Strike Anywhere Matches, iodine crystals, and much else besides. It is ironic that just about anybody can get what they need from a reasonably well-stocked cattle or horse supply store.

Lovett made the observation that by 2005, Arkansas' Washington County had established its own Drug Court, usually reserved for first-time offenders. First-timers, he explained, were seldom sent to jail. Sometimes even second- and third-time offenders would have their probation revoked, only to have more probation time added.

"Right now, the thinking on these issues seems to be that sending an individual to prison for a drug offense is the last resort. And if the drug is marijuana, it won't even get on the docket. The paper trail to court is too onerous, and if the case isn't thrown out, it'll come up as a misdemeanor."

There are other consequences to methamphetamines that can sometimes affect the entire community.

Once a lab has been taken down and the people involved are in custody, the police are required to contact a hazardous materials or HAZMAT Team to come in and clean up the mess. As he says, the closest HAZMAT unit when he was working in drugs in Arkansas was four hours away. And it costs money.

"The bill, charged to the department making the arrest, always runs into thousands of dollars. While the average cost for a cleanup is about $5,000, it can quickly escalate to as much as $25,000. Much depends on how large the lab is and a host of other factors, like the amount of time the place had been used to produce the substance. It's the level of contamination that counts with these people.

"There is not a surface in a house where somebody has been cooking meth that does not have some of this stuff on it. It permeates everything, your skin and hair . . . You become your own walking drug lab."

Most local police departments like to have DEA officers tag along, so this federal authority can pick up the bill for the cleanup. But, they'll claim the case for themselves. And since the feds also list the bust as one of their cases, in the D.C. numbers game, one drug raid becomes two.

There are other, more fundamental issues, says Lovett. The local health department usually arrives afterward and can claim that the location is now what they like to term a *hazardous waste site*. The property is condemned and, as a consequence, you can kiss the house good-bye.

"Not only that, when there are drugs involved, then property values tend to plummet. Living next door to a hazardous waste site is not the most attractive selling point in real estate.

"This wasn't the case too often in our area, but some of the larger cities use this system to send a message to property owners who might have turned a blind eye to their tenants. And, if the owner was involved, then the property is seized.

"Over recent years this trend has slowed, due largely to the size of the labs going from large and intricate to small mom-and-pop operations in the kitchen."

---

[1] Al J. Venter, *War Dog: Fighting Other People's Wars* (Casemate Publishers, 2006).

CHAPTER 5

The Vest Faces Its First Critical Test

Richard and Karen Davis cut the template for the first sets of concealable body armor on the kitchen table of their small, low-income-area town house in Detroit. For fifty dollars they were selling a complete set of body armor—front and back panels. Initially there were few takers. Hardly anybody was aware of the remarkable potential of concealable body armor and its purpose. Somehow, the Davis family had to find a way of getting the message across.

By the time Richard Davis' invention was in everyday use by law enforcement, he'd turned the gun on himself more than a hundred times. That number had reached the two hundred mark by 2006. By then Matt, the youngest of the Davis sons, had taken on the role of official target. Father and son appear in a photo taken for their new company, Armor Express, also of Central Lake, Michigan, which they launched in 2005. The picture, a time exposure, shows the team shooting themselves with .44 magnum revolvers.

Turning a gun yourself has never been easy. Loading a .44 magnum revolver with Black Talon ammunition presented its own set of imponderables. Not only was this a "super load," but the bullet mushroomed on impact, presenting to those who were required to dig it out in the emergency room an irregularly shaped, jagged-edged chunk of metal around the core of the bullet. If Davis was not properly protected, he—or anybody else trying the demonstration—could be seriously hurt, or as he also quips, "seriously dead!"

For all that, he was able to demonstrate that he could not only survive the strike, but an instant later he could turn, draw his pistol, and spectacularly knock down a stack of Coke cans. These were usually placed on a table ten or twelve feet away.

To eliminate any question of fake or illusion, he would customarily have a local cop, one who had his own .44 magnum, load the six-and-a-half-inch Smith & Wesson M-29 and spin the cylinder. After the demo, he would let the same cop unload and keep both fired cases together with the unfired rounds and show them to anyone who might be interested.

The message was clear. He could take a powerful hit that was pretty painful and—as they were to see afterward—left a huge welt, but he was in no way incapacitated. He could immediately retaliate. That impressed a lot of people.

"Despite the shock from the bullet hitting my stomach, I showed that I could not only react quickly but with real purpose. This is the sort of thing that law enforcement officers—county, state, federal, or local—like to hear," reckons Davis.

The Davis family made their first sales of concealable body armor from their apartment in the fall of 1972. Richard had meanwhile sold one to Ronald Jagielski of the Detroit Police Department who was working undercover narcotics at the time.

In May 1973, Officer Jagielski and several other officers entered a residence being used by a drug gang. They had barely arrived at the target apartment when a shot rang out. A hot-load .38 was fired from inside the building, pierced the flimsy wooden front door, and hit Jagielski in the chest. It was later found embedded in the folds of his body armor.

Jagielski's hit went into the record books as the third recorded Second Chance Save. It was also the first time that a bullet had been stopped by the new invention. The first two were from sharp objects, including a knife attack on Larry Lindstrom of Rockford, Illinois (Save #2).

Reports of the so-called "miracle save," as one reporter dubbed it, rippled through police agencies, especially after details of the incident aired on television. The fact that a policeman had been hit in the chest by a relatively heavy bullet and not been injured was suddenly very newsworthy. But it was still not enough to generate either the kind of interest or sales that might make the body armor business viable.

Until then, Davis had been hanging around several Detroit police precincts. He'd show his product and pass out brochures that explained the potential of body armor. There was interest, obviously. Anybody claiming to have developed a lifesaver is going to get some attention. But there was also skepticism, and lots of it. At the time, flak jackets relied on steel plates in front of nylon—which was a bulky, uncomfortable combination.

Most officers simply couldn't accept that sheets of soft and pliable nylon material (Kevlar was to come two years later) could stop the force of a bullet in full flight. It hadn't happened, said some. Others declared that it could *never* happen!

Eventually Davis made contact with Carl Parcell, then president of the Detroit Police Officers Association. A maverick, Parcell took good care of the interests of police in this semi-lawless city where homicides in the past have hit double digits every day. He was not averse to threatening the city fathers with an epidemic of "Blue flu" if they wouldn't see their way to giving members of the already underpaid police force an extra buck or two an hour.

He would tell his bosses, "Ignore my demand and we'll see what happens when five thousand police officers go off sick with the flu. You'll have no police on duty and you all know what that means; it will result in anarchy in the streets of Detroit. Try me on that one and let's see what happens."

After the usual bluster and grandstanding by the authorities, the force would get its belated raise, which would still be below the national average. But at least he'd gotten something for his guys. A year later he'd be back again, seeking something different, this time perhaps a better health or retirement plan for his officers.

Parcell, recalls Davis, "had the kind of skills in achieving things that you didn't learn in school. He was the original rough diamond, swore like the proverbial trooper—but he got things done.

"Did so for me too, though he wasn't happy. I went to him, told him what I had. I cited the save on Jagielski, and said that I'd like to shoot myself in the stomach. I'd do so in his presence to prove that I really had something that could save the lives of cops. There was a Detroit policeman losing his life every two months, and it was happening almost as if it were on schedule.

"To begin with, he was utterly incredulous . . . wanted none of it. Said I couldn't do anything like that while he was around. But if he wasn't there, he suggested—wink-wink, nudge-nudge—then maybe it might just be possible."

The date was set for the bimonthly meeting of the Detroit Police Officers Association (DPOA). Two thousand police, almost half the Detroit Police Department, arrived at Detroit's Slovene Hall for the demo. The word was out: some lunatic would shoot himself in the gut with a .357 magnum and it was almost as if Barnum & Bailey had come to town. In fact, recalls Davis, there weren't many officers present who didn't believe that the live firing exercise would end in a visit by his family to the morgue. Nobody had ever tried anything like this before, and certainly not in front of every other police officer in one of America's biggest cities.

In the meantime, Parcell, having been involved on the fringes of what he called this ridiculous thing, introduced Davis to the crowd. "He told this very substantial gathering that I was some guy with a vest or something that could stop bullets. His body language exuded neutrality. He said that he didn't know much about what was going to happen, then he left the stage.

"Meantime I'd put on the vest, and, to be additionally safe, I'd discreetly inserted one of the very first steel plates into the front panel. It was very thin, but once I had on my shirt, you couldn't see that I was wearing body armor. I just looked like a normal guy.

"Gary Lee, one of the policemen and vice-president of the Detroit Police Officers Association, came forward to help me. He probably thought he'd have to make arrangements to cart away my body and contact my wife afterward. But he was helpful and stood to one side while I got ready.

"I took out my four-inch .357 magnum and called for some rounds. Christ! We were showered with hundreds from the front rows. There was a rain of bullets that came pouring in. 'Enough, guys! Enough!' I shouted. 'Save some for the criminals!'"

Davis picked up a handful of rounds, loaded six into his revolver, looked at the ocean of eager uplifted faces for a moment, and then turned the gun inward. Thumb on the trigger, he shot himself in the chest.

"There were six loud reports: *Bam! Bam! Bam! BOOM! Bam, Bam!* One of the rounds was a reload with a much more potent charge than the others. I could *really* feel that one when it hit me," he recalls today.

With the demonstration over, Davis' shirt was ripped to smithereens mostly by the six heavy muzzle blasts. But he was standing tall. The hall went wild with a frenzy of cheers, whistles, and catcalls as the crowd realized that this Davis guy really had the answer to cops being shot to death.

"Carl Parcell came up to me five seconds afterward and had his arms around me like I was his son, waving to the men with his other hand. The event certainly underscored the old Chinese saying . . . 'Success has a thousand fathers while failure's an orphan,'" ruminated Davis.

"'Is this really going to stop three-quarters of the killings?' one of them asked, and I reckon that everybody there that afternoon believed it could. On the other hand, had I dropped dead, you could have been sure that they wouldn't have seen anything . . . 'Some idiot, you know.' But it didn't happen that way.

"Another cop came up and told me that I'd fired one of his hand-loads. I told him I knew. Said it was pretty damn powerful. I was pleased that the vest held because it really showed its potential as a bullet stopper. That was something else we spoke about afterward."

Also in the crowd that summer afternoon was Jerry Zufoli from Burlington Industrial Fabrics Division from New York. It was he who had sold Davis the nylon fabric he'd used for the test. Zufoli was as eager to see the outcome of the demo as the rest, only he wasn't as confident.

"I'd picked him up at the airport earlier and we drove together to the hall. Just before I went on stage, I threw my car keys to him. Said something about 'Just in case things don't go right . . .'"

Zufoli's report to Burlington resulted in that company setting up its own body armor company, without consulting, or even telling the inventor. It fizzled within months because they had none of Davis' expertise. They also lacked his marketing ability and his technical know-how about ballistics and firearms. He refers to Burlington Industrial Fabrics today as, "the first company that tried to steal my idea . . . the first of many."

Once Second Chance had gotten off the ground and started producing vests in quantity, Burlington approached Davis again about weaving the DuPont nylon for the company; somewhat characteristically, he told them in the nicest possible way to get stuffed.

While Davis' vests didn't exactly sell by themselves after the demo, sales began to pick up. Marketed at $50 each without any intermediaries, they made a gross profit of about $15 per item after advertising and taxes.

"I now realized that with the orders starting to come in—we were then averaging about two sales a day—that we could actually make a living out of this thing. Somehow, we'd have to get to the bigger market. I just knew that there were police officers in every state in America who would be interested. Even more important, exactly the same applied to their families.

"I discovered afterward that many of the orders placed in those first few years came from the wives and girlfriends of law enforcement people. And, of course, their parents. There were very few moms and dads in that age of escalating violence who weren't concerned for the safety of their kids.

"It took me only about a month to decide that we had to go national. Though we couldn't scrape together the $660 that we needed to place an ad in *Law & Order*, the biggest police magazines in the country, we went ahead anyway.

"It was the world's first ad for concealable body armor. I still have a copy of that edition: it appeared in March 1973. Illustrated with a series of photos of me getting shot, the headline read:

At last: Somebody does care. Something has been done:
They don't have to die anymore.

"The advertisement appeared as a full-page bleed and we did it all by mail. Though it really put us on the line financially, it was a chance we had to take. And it worked. By the time the bill arrived in the mail a couple of weeks later we'd sold enough vests to pay for it. That old British seer John Donne was right when he wrote four hundred years ago that 'There comes a time in the affairs of men when taken at the flood can lead on to fortune . . .'"

Law & Order told Davis that following their having run the ad, they received more than six hundred inquiries from across the nation. It was a record number. More than three decades later that first Second Chance advertisement still stands as having initiated the most applications for more info for a single insertion. A typical ad back then, explained one of the magazine's editors, generated perhaps five or ten responses. Twenty was doing just fine. But six hundred! Interested parties would fill out a card in the back of the magazine and check off the item they wanted to know more about.

"All these inquiries about body armor would arrive at my door a week or so later and I'd send each of them my new four-page brochure. But I went a step further.

"Each of our brochures had an emotive photo of Karen holding baby Andy on her lap. The caption across the top read: 'Will this be the night that he doesn't come home?'"

While all this was going on, Davis knew he could do more. He followed the *Law & Order* ad with a gimmick linked to the old reliable hook of sex and violence.

"I kept saying to Karen that we needed to produce a glossy four-color brochure with a girl in a bikini prominently displayed on the cover. She had to be really stunning, I ventured: we needed to draw attention and this was a way of doing it. I grant you, it might have been a bit below the belt, but I slashed the slogan across the top of the first page: 'Sex and Violence: If you don't survive one, you can't enjoy the other.' I thought it was pretty nifty at the time.

"Inside, I had more photos of me being shot, and I told the reader all he needed to know about our new body armor. I went into a lot of detail about what it could do, how it saved lives, and what it cost."

It was a pretty classy production, Davis added. Moreover, it got the attention of that section of the community he was aiming at. Also, as he was to find out later, cops and their families not only read it themselves, but they passed it around. They then began getting inquiries from police departments.

Davis had meanwhile accumulated about a thousand addresses from people who had bought, or been asking about, body armor—or had perhaps been sent brochures. To each he dispatched his new "Sex and Violence" brochure and to everybody's surprise, the reaction was stupendous.

"From a few orders a day, suddenly about half of the people who got the new 'Sex and Violence' brochure ordered vests. There were pretty close to five hundred of them," said Davis, adding that all sent money with their orders, which was an added bonus for the cash-strapped young firm.

More important still, almost overnight, Second Chance Body Armor had created for itself a niche in law enforcement in the United States. At that point, he told his wife, there was only one way that they could go—and that was up.

In the meantime, Karen's parents, Beverly and Anthony Troskey—both of whom were skeptical of Richard's ability to make a proper living, or even his ability to provide a home for their beloved daughter—were not yet aware of the turnaround. They thought many of their son-in-law's inventions were goofy. In a sense, they were right. As Richard has said, laughing, while the concept of body armor might appear to be ridiculous, the product did what it was intended to do, and that was to save lives.

From visits to the Davises' lower-middle-class town house in Romulus in southwest Detroit, the Troskeys were aware that Richard was shipping an occasional batch of vests. They could hardly miss the pizza boxes, in which he shipped the product, scattered around their daughter's house. They'd also seen Richard load two or three at a time and then head for the post office. Usually they'd smile indulgently. It was a phase he was going through, they reckoned. He'd get over it with time and get himself a proper job.

Karen's dad visited the house one afternoon just as Richard emerged from the house with his arms piled high with pizza boxes, six or seven of them. All were labeled and ready for mailing. He was headed for the car when her dad asked: "You got this week's production there, Richard?" By which time the father-in-law had opened the passenger door to reveal the front and rear seats stacked high with more. There must have been at least fifty vests due to go out in that batch.

"No, not this week's," said Richard nonchalantly. "That's just today's. And a few from yesterday. We still have to process the orders that arrived this afternoon. And that's even more than this lot."

Mr. Troskey's jaw dropped. As Richard said with an evil glint, "He's realizing that, 'God! my ne'er-do-well, crumb-bum son-in-law, pizza delivery boy that my virgin daughter married is now making twice as much money as I am . . .'"

It also bothered Karen in a funny way that they were doing better than her parents. Her father was an insurance agent and they lived in a very nice house in a pleasant neighborhood up in Bloomfield Hills. It was a lovely place, but

Karen suddenly felt guilty, as though you're not supposed to have more money than your folks until you get older. She and Richard were still in their twenties.

The rest is history: the move to Central Lake in Northern Michigan; the making of more vests, but with it, more difficulties tied to quick growth; hiring Diane Erickson, the local postmaster's newly graduated daughter as their first member of staff; the arrival of little Matthew, their second son. All this was coupled to a really bitter winter in an uninsulated lakeside cottage, where the only heat was from a single oil stove that needed filling every night or the pipes would freeze. Then the banks refused them loans on what was regarded by their financial "experts" as a perilously risky commercial option. Gradually, though, things began to work out and the company prospered.

One notable event stands out. By the time the company had a staff of twenty, they were able to consider building their first factory.

As Davis explains, they intended to build it forty feet wide. "So I asked everybody to tell me what space they thought they'd need so I could figure the length. They came back and said that, in total, they wouldn't be needing more than eighty-eight feet. That included office, cutting, design, and factory space.

"I thought we should increase that by forty feet. Karen and the others thought I was crazy. 'What are we going to do in a hundred-and-twenty-eight-foot-long building?'" they asked. "They humored me and let it go. Two weeks after we'd moved in, the place was already crammed full and we had to start thinking about building an extension."

Keeping pace with orders was always a problem. While Richard made his first vests in the basement of their Detroit home, production for what was largely a fast-growing home industry was being farmed out to individuals in the neighborhood. At first one or two people were involved; eventually it became dozens.

Each item of body armor demanded close attention. From the gun tests that Davis had conducted in his basement, he'd established that to be effective, each vest—front and back—would need to incorporate nineteen sheets of nylon. Anything less and the ballistic nylon might not stop all the bullets it claimed it would; anything thicker would make the vest stiff and uncomfortable, especially when it was hot.

In addition to the nylon (and afterward, Kevlar) sheets—cut on templates according to the customer's size, and then stitched together—the finished product needed a durable cotton cover. There were also straps that had to be manufactured and fitted with Velcro.

"So I suddenly had to find someone who could do industrial sewing," Davis explained. "I eventually made contact with a wonderful woman, Marge Sipenko of the Detroit League for the Handicapped. Her son was a policeman in Dearborn Heights, so her interest was high: she gave him one of the very first vests that we produced.

"Marge was old and frail, but, my goodness, she was a dynamo in organizing her charges to do work for us, because, as she told them, they were not only getting paid good money, they were saving the lives of police men and women. At the time her ladies were also working on newfangled things called air bags, but she'd been made acutely aware by her uniformed son of the problems faced by the police in the big bad world outside their front door.

"So she gave us a priority on every one of our orders. Eventually the League started working for me on an industrial basis. We had Marge Sipenko and her girls cranking out several hundred vests a week, and they did a pretty good job. There were very rarely any complaints about quality."

Karen Davis quickly assumed the role of general factotum for the new body armor company. She was the secretary, handled the phones (sometimes well into the dark to cope with West Coast interests), and took care of the mail, which meant both incoming and outgoing. At this point Diane Erickson, an eighteen-year-old high school senior who began work in March 1974 (and ended up staying with the firm for the next thirty-one years), had joined the husband-and-wife team.

Karen, a math major and former bank teller, had the responsibility of finances. Most important, with all the bustle and fuss of a modest home that had evolved into a full-blown improvised factory, she had to attend to her duties as wife to Richard and mom to little Andy, both of whom needed a lot of mothering. Never mind still having to feed them both. Once Matthew, their second son arrived, her time was in ever greater demand, but by then they'd moved to Central Lake.

"When Richard first started out with his body armor thing, I told him that he'd better make this one work because if he didn't, we were going to be out of money," Karen told me when we spoke about the early days. "It was plain and simple, I stressed, trying not to sound like the nagging housewife. If this one flopped, he knew I'd have to go back to working at the bank. Then we'd have to find somebody to look after the baby.

"Being the inventor he was, Richard was always full of ideas. But it sometimes worried me that he didn't follow through with everything he started. Just before the vests, he'd completed a computer course, and that cost us what little spare cash we had—at a time, not surprisingly, when we had no spare cash at all. Then the glitz of being a programmer wore off and we were back to square one.

"It seemed he'd always get distracted and start with something fresh. It concerned us all. But then again, I knew that he had an incredibly active mind. He neither smoked nor drank—nor does he, to this day. He'd read voraciously and show an interest in just about everything in creation. Eventually, I knew he'd find something to which he could devote all his energy, which was boundless. He sublimated some of that by lifting weights, which meant that he was also well above average physically.

"Ultimately, that something was body armor, and from the start he went at it like a demon. He took a lot of knocks there too, but, like they say in the song, he'd pick himself up, dust himself off, and try again. You could describe him in those days as the archetypical, always-broke American entrepreneur.

"One thing about Richard, no matter how hard it was, he'd always have a smile for us . . . it was part of his make-up, the eternal optimist. In the end, his application to this new thing, the dedication and time that he put into it, paid off."

For a time, Karen Davis thought the pizza parlors would work. But they didn't because the staff hired for the other two were so erratic. In fact, from owning three pizza shops to owning none was a fairly rapid downhill transition after the enterprising inventor was shot and wounded.

One of his pizza outlets burned down, and though the police took an interest in how that happened (there were some who thought he might have set the blaze), it came to nothing when it was found that neither the building nor the business were insured. They concluded that he couldn't be stupid enough to destroy something on which he couldn't claim a penny. Karen Davis believes that a disgruntled former employee started the fire.

"I was pregnant with Andy at the time and Richard was doing this and that. Eventually he got a job as a security guard at an industrial site, working nights.

"He wasn't all that happy with the security situation. It was in an industrial park and the area had a lot of crime. That set him to thinking about what to do if someone attempted to shoot him again. Remember, he'd been shot twice before," said Karen, his first wife.

"He came home one morning and said he'd been thinking about getting something to wear under his shirt that nobody would be aware of. He figured if they didn't know he was protected and they shot him, he'd have a 'second chance.' What was important, he explained to me at some length—because he knew I was interested—was that whatever the 'protection' was, it should be discreet. Undetectable, he suggested. That's why we eventually called it concealable body armor.

"He ended up getting two thin steel plates. I fashioned a cotton holder for them, which he could slip over his head. That gave him front and back protection, and I suppose he took it from there because he'd been reading about what was then called *ballistic nylon*. Kevlar hadn't come onto the market yet," Karen Davis related, three-and-a-half decades later.

"He kept talking about it, and at one point said he wanted to investigate some materials that could be used for something like that. Meantime, he's still reading up on guns, ammunition, ballistics, and that sort of thing; he'd actually become extremely knowledgeable in that department. He's still a leader in that field."

At the time, Davis was aware that the kind of military flak jackets then being produced—some of which were then being used in Vietnam—were thick, heavy, and impractical for the purposes he had in mind. Crime in Detroit just then was endemic and most criminals had firearms. In any event, he was aiming at something a lot thinner. Also, there was the concealability aspect.

Karen Davis: "So he comes to me and says that he is going to have to spend seventy dollars for a roll of material from the Burlington company in New York. I argued that we didn't have that kind of money to spare. He didn't give up on the idea though. In fact, he persisted and actually took some extra work. It was a really big decision to go ahead—by which time he had been doing several other jobs, like driving a taxi, roof repair, and of course the security thing.

"He got busy in our basement and started cutting up this cloth, layer by layer, fashioning it into a primitive kind of ballistic vest. He used an awl to stitch the layers together by hand. For the first one he cut the extra back seat belts from our car to use for shoulder straps, which I didn't mind because it saved money. But it does give you an idea of how determined he was. He was onto something and he sensed it. Richard said all along that he had a good feeling about this one.

"Neither of us knew what to call it yet. We thought initially, because of its firearm connotations, of using the name Point Blank. But that name implied that you could stand in front of any artillery piece. Then we settled on Second Chance.

"It was a good choice. It said that our body armor would improve your chance to survive a gunfight. At the same time, the brochures we sent out were also precautionary. There was always a proviso included in the text that indicated that while body armor saved lives, absolutely nothing was certain."

When asked by his police friends what it was all about, Davis would explain exactly what he was doing. Then he'd always add the rider: "I'm giving all you guys a second chance in life." It was a powerful argument.

During this period the Davises were also using their basement as a shooting range. Richard needed to establish the parameters within which ballistic nylon would stop a bullet from penetrating all the way through. It was delicate, complicated work because he used many different kinds of firearms, calibers, bullet weights, and charges. Months of tests followed, months of trial and error.

The neighbors weren't amused. One couple claimed they had to keep their kids inside because they feared they might be shot, which was nonsense. Davis told them that because he worked below ground, that was impossible. He invited them to come and see what he was doing, but there were no takers.

Some viewed him as a halfwit. Others regarded him as a dangerous gun nut. That he was a pretty powerful man didn't help his case: everyone was frightened of this otherwise gentle giant.

The community eventually got together and tried to organize a petition to have the Davises evicted, but as Karen Davis commented, "by then we were already making good sales and one day we just decided to quit and move to Central Lake." Until that happened, production went ahead in their modest home in Romulus.

"Richard would be doing his thing in the basement and I'd be sewing in the upstairs room. It was early days and all very crude of course, but we were turning out a couple of vests a day and the market was coming along nicely.

"By then we were able to afford rolls of ballistic nylon and also Velcro in bulk from the people that supply Detroit's motor industry. I'd sit upstairs and sew the stuff together. I'd finish one set of straps and I'd ask little Andy—he was then about two years old—to take the finished product to his daddy in the basement.

"He'd go all the way down two flights of steps, give it to him, and then make his way back upstairs again. A short while later I'd repeat the process. At least it kept the little guy busy and also gave him a strong pair of legs. He was a child that seemed to like to do things for us . . . made it all rather helpful."

Then came the demonstration at Slovene Hall. Davis never told his wife that he'd be turning the gun on himself in front of a couple thousand Detroit cops.

"He came home one evening and opened his shirt and said, 'Look what I did.' Of course I was very upset. But he was there, right in front of me and safe. In fact, he wasn't hurt and, as he explained, he'd achieved what he'd set out to do. Had he warned me beforehand, I'm pretty sure that I would have done everything I could have to stop him.

"Goodness, he was a family man now, with a wife and child. Giving it to me as a fait accompli somewhat lessened the blow. Then he went on and did it quite regularly after that. You kind of get used to anything after the first few times.

"About then we also started to work on our brochures. It wasn't long before the entire house was stacked with pizza boxes, sometimes up to the ceiling, which we also bought in bulk because it was cheaper. When we'd take an order, we'd write it on a pizza box, so it wouldn't get lost, and none ever did. My parents were appalled that we could live like that.

"We'd also have cops who were impressed with what we were doing, and they'd take several vests and sell them out of the trunks of their cars, usually after work, or in the locker room. Or a bunch of them would get together and discuss the pros and cons, and you'd always have one or two putting their hands into their pockets and getting themselves this new protection against bullets that everybody was starting to talk about.

"Those were the days before police departments began to buy vests for their officers and long before any big sales happened, like they do today."

As Karen Davis said, the biggest publicity of all came from the saves themselves. Richard would keep in touch with everybody who got shot wearing them and also with the people in the business that were starting to market the product.

"Each time he produced a new brochure, he'd send out batches, and before long they were being read all over America. It was truly missionary work.

"He'd never dispatch one brochure at a time, but rather, two or three or more. He'd ask the recipients to pass them on to their pals and partners, which they invariably did, together with details about the latest survival story linked to a shooting or someone stabbed. The same went out with vests that had been sold. Extra brochures would be included in the pizza box."

Richard Davis reckons today that in the early days, just by getting the word out, and by keeping the police abreast of what was happening in the business, they were routinely doubling the number of saves. At first this happened every month. Then, as more vests entered the market and he gained a wider audience, it would double every quarter. Finally sales would double year by year.

It is significant that the number of saves leveled off at the end of the millennium at about one save every eleven days or so for Second Chance alone. The rest of the body armor market together had about the same number.

By 1976, he was pushing out as many as five hundred sets of body armor a week. A decade later, this had mushroomed to fifty thousand a year, all of it from the Northern Michigan plant. Eventually, the company expanded to more plants—in Alabama and Massachusetts, and a major factory in Casablanca, Morocco, that catered to the European Union demand for body armor.

From that unit, more than seventy thousand sets of body armor were supplied to German security services alone. Karen Davis explains.

"Gradually the word about soft, concealable body armor got out and we are able to start building up what later became a pretty extensive dealer network. People would come to us and say that they believed we had potential. They'd intimate that they wanted to be a part of it, this miraculous new product, as they'd call it. We'd talk percentages, and they'd go home and do their thing for themselves and, naturally, we'd all score.

"It was modest to start with, which underscores the maxim that you should never forget the little guy. He could end up becoming the big guy—

and in a number of cases that actually happened. People grew with us. They flourished, just as the company began to become profitable and here we're talking of annual turnovers of about sixty million dollars a year when we were at our best.

"Many of these outlets were police supply companies, which you find in every American city. These people looked at our product to begin with, and though they might have been a little skeptical initially, that changed as saves multiplied into the hundreds.

"Then we'd invite them to the annual Second Chance Shoot in Central Lake, which eventually became a bit like a yearly body armor and shooting festival. Richard organized various types of competitions, very similar to the national championships. There were also ancillary events like trying to hit five bowling pins in a row, where accuracy and power counted as much as placement, especially if you were trying to knock down heavy wooden items.

"At one stage Richard was giving away tens of thousands of dollars in prizes. And with time, there were few manufacturers of law enforcement–related products that didn't supply their own prizes for the event. It became a very prestigious occasion indeed, with Richard always master of ceremonies: he'd wear a T-shirt tuxedo with short pants and that always made a fun impression.

"New people arrived each year. Eventually it became mandatory to do what almost everybody regarded as a kind of body armor pilgrimage. You were not in the loop if you hadn't been to a Second Chance function at least once."

All the while, interest in the role of body armor increased, to the point where some of the larger police departments started making inquiries.

But that was still decades ahead. The first serious order for Second Chance Body Armor came from the federal body that preceded the DEA, the Bureau of Narcotics and Dangerous Drugs, or BNDD. The head of the Detroit office was a redheaded, freckle-faced agent named Harold Davidson.

Richard Davis: "He was an incredibly good shot. Ended up number one in our first bowling pin shoot that we had on the farm. Must have been about fifty competitors and he outshot them all. Anyway, he went ahead and ordered fifty of our vests. That was way back in '74, so it was a brand new thing.

"The funny thing is that none of our vests had labels on them. It was all very secret, and it remained so for the first decade. I'd avoid talking to the press after there'd been a save . . . We didn't want publicity . . . We didn't need it because the product generated its own mystique, and everything remained sort of 'in house,' between us and the police community. We'd keep them all informed and that was about as far as it would go."

The next order of any substance came from a Detroit police agency called STRESS (Stop the Robberies, Enjoy Safe Streets). That brought in quite a few thousand dollars for the fledgling company. STRESS worked undercover and was so successful that there were more than thirty gun-toting criminals killed. The crime rate in Michigan's biggest city went down for the first time—way down.

Soon after, Philadelphia followed. Then came New York, with its Stake Out Squad, mainly used inside stores that were being robbed, though they worked elsewhere in the city as well. They had the same effect of lessening crime. Then really big orders came in: twelve thousand from the Chicago Police Department; another fifteen thousand went to the LAPD; five thousand to the Detroit Police Department; and so on around the nation.

What made the difference was that it didn't take the government long to accept that body armor was an answer to many of the killings of police officers, which had become a serious problem in every American city by the mid-1980s. So Washington stepped in and made a deal with the cities, saying that they'd pay for half the cost of any body armor that was acquired, which was a huge saving for the authorities involved.

"Obviously we didn't have a monopoly on saving lives. By the mid-1980s there were several major companies competing for the business, including Safariland, Point Blank, PACA, and Armor Holdings, which owned American Body Armor.

"But what it did," said Davis, "was that these government grants became a significant incentive for the entire body armor industry. In its own way, human nature played a role as well.

"With the government paying half the cost, you'd get people who would go to the suppliers and because a 'rich uncle' is picking up half the tab, they'd usually gravitate toward the best vest available. For a long time that helped us to market our top-of-the-line Ultima II, which eventually became the standard for concealable body armor on the American market."

It stayed that way for some years.

Richard Davis likes to sound off occasionally about the way his competitors "jumped" his patents. By then, he'd had four patents granted by the US Patent Office. Looking back today, he reckons he might have done something about it.

"But in the early days, what could I do? It took us years to get established. Some of the guilty parties, like American Body Armor, had unlimited funds. They were owned by wealthy financiers, or had gone public. To take them to court would have resulted in endless rounds of litigation, not to mention legal costs. That alone would have been formidable and cost millions.

"Of course the lawyers would have had a field day. Eventually we would have nailed each one of them, but at what cost? What was there to stop a transgressor [from] closing his factory and starting another under a different brand name, another company name?

"We gave it a lot of thought. But in the end we were doing well, and we all reckoned, what the hell. The best recourse in such a case is simply to do a better job for less money.

"That's what we did and in the end, that's what worked."

CHAPTER 6

"Let's See How Many People I Can Shoot Today"

> There is nothing quite so scary as coming face to face with your own principles. Evil, violent men must be confronted with righteous violence. Only violence will do. Nothing else works. Nothing else will get their attention. The current generation of naive grass eaters insist that *all* violence is bad. They are wrong. They have always been wrong. Even Einstein was able to see that!
>
> —John Farnam

Reginald Sutton—Reggie to his pals—agrees. The only difference, he says, is that no cop gets up in the morning and says, "Let's see how many people I can shoot today."

As he maintains, the last thing a cop wants is to be shot or to shoot somebody. "You don't want to take somebody's life, because you then have to contend with the reality of that event forever. It's something that never goes away. Remember, the person that you kill has a family. Even though this lawbreaker might be the meanest bad guy on the block, there are still people out there who love him. That's how I look at it.

"But if I really have to do the necessary, then I will do what I have to. I speak from experience, having been hit by four bullets on a drug raid."

Sometimes, he added, there is absolutely no choice. "Then it's him or me," says the New Haven Police Department (NHPD) detective who had been in five shootings by the time of our interview.

Before Reggie Sutton earned his badge, he served four years in the US Marines. He was actually due to be deployed to Lebanon prior to his discharge and lost friends when Hezbollah terrorists drove a truck into a five-story structure used as a barracks by the Marines in Beirut. The suicide bomber detonated a ton of explosives and killed 240 American servicemen.

He's proud of his time in the military and keeps all the old badges and mementos. He has a US Marine flag and his unit insignia hanging on the walls of his home. *Semper Fi* (Always Faithful) means a lot to this detective.

Since then, he has conducted numerous drug busts involving firearms. He is also twice married and the proud father of four lovely kids. Through it all, he has taught unarmed combat to youngsters of all races in one of the best dojos along the Atlantic seaboard.

Working out at Elm City Judo, this second-degree black belt with almost three decades of experience has helped produce nine juvenile state and northeast open champions, one of whom is his son, Maurice. More recently, some of his protégés excelled in the 2004 Special Olympics.

His students range in age from five to their late teens; they are black, white, Hispanics, and everything else. He teaches Kodokan judo. Sutton also trains in tae kwon do.

Born, as he calls it, "on the wrong side of the tracks," young Reggie was three when his parents moved to New Haven. He learned very quickly to use both fists and guile in Fair Haven District, the Eastern Circle housing projects, one of the toughest neighborhoods anywhere. He concedes that much of what he assimilated about the hard side of life as a black teen—growing up in a society riddled with violence, racism, drugs, and gangs—he applies to his work today.

"I come from there. I know my own people. I understand why they do this or that, even though it might appear illogical to people who have never known hard times. Even the worst criminals who know me are aware of my principles. They understand what I stand for and from where I come. Also, it says something that they display courtesy and respect when I'm around, perhaps by walking on the other side of the street, or disappearing during my tour of duty."

After almost twenty years in the force, Reggie Sutton's life has changed in other respects as well. Being a detective in New Haven, he declares, is a responsibility that needs to be experienced up close before it can be properly understood.

"A detective in this city has his job cut out for him because they throw everything at us. What I do during the course of my duties is basically the next level of police work. It is somewhat different from the undercover plainclothes duties I had before, and a couple of notches up from patrolmen, who, as we all know, are the backbone of any police department. They set the foundation for detective investigations.

"What is different is that we take the investigation right to the very end, to the courts, trial, verdict, and sentencing. Ultimately, if we detectives are successful, we get to know that a criminal is going away for a very long time. Bottom line, the work involves lots of sweat, frustration, and heartache."

As Sutton explains, there are no half-measures to his role in law enforcement. "You need to dot all your i's and cross your t's, because a single mistake can cost you dearly, and it can be much more than a criminal going free. You've also got to accept that a slip-up could result in an innocent person being incarcerated. Those things are compounded by the fact that no matter how well you do your job, you still may be sued and you and your family could lose everything.

"Remember too," he added, "this is no ordinary place. On the one hand you have a city with remarkable amenities, a lovely setting on the ocean, and some of the most beautiful neighborhoods in the region.

"It is also Ivy League and there are very wealthy people here. Much of it is big money. There's also old money, with many residents commuting to and from New York. Others shop there. Some have second homes in New Haven, or the principal residence might be here and they own an apartment on Fifth Avenue.

"In sharp contrast, you've also got some places here that are among the poorest in the land. It's here, in the streets and alleys, where crime is commonplace and that's where trouble starts, what we're up against. Some of those people are young and desperate. You only need to give some of these criminals half a chance and they'll turn on you.

"Let's face it, they're at the lowest rung of society. Many times this is not of their own making, so they believe they've nothing to lose by letting it rip. In fact, they are of a mind that they've got everything to gain if they disrupt the status quo and like it or not, it's our job to maintain some kind of equilibrium."

Yale University's position in the heart of New Haven—as with Harvard's in Cambridge, Massachusetts, farther north—has created an unusual security situation for the city. With the high crime rate of the past coupled to a very substantial student and academic influence, the city fathers long ago decided to adopt extraordinary security measures.

The result is that New Haven—which once had almost as much crime as New York City—is protected by three security establishments (plus private security personnel). Detective Sutton explained that Yale has its own police force. The Yale Police Department patrols both the university and the streets surrounding the campus. "So going into Yale itself is very safe. There are only so many ways of getting in and out, and those routes are all very carefully monitored.

"Then there is our Metro or Downtown Unit. They're geared for the business and commercial parts of the city.

"The New Haven Police Department, my lot, is a much larger force than the other two. It takes care of the rest, which includes all the housing projects, suburbs, and outlying areas. That's where my colleagues and I come in."

During our interview, Reginald Sutton let his guard down only once when he admitted that what he did was hard not only on the mind, but also on the body and the soul.

"You see things which, if you're not careful, can make you hard and uncompromising, not only in the department, but with ordinary people. Each of us has to watch for that, because if you lose your objectivity, your balance, then your judgment goes. And so does trust.

"You must never get complacent, because there's just too much at stake," he declared with his customary open-faced smile.

"When I really think I've had it rough, then I think of my daughter, little Jo'Anna, who is ten years old. I go home, and I leave all this behind. She and the other three don't need to know anything about all this until they're ready for it, which will come all too soon.

"Right now she thinks her Daddy is one big teddy bear. I want to keep it that way. I try not to take home some of the feelings I have at work. But sometimes the things you do and see are locked in your brain. Sometimes it becomes difficult to be detached when you've closed the front door behind you. Suddenly you become father and husband.

"Trouble is, the average American really has no idea what we police are put through in keeping them secure. They take a lot for granted, but I suppose that's the taxpayers' prerogative."

A few hours talking to Sutton leaves one with an image of an intense, dedicated professional. New Haven is fortunate to have this detective and a lot more like him in that gray-faced concrete structure in Union Avenue close to the railroad station.

My son and I got an insight into one of the problems that face this police department. I'd gone to New York on business, and Luke was waiting for me outside the main railway station when a young man—probably a student at Yale—walked up and secured his bike to a steel pole in the concrete on Union Avenue. He took no chances, locking a heavy-linked chain through the frame of the bike and all the way around the steel support. All this took place a short stroll from Detective Sutton's office, which should have been another plus.

A short while later, two Hispanic youngsters, probably fifteen or sixteen years old, ambled by. They took a long hard look around and then stripped the bike to its bare frame. From start to finish, this effort took about forty seconds.

As Luke commented afterward, there were a lot of people who observed this action but nobody did a thing. Nobody wanted to get involved. "Probably didn't want to get stabbed," he suggested, which was probably the nub of it . . .

Reggie Sutton's career with the New Haven Police Department started, literally, with a bang. He'd completed the Police Academy, and one of his first duties was at a rap concert at the New Haven Coliseum.

The gig had just started when a report came of a young man having been stabbed in the neck, "and that resulted in the biggest brawl of the year. There was fighting everywhere," he explained. "Also, there was no controlling it. The mob was on the rampage."

The concert that December night had drawn a huge number of undesirables. At that time New Haven was the crime capital of the region.

Sutton: "There were more gangs than the authorities cared to count, or even admit to. We had a homicide every ten days or so." Out-of-towners had descended on the city that evening, from New London, Stamford, Bridgeport, and elsewhere. That complicated security issues still more.

"So here I am, with another rookie, Officer Monquie Cain, and we're faced with this situation that we've never experienced before, because it was only six months since we left the Academy. We took responsibility for the kid because we were the only ones there who were interested in his welfare: my God, he was dying and nobody else would touch him!

"You'll recall that's when AIDS first became rampant. Everybody was terrified of being infected. At first glance we could see that his wound was bleeding like there was no end to it . . . looked like the main artery had been severed.

"So I did what I was trained for, got on the radio and gave our location. But as fate would have it, the streets around the Coliseum are all one-way, and the paramedic unit overran us. With everybody rushing to get away from the rumpus, traffic had suddenly become overwhelming. The result was that the ambulance was unable to back up and I had no option but do something drastic or this youngster would really die on us.

"First I had to stop the bleeding. I thought the best would be to use the sleeve of his coat and wrap it around the wound, around his neck. And because we couldn't chance waiting any longer, I just picked him up and carried him up a flight of stairs to the main exit, where the medics said they'd pulled up.

"We got him to the top of the stairs, I put him down, legs raised, like they'd taught us. Just then a couple of the medics came around the corner, but it was too late. He died right there on the sidewalk . . . shook me up for days afterward. What a waste of a life! He was certainly some mother's boy."

On another occasion, sitting with three other officers in what is today called District Eight, a housing complex previously known as Farnham Courts, Sutton and his colleagues suddenly came under fire from one of the nearby buildings. Gunshots reverberated among the buildings, and there was no mistaking the rounds as they ricocheted off the pavement around their cars.

"The bastards were taking pot shots at us, but it didn't take us long to zero in on one of the roofs across the street. A mad scramble to get up there followed, with back-up teams giving support. They conducted an extensive rooftop search and two long guns were found. We were never able to work out what that was all about, except that the people responsible probably hated cops."

This was one of five times Detective Sutton has come under fire while with the NHPD.

"You know, coming out of the Police Academy, one of the instructors said some of us would never be involved in a shooting incident in our entire careers. He added that some of us may never even remove our weapon from its holster in reaction to a threat. In contrast, he said that there would be one or two of us who would possibly be involved in exceptional circumstances. I suppose he was right, because some officers with whom I came on the job have never faced any real drama in almost twenty years of police work.

"Yet two weeks after we started work here, my best friend Sammy Cotto and I found ourselves with our guns drawn as we initiated the arrest and apprehension of several subjects in possession of seven handguns and rifles. This arrest netted us the first commendation of our careers.

"On the night I got shot, I remember Sammy coming to my hospital ward and saying to me, 'Don't worry Reggie, this will never happen again. You're home free now. You remember what the instructor said: we've had our experiences with people with guns.'

"Then a couple of weeks later, he goes out and is involved in another exchange of gunfire. It's a tough new world out there."

A still youthful lawman in his forties—who, his friends all say, hasn't aged a day in a decade—Detective Sutton has strong views about wearing concealable body armor.

He admits to taking heat for this initially; some of his colleagues objected to his wearing a vest. They claimed that he was trying to "jinx" them. Others said that body armor was "sissy stuff." Still more believed that to wear a ballistic vest was a bad omen, that it was inviting disaster.

"I'd get my balls busted, because I was one of the few who would never go out without my vest. I didn't tell them that my mother had originally bought it for me when I graduated from the Academy. We weren't exactly poor, but there was never enough cash to go around. Also, the department didn't provide us with body armor like they do today.

"So I kept my side of the bargain and wore it under my sweatshirt, T-shirt, jacket, anything. The night I got shot, that same vest took two slugs. Saved my life.

"That changed everybody's thinking. Some of the old timers started looking at body armor a little differently. Gradually the perception swung around to the way I'd been doing it all along. These days most of the officers wear them, and if they don't when they're on duty, they're in trouble.

"Seems I started something there too . . ."

The night of March 12, 1993, when Detective Sutton became a shooter's target, he'd been on the three-to-eleven shift for about a week. Things had gone smoothly until an hour before they were due to clock out when word came down about a last-minute job. It had to be done that night.

They were to raid an after-hours place, the Unity Social Club at 4 West Street. The word was that crack cocaine, crystal meth, and marijuana were sold there; there had been shootings; there was also illegal after-hours liquor. The club needed to be shut down and the order came directly from the mayor's office.

Eight officers—including Sutton—were chosen for the job. Judge Joseph B. Clark signed a search and seizure warrant and the group was briefed. The men accepted that it wouldn't be easy: although it was almost spring, it had been snowing heavily and there weren't that many cars on the street. The men were warned that getting close undetected would be difficult. Also, their unmarked cars had been in the department for a long time and there were few criminals in the city who didn't recognize them.

Sutton: "But I had a problem. I hadn't eaten much until then, and because I was in training, I liked to get something in my stomach, perhaps four or five small meals a day. I needed to keep my energy level up. So I told my boss, Archie Generosa, that I had to get something before we went off or I wouldn't be able to function well. He agreed, but reluctantly.

"I shot out to the local hamburger place. Leaving through our reception area downstairs, I spotted two women I'd seen there earlier in the day. They'd been robbed of everything they had and had come in about lunchtime to report their loss. Almost ten hours later they were still sitting there. Being from out of town, they told me that they were waiting for their ride. I knew they had no money.

"I rushed back to the station, because Archie had called me on my cell phone and told me to hurry up. But as I passed through the main door I saw the two women again. Hey, I knew that they'd had nothing to eat all day, so I gave them my hamburger and fries. Hang it, their need was greater than mine. I suppose you could call it my good deed for the day, and I'd like to think it paid a few dividends."

Split into two teams, the cars pulled up a short distance from the club and the cops poured out. At this point they were spotted by a lookout that ran inside and slammed the door shut, bolting it.

Detective Sutton takes up the story: "I come out of the driver's seat. My job was to carry the two-man battering ram for knocking down obstacles like locked doors. I ran up, hit the door hard just once, and it flew open. Then the fun started, with me being the first one in. I'll never forget it, Sammy Cotto was right behind me and he went left. Frank Roberts took the right.

"What threw us immediately was that only after we'd entered this place did we discover that this was actually one fairly large room. We'd expected something else, which underscores the dangers of going into any situation unprepared. They'd switched off the lights and all the illumination we had came from the streetlights outside.

"Also, we were completely disoriented because the entire back wall of the place was one giant mirror. It was huge. So it made the place look much bigger than it really was.

"Meanwhile, we could see that there were people there, all of them like shadows, moving about. We couldn't make out much detail, except that we know some of them were women. We ordered everybody down.

"At that point I was alone, weapon in hand and walking toward the center of this place. Then a shot rang out, which hit me in the arm and continued right through. It was a flesh wound through my triceps, but the bullet grazed my body and made holes in my shirt and jacket. It came out on the other side without touching my torso. Now I'm hurt and I'd like to retaliate. But I can't see the guy with the gun."

Unable to react because of bad light and the many people in the building—some of whom might have been innocents—the squad was obliged to hold their fire. Sutton accepts that this might be just as well because the mirror confused everything. They initially thought there were a hundred people there. In fact, there were nineteen.

"So I turned toward where the shot came from and two more shots rang out, both of them 9mm Para. This time I was hit in the chest, but I was saved from further injury by my body armor. In retrospect, my vest kind of acted like a pitcher's mitt. The shock caused me to spin and hit the floor.

"The next thing I knew this guy was shooting at me again. He'd walked right up, almost standing over me with his gun. Then he started firing again, and when he was done he'd shot seventeen times altogether.

"There was I, face down, bullets everywhere. I'd turned my head to the left and the next minute all I see is pieces of metal flying up next to my face. That didn't make sense, because I thought the floor was made of wood. We found out later that it was metal, which was why the bullets were bouncing off.

"He missed with every shot except one more, which shattered my thumb. That was on the hand that I'd hoped was covering my head. By now, my guys had begun shooting at this felon, who, despite hitting me, was probably the worst pistol shot in New England.

"I'd taken four of his bullets. Lucky for me, Sammy Cotto returned fire. That allowed me to get my bearings as the subject scrambled for cover and I was able to return fire before finding my way out the door.

"It ended immediately afterward. Seeing more cops coming through the door—there were patrol groups on their way anyway—the shooter disappeared toward the back of the building where he was arrested soon afterward, but now without his weapon in hand.

"Though I wasn't around when our guys began to clean up, they found eight guns on the premises, including the 9mm that was used to try to kill me. I reckon this kind of underscores the wisdom of my decision to go in hard and fast: if we'd waited for back-up we might have had a reenactment of the OK Corral. Very likely some of those people inside the club would have used all those guns against us, which, in such unhealthy circumstances, mirrors and all, would definitely have resulted in more casualties.

"Tactically, they had the edge. They knew the layout of the place, and we didn't.

"Also, the mirror proved to be deceptive. In fact the image that Sammy Cotto thought he was shooting at initially was actually the reflection of the gunman in the mirror. Afterward, when we discussed the raid he said he couldn't understand why the guy didn't drop because he knew he was on target. It was like that dream all cops have about the bad guy that you just can't stop.

"As it was, two of the women who were on the floor ended up getting shot in the legs. Nothing serious; some of the ricochets hit them."

The suspect, Michael Allen, who'd fired seventeen shots at a New Haven detective, was never charged with attempted murder. He'd ditched his gun inside the building and the police found it afterward, together with the others. But in such poor light, Detective Sutton had to admit in the line-up that he couldn't be absolutely certain who it was that had shot him.

And since he wasn't going to send an innocent person to prison—even though they took in everybody who was there that night—he couldn't testify that he was 100 percent certain that Allen was his man.

Though he slipped through that time, the police knew exactly who the shooter was. They got him in the end, and he's in jail today, serving a thirty-year sentence. But, as Detective Sutton told me, he left a destructive trail behind him, including one or more murders.

Having lit the club up afterward—with enough big lights to illuminate Yankee Stadium—the police spoke to everybody in the building. Two of the girls who were there when the cops arrived fingered the shooter. One of them discreetly pointed him out at the station while he was being interviewed. Both women said that they were prepared to testify.

Sutton: "One of the girls was part of a group called Elm City Nation and they came to see me in the hospital. They actually waited until they could speak to me alone. She said they'd be happy to testify against that crooked slob.

"They also explained why we couldn't find him when he was firing at us. He'd apparently slunk down low, next to one of the girls on the floor. He'd actually used her as a shield. So there was I, looking for someone at normal height and he was down there on the ground.

"Then, two weeks later, this young woman was coming to her house back from the corner store with a family friend and someone killed her as they drove past. Shot her several times. Though we had everything she'd told us on tape, she still had to come back to the station and sign the statement . . . never got around to doing that, and the man walked."

It was alleged that Michael Allen was a member of the Elm City Nation and that they were behind the murder of the witness. "So when we got to court, he got time for narcotics and weapons charges, and then got out of jail on bond, which I found inexplicable because of the serious nature of the charges.

"He'd tried to kill a cop, and we in law enforcement take a very dim view of that. We don't forget, so we kept close tabs on him once he got out of prison. We always do that with people we know are hardened criminals. In a way, it's a kind of life insurance . . . We monitor everything he does, who he meets, where he goes.

"Not very long afterward, a robbery took place. It was a gang job and we were running around locking up people we knew were linked to drugs. Didn't get him then, but we had info that he was riding around in a Mazda MPV, which was stopped shortly afterward. And what a pleasure it was when a handgun was found under his seat.

"This time he went to federal court. Because the rules are different there, I was able to come in and tell them everything. Also, the feds go much further than we do because their tolerance is somewhere between zero and nothing, with the result that he got his thirty years."

This brings up a major challenge faced by US prosecution authorities: witnesses threatened with violence or death, before, during, or after a trial.

The intimidation or killing of a potential witness, Reggie Sutton said, is hardly a recent phenomenon. This is much more widespread than some police authorities concede. It is worse in the depressed, low-income societies that blight every American city. There everybody knows just about everybody else, criminals included, as with the young woman who was prepared to testify against Michael Allen.

Barely a month goes by without reports appearing in police journals such as *American Police Beat, Law and Order*, or *Law Enforcement News*, of witnesses being intimidated. This situation has become so bad that some district attorneys have urged their state legislatures to provide better protection for witnesses. They have also asked for greater punishment for injuring, intimidating, or even killing those who would prevent them from taking the stand.

One such authority, District Attorney Daniel F. Conley of Suffolk County, Massachusetts, disclosed that in cases where violence, guns, and gangs were involved, about 90 percent of the witnesses were intimidated. And if they weren't, their families were.

He remembers one woman who summoned up enough courage to testify against a felon, and then promptly fled the courthouse after she watched bench after bench in the courtroom being filled by the defendant's fellow gang members. Conley said that her comment afterward was that if she had gone ahead and testified, they might as well have painted a bull's-eye on her back.

It is DA Conley's view that this problem is on the increase. He feels very strongly that the issue simply does not get the attention it deserves.

Having been in one major shootout, Detective Reggie Sutton these days has a very different, more tactical approach to running into buildings where some of the occupants might be armed.

Though he hasn't been shot at again, he's had some close encounters. On one occasion, after the social club affair, he and his team went into a building, again on a search and seizure warrant. This time, he was number three to enter.

"We came in through the back door. While the others veered off ahead and upstairs, I realized there was a room off to the left that nobody had bothered to check. I moved gingerly past it, and because the door was open half a crack, I see a guy get up off the bed and take a gun out from under his pillow.

"Now this is a pretty small room, only big enough for a bed and a cupboard. Very quietly, very deliberately, I entered and got the drop on this guy. Now we were four or five feet apart and I was at the foot of the bed and we both had weapons.

"I told him to drop it, but he didn't react. He kept the gun in his hand, but it was pointed down, by his side. So I said again, loud, so there could be no mistake, 'Drop it!' This time he looked me dead in the eye and he saw I meant business. This was for real . . .

"I would have shot him without a doubt, but fortunately two other cops heard me, and they ran up to give cover. We had ourselves a criminal with this illegal firearm he'd probably have used if I'd given him half a chance. He was one mean mother."

Detective Sutton thought about that event afterward. He was probably just as afraid as the other man. Shooting him, he reckons, would have been the last option, though it would have had to be a split-second thing.

One of the final words on this subject is from Richard Davis, who has spoken to hundreds of cops who have been shot and survived. "This is typical of the conundrum that sometimes faces the modern American law enforcement officer. They have to make a decision that is immediate. Do they shoot—or don't they?

"Most times they have a micro-second to make up their minds whether the situation, in the darkened confines of a building where they've already established there are children or elderly people present, is life threatening. If they're wrong one way, they can face serious charges, sometimes including that of murder. If they're wrong the other way, they're dead meat.

"Even if they're proven to have been correct in using their firearm, the news media—which is almost always anti-law enforcement—together with a bunch of self-serving politicians who rarely take the trouble to check the facts, will attack and second-guess them.

"What's more, that is all invariably done from the comfort and safety of their offices."

Detective Sutton is outspoken about most things, the most striking being the need for his people to drag themselves out of the quagmire in which so many of them have found themselves. And they need to do so by their own bootstraps, he forcibly states.

He long ago determined that there are ways of combating the hopeless poverty and lethargy that has beset so many minority communities. He points to his own role in taking young people off the streets and helping them make something of themselves.

"I work the worst areas in the city, only because I feel that is the place that needs the most attention. I understand the people there. I come from where they are, which is one of the reasons why I am genuine about what I do when I'm there.

"I go into these poor districts and I see much that can be done to change things for the better. It's not just education. It's also financing, and perhaps altering the landscape in some of the worst areas, something that I've actually witnessed . . . I've seen it happen.

"We had Elm Haven, which was riddled with drugs and shootings and every other crime you could imagine. They tore down that cesspool, and completely rebuilt it with single-family homes. Then they gave the people who moved in the opportunity to own their properties, which were modest and low cost. But the operative word here is to *own* your place and not rent it.

"Even though these apartments are way below market value, the people who have them now know that they're theirs. That's a whole different feeling, going into that neighborhood, compared to somewhere that's federally funded. It's got an altogether other feel to it . . . the first being that people actually care.

"They are concerned about themselves. They worry about the welfare of their children, the place that they have put down roots. So it costs them money. Then they go out and they find themselves jobs to meet that demand. Soon you have an altogether other kind of person, another kind of community that is responsible, and, yes, very much more caring than before.

"You know, at the Police Academy one of our instructors talked about what he termed the 'broken window principle.' It basically centered on the effect that a single broken window might have on a community. So you have a situation where nobody repairs or replaces that one broken window. Soon there are two broken windows, then three, and so on[1].

"What they did for Elm Haven, basically, is that they fixed that broken window. The result is that you don't have a fraction of the problems that we had in the past, though let's be realistic, because where you have any kind of human influence, there are some problems that never go away."

It was also Sutton's opinion that making the society more responsible, by giving the people something, as he puts it, "to fight for" was another way of fighting drugs. With time, the citizens of Elm Haven had become a responsible element within the community. More important, they had also become responsive to change.

"Obviously the place still had its problems . . . some people never change. But given the opportunity—and I'm not talking about handouts, which are always counterproductive—many of them do. I've seen it happen, with home ownership having the effect of creating a social awareness among people who had little or nothing before."

[1] *Broken Windows*, the book by George Kelling and James Wilson, had a major impact on revolutionizing law enforcement in the United States in the early 1980s. As Ed Sanow, editorial director of *Law and Order*, pointed out in the September 2004 edition, "Every police management course has included the profound tactic that we can actually manage the big stuff by managing the small stuff . . . fix the window and prevent a murder." Or as it is bluntly phrased, "Arrest a small-time punk and prevent a big-time crime." Sanow goes on to make the point that a quarter century on, America's law enforcement establishment seems to have forgotten what *Broken Windows* was all about.

CHAPTER 7

Shot, Wounded, and Retired from the Force

Young and ambitious, Officer John Aguiar took two hits in the line of fire. As a result, his life was forever changed. He not only underwent a dramatic personality change that tested the strength and fortitude of his marriage, but his days in the force were over. With the help of a psychologist—who, Aguiar says, "knows cops and understands the implications of post-traumatic stress disorder"—he was able to pick up the pieces, but it took time. Aguiar provides an unusual insight into the aftermath of this tragedy.

John Aguiar, a dynamic thirty-something former policeman from Hoboken, New Jersey—Frank Sinatra's hometown and the birthplace of baseball—suffered an immense post-traumatic stress disorder (PTSD) attack after he was shot twice by a felon on the run. He acquired three holes in his body in that confrontation. The bullet that hit his shoulder was a pretty straightforward in-and-out flesh wound. Another hit his vest, directly over his heart.

The shooting occurred on April 2, 2003. As he is able to recollect more than two years later, the implications of post-traumatic stress problems only became manifest six or eight weeks later. Ultimately, they were serious enough for him to leave the force.

Six feet tall, dark-haired, and personable—good looking enough to become a Second Chance poster boy after his shooting—this otherwise fit and agile young man who today plays soccer for an amateur New Jersey league talks easily about the debacle.

"Debacle it was," he admits. "It was an experience like no other because the wounds I suffered in those critical ten or fifteen seconds went on to prevent me from doing the one thing that I'd always believed I was best suited for. That was to be a cop.

"That cretin deprived me of something that was rightfully mine," he said after we'd met in downtown Hoboken within a couple of hundred yards of where it all happened. But, he adds, "Life has a way of changing, of sometimes presenting the unexpected," he told me as we looked toward the now-depleted Manhattan skyline across the way.

John Aguiar accepts that the decision to be retired from the Hoboken Police Department was correct. It was reached by Dr. Eugene Stephanelli, the psychologist who treated him throughout this difficult period, and by Aguiar himself.

"I didn't like it, obviously. But I accept that PTSD can be a liability. Nobody really knows how I might react if the same thing happened again, and, let's face it, in New Jersey that's always a possibility."

As he points out, it need not be a shooting that triggers the syndrome. The high stress level of many different situations in which police officers find themselves just about every other day can result in an unwarranted response. That, he suggested, has potential for harm.

"I believe PTSD is the mind's way of assuring survival. Where once there was a passive awareness of one's surroundings, now the body and the mind overly react, in such a way as to assure that they won't be harmed. This is potentially disruptive, especially since the very essence of being a cop is to move toward a threat [and danger] and not away from it. Split-second decisions are being made all the time. A wrong one can cost a life or worse.

"I am also aware that my personal feelings about the shooting are still there. I look in the mirror when I shave. I see the scars left by the bullets.

"Make no mistake, these are strong impulses. They might be sublimated somewhere in the back of the mind, but they're there all right. So perhaps, I thought at the time, it is best to move on. And anyway, I'm doing something today that brings me into regular contact with my old pals, in and out of uniform. I see them regularly, only now it's as a consequence of the business I'm in."

Together with some old school friends, John Aguiar these days heads a computer firm specializing in software for law enforcement units, police departments, EMS, fire fighters, HAZMAT, and others. His company creates programs that are useful to them all. "We know how these people work, what they need, and we set about providing it."[1]

Despite the emotional drama, Aguiar doesn't mind talking—either about the event or subsequent developments that, for more than a year, cast his mind and life into turmoil. There's still some of it that he doesn't understand. "I took hits that put me in the hospital. That makes me one of the fortunate few. There are others who were not so lucky. So I am blessed. My family [is] as well, obviously."

About the shooting and how it affected family life, John Aguiar talks warmly about his wife Anna, a nurse at a local hospital. Originally from Poland, she arrived in the States with her parents and two siblings as a child (though her family has since become six). Overcoming the language barrier, Anna Aguiar graduated with a bachelor's degree in nursing at Long Island University.

Also constantly on his mind are John Aguiar's two children. At the time of writing, Sebastian was three years old and Kayla was not yet a year when we got together to chat. He calls her his Second Chance baby. She wouldn't be around today if he hadn't been wearing his body armor on that spring night on the south bank of the Hudson River.

Second Chance Body Armor has a hefty file on children who came into the world after their fathers had been saved because they wore body armor. That tally is today somewhere near the four hundred mark, with a smattering of grandchildren from some of the earlier saves.

"When I got out of the hospital once it was all over, I was fine. I'd survived a major shooting, my wounds were healing, and life was great. Then, about two months after getting back to the real world, a slew of problems arose.

"What happened was a slow but also a distinct and identifiable process. First I found that I couldn't sleep, or I slept badly. I became argumentative, not only with friends and family, but also with my wife. Now this was a huge change, if you realize that we'd been together for more than ten years. We *know* each other well enough to understand our shortcomings, and, let's face it, we all have them. Even more important, in all that time, we'd had only one honestly bad argument, and that was it. Then suddenly we're butting heads on a daily basis." He also found himself constantly yelling at the children or being easily annoyed by them for nothing more than what kids do every day of their young lives.

Aguiar had not yet gone back to work and he did not yet know that he would never be a policeman again.

He explained that as part of the process—or what he calls departmental policy—he was kept out of the office. Apart from having his physical wounds needing to be seen to, he was instructed to seek psychological help, not because anybody felt that he might need it but because it was the way things worked in the force. "Essentially, they wanted to make sure that everything was fine; it was an approach that came from years of experience.

"So I saw a shrink, and on the surface—to my mind, anyway—it seemed okay. Then these *things* came crawling into my life.

"There were no dramatic flashbacks like you see in the movies or that kind of stuff. But when I went out in public I'd feel myself retreating into a state of paranoia. It was as if I was waiting for somebody to pop out and start shooting again."

During this period Officer Aguiar didn't have any body armor to wear either. The vest he'd had on when the shootings happened—and which absorbed the chest bullet—was taken from him by the prosecutor's office for ballistics and evidence.

"So this whole time I was in physiotherapy for my shoulder and seeing my psychologist once a week, going from one to the other. It was all routine. But meanwhile, I have a problem with my mind and it's not getting better. In fact, it is worsening."

Eventually Aguiar's psychologist, Dr. Stephanelli, put the young officer on medication for anxiety and panic attacks.

"This doctor had done a lot of work for the Police Benevolent Association and was a real angel. He'd worked a lot with police officers. He understood the kind of problems they'd faced in the past and were facing now. Essentially, he understood cop mentality . . .

"If I had gone to any other kind of doctor, one who had never seen this sort of thing, I doubt whether I'd have had the same understanding. Dr. Stephanelli, in contrast, comprehends fundamental realities. He understands full well that the mind of the policeman is very different from the run of the mill out there, and I was fortunate to be able to work through all this with him.

"Our minds work differently, and you have to look at what we're up against to understand why this is so. Hell, our wives wave us goodbye and there's not one among them who hasn't been fearful about whether they'd see us again at the end of the shift . . . It's that kind of existence. It can be tough.

"Being a cop, we are held to inordinately high standards of professionalism by society. People expect us to be exemplary. Then, when we're insulted, usually in public, we have to smile and pretend we didn't hear or didn't see it. So too when we stumble, and believe me, it happens. You read about it in the press, and situations are often taken out of context.

"Let's face it: the world out there very often views us with contempt, if only because the mechanisms that we, the enforcers of the law, are obliged to use. We are often seen as obstructive, or possibly out of kilter, compared to how the rest of an invariably judgmental community might handle something similar. But man, when there's a problem, *are they our friends*?

"There is a lot of hypocrisy out there . . . We are the true outcasts of American society and we have only each other for comfort.

"We use different techniques to combat the everyday stresses of the job, and Dr. Stephanelli—with years of experience in these kinds of cases—took all that into account. He just sort of kept on top of me . . . made sure that I was okay . . . even brought my wife into it for counseling sessions.

"At one point I actually went physical. I put my fist through a coffee table, which was something that I'd never done before. I must have been a tough nut to handle."

The problems at home took time to subside. Aguiar felt he'd become totally isolated from everybody. "Anna went to pieces, because she wanted to find out what she could do for me, and at first she couldn't do anything . . . at least until Dr. Stephanelli's approach started to take effect.

"That was a bad time, a really bad time. I didn't even want to go out, like take a break and the two of us go to a restaurant or to movie. I couldn't be bothered . . . didn't want to see or meet people, even old friends. Then, with treatment, things did begin to improve. But it was no overnight thing.

"We had to take it step by step, day by day. I'd relapse and we'd begin again. And Anna, bless her lovely heart, she was there for me. She was always there for me. The kids too. And when you have them around, you begin to get things a little better into perspective. You have two hard choices: you give up, or you take a stand. So you say to yourself, I need to move on. And I did.

"I've always maintained a barrier between the two lives I led, the one at work and other at home, though that can be difficult. Being behind closed doors with Anna and the kids provided me with an escape from the harshness outside. For some of us, I suppose, it's essential to lead a double life; like oil and water, the two just don't mix."

More than two years after the shooting, former police officer John Aguiar is not yet out of the woods. He says that even today he's not yet 100 percent.

"But then, I suppose I must also pose the question, who among us is really 100 percent?" He gave me his million-dollar smile, one that appeared in all the major law enforcement magazines in Second Chance Body Armor advertisements, including *Law and Order* and *American Police Beat.*

John Aguiar's story began early one April evening when reports came in of a cab driver having been shot on Washington Street, Hoboken's main drag. Dispatch gave out details of a suspect who had taken off running westbound on Fifth Street. Since there are only so many ways in and out of the city, the police quickly set up a perimeter that covered most exits.

The criminal was later identified as Abraham Santiago and he was reported headed west. That was troubling, since that area was lower-income with high crime; then add the fact that it bordered Jersey City. Nearby was a stretch where it was possible to duck into the woods.

Initial descriptions of the perp were vague, Hispanic male in his twenties. He wore a black jump suit and a baseball cap, which, Aguiar said later, would have fitted the description of about 60 percent of Hoboken's youthful Hispanic community.

The authorities were dealing with someone who might prove impossible to trace. But they hadn't reckoned on the man himself. As they discovered afterward, Santiago had been in depression for some years. On the night in question he had told friends he was going into town and mentioned something about "kill or be killed." He was reported to have been trying to join a gang and there are indications that he might have wanted to prove that he was a recruit worthy of their attention.

Not all of this makes sense. Prior to the first shooting, he walked up to a cab, got in, and asked the driver to take him to Jersey City. He actually gave an address, which he wouldn't have done if he'd been thinking properly. Especially if he'd intended to kill somebody.

Then the driver told him he couldn't take him anywhere. He already had a fare, he said, adding that he was parked where he was because he was waiting for him. A noisy altercation ensued, ending with Santiago trying to kill the driver with his .45 ACP automatic pistol.

Clearly not the best of shots, he grazed the cabbie twice, once in each leg. Then he took off running. Aguiar takes up the story:

"I was in my cruiser and started to look around about a block away from where the shooting went down. I drove around several city blocks, moving in concentric circles to see if I could spot someone fitting the description. Remember, we had no name yet, only a description.

"I'd gone about twenty blocks when I spotted somebody who looked likely. He was walking fast and he looked spooked. Also, he had on the trademark cap and, as the first report had described him, his clothes were dark. So centering my attention on this guy, I decided we had to talk.

"I circled the block again hoping to come on to him suddenly, perhaps as he got to the far corner. One of the reasons I wasn't able to follow him directly was because he moved against the flow of traffic. It was probably intentional, aware that a police car couldn't creep up on him from behind."

Just then, to Aguiar's surprise, on the corner of Adams and First streets Barbara Cahill, his sergeant's wife, came out of her dojo where she'd been working out. She greeted the young cop with a wave. Normally, when things are slow and cops on patrol run into the wives of colleagues, they might offer them a lift. But not that night.

"I was going at about five miles an hour and though I gave a nodding hi to Barbara, I just kept on going. She could see I was on the lookout for something.

I'd focused all my attention back to the area ahead where I expected to see the suspect come out, but he wasn't there."

Officer Aguiar kept going, now checking both sides of the street. Going past side alleys, he looked to see if the man he was looking for had ducked in, or was perhaps hiding between cars.

"I'd gone halfway down the block when I spotted him again. This time he was coming out of an entrance from between two cars and I realized with shock that he was heading straight for me.

"The only thing I vividly recall about those initial few moments was making eye contact with the man. He was fairly close. What I saw was a face and a pair of eyes that registered absolutely nothing. His entire countenance was a total void, if that's the way to describe it . . . a blank stare that I'll never forget if I get to live to be a hundred.

"In a fraction of a second I became aware that he was moving with serious intent, as if he was on a mission. Now, this was a pretty big man, about six feet tall, two hundred and twenty pounds, and you couldn't mistake it. 'A real mean mother,' as somebody had once described him.

"From that moment, everything happened fast," said Aguiar. As their eyes met, the suspect reached into his waistband and drew his pistol.

"I'd stopped the vehicle by then and was momentarily caught short by the abruptness of it all. I did what I thought at the time to be the only logical thing and screamed at him to show me his hands. At the same time I tried to draw my own firearm but I wasn't getting it right. I tugged, pushed, pulled, but it was stuck in the holster. I couldn't get to it."

As Aguiar explained afterward, what worked against him was the holster's standard safety device, designed in such a way as to prevent officers from being disarmed from behind. Essentially, there are three motions, the most complex of which involved rocking the gun forward and then sliding it out.

"But I'd chosen the lowest level, which meant that I had to draw my weapon, a Smith & Wesson 9mm, straight up and out. That's easy enough when you're standing on the range. But just then, seated in a car that was cramped with a laptop and a bunch of gadgets, a lot of new police technology, it wasn't doing its thing for me. The gun stayed put.

"So he's already got the jump on me, and there's absolutely no hesitation on his part. He lets rip with four or five rounds. In a reflex action that I suppose is absurd, I put my hands out to deflect the bullets. It was desperate, but what else to do?"

Talking about it afterward, Aguiar reckons that the episode lasted a second, maybe two, but certainly no longer. By then he'd gone back to trying to get his firearm out and this time he succeeded.

"But I'm not home yet. I get off a single shot, and the pistol jams. It couldn't have been worse situation if I'd planned it!

"By now Barbara, the sergeant's wife, is fifteen or twenty feet from me. She's witnessed the entire catastrophe and starts to scream, which, I honestly believe is why I'm still alive today. As soon as she began yelling, the perp stopped firing. Gun in hand, Santiago started to run right at her, as if to silence her."

Barbara Cahill didn't hang around. She shot back into the dojo, which was owned by a fellow Hoboken police officer. He'd heard firing and called in a shots-fired report and then grabbed his own pistol and ran into the street.

Aguiar: "As soon as Santiago took off, I exited my cruiser. I knew I'd been shot, but right then I was so pumped up that my wounds were of secondary concern. I had a gunman on the loose who'd already proved *twice* that given the chance, he'd kill."

Radioing his position on his lapel mike—and the fact that he'd taken two hits—Officer Aguiar went after the criminal. He tried to give a description over the radio, but the on-air staff was all confusion. He could hear officers coming through, asking for his position, but because it was possible to hear only one transmission at a time, the result was little more than a scramble of words.

To compound matters, what was coming in was a mix of details that not only conflicted, but made little sense. All the people in charge could make out was that one of their cops had been shot and that the gunman had gotten away. They had no way of telling where this hullabaloo was taking place. Somewhere in Hoboken to be sure, but it's a big place.

The confusion was caused by an officer with a radio system superior to the one installed in Aguiar's cruiser, which the police called a *brick* because it was an earlier generation set and actually looked a bit like a brick. When the fracas started, he was calling in his position from the Hoboken train station.

Though the other radio was a bit more powerful than Aguiar's brick, the young policeman still managed to cut him off while he was transmitting, and he did so in mid-sentence. What came out to those trying to make sense of it was a message that Officer Aguiar was at the rail station, whereas he was actually at the other end of town.

"Meanwhile, I'm chasing the guy. At the same time I'm trying to unjam my gun, which had a round lodged in the slide.

"We'd been taught at the Academy that we should tap the butt of the pistol, rock back the slide, and it would eject whatever was jammed in there. But that wasn't working. Eventually I had to put my index finger into the top of the chamber and rip out the cartridge.

"So, my gun is cleared and Santiago is now ahead of me by twenty or thirty yards and I'm on the run after him. Hard! I must have been impervious to the pain and the blood, because I seemed to be performing pretty well, which I've since been told is the way it sometimes goes when you've taken a hit.

"As I make the next corner, I see him running down Jefferson Street. To avoid being ambushed—because I could see Santiago turning his head now and again to check whether I'm following—I crossed over to the other side of the road and began to use parked cars and vehicles coming toward me for possible cover.

"He must have seen me, because moments later he runs up to a Ford Explorer, puts his gun to the head of the driver, and tells the poor man to 'get out of the fucking car,' which he does, hands straight up in the air. I now try and take a shot, but since the ejected victim is in my line of fire, I shout for him to get down. He immediately complies and takes a header straight into a driveway."

Aguiar took one more shot from Santiago but it missed. He managed to get five hits into the Explorer as it pulled away, but none hit the target. Since the Explorer's cab sits fractionally higher than most, he couldn't aim upward because there were numerous first floor apartments in his line of sight.

"Couldn't take a chance of hitting somebody else. So I aimed low, and, of course, it didn't do the job. I would have liked to stop him there, but it was no deal.

"Suddenly I'm starting to feel the effects of my wounds and I'm groggy. Shock, though delayed, had started to set in, and I was going in and out of tiny blackouts. They came at split-second intervals and there was no real loss of consciousness, but I was aware, too, that it was no longer safe for me to discharge my weapon.

"I kept chasing for a little while longer. Even got a partial plate of the vehicle, which I radioed in. This time I got through! Dispatch had cleared the air of all unnecessary transmissions because this Santiago thing had become big. Also, they had on their hands a cop who'd been shot and they still had to get to me.

"At which point I felt my body literally start to shut down. That frightened me. I had to go down on one knee to stay with it when two guys came running up to me. Still to this day I don't know who they were, though one of them kept asking me to holster my weapon. I didn't do so at first, because I wasn't registering properly. The other guy was saying over and over again that help was on the way . . . they really thought I'd croak on them. Shortly afterward, the cavalry came in.

"None too soon either. By then I was in a pretty bad way and I'd lost a lot of blood."

They got Abraham Santiago. He was stupid enough to give the original cab driver his address in Jersey City.

From his hospital bed, Officer Aguiar was able to tell dispatch in which direction the perp had taken off. Since they figured he was going home, the police in Jersey City were radioed with details about the vehicle, its tag, as well as a more accurate description of the man.

Santiago went home, apparently to reload his weapon. He told his mother he'd shot a cop, and that she wouldn't see him for a while. Possibly a long while, he suggested.

As he was leaving, he met two sheriff's officers and exchanged gunfire with them. Then he took off again.

A seven- or eight-block foot chase ensued, during which time he shot another officer in the stomach. It was a clean wound into the abdomen and out the back without damaging vital organs. In fact, Aguiar heard afterward, the man recovered fully and was back in the force.

The man who got Santiago was Sheriff Deputy Mark Borcherts, whom John Aguiar refers to as a tough, stocky, five-foot-nothing fighter "who is one of the greatest guys you'll ever meet." Borcherts shot Santiago only once in the torso and he'd bled to death by the time he'd reached the hospital.

"So at least I got closure," Aguiar said with a measure of satisfaction, his big smile dominating.

He confided that that was more than a female police officer with the Washington State Patrol achieved after she'd been badly wounded in a shootout with a felon who had applied for parole several times. The worst of it, he said, was that the criminal was likely to get out of prison eventually.

He'd met the policewoman at one of the Second Chance Save reunions at the plant in Central Lake.

The late Abraham Santiago was not unknown to the police. He'd been arrested numerous times for aggravated assault. Being big and strong and a bully, he seemed to revel in thumping people. He also had charges for receiving stolen property on his rap sheet.

Aguiar heard later that people in the area where he lived knew Santiago had guns. He'd discharged them in the middle of the night and that worried some of them. It was also suggested that he might have been involved in a couple of liquor store robberies in the vicinity. A .45 had been used in all of them and he matched descriptions given to the police. The gun itself had originally been stolen from a sports shop.

Though he kept to himself a lot, Santiago's antics worried his mother, who, though having lost her son, was apologetic to the Aguiar family. It was then that all Santiago's "depression stuff" came out, with revelations about his having painted the walls of his bedroom black and decorated it with all kinds of cryptic sayings: It is Time to Go! and A Time to Kill and a Time to Die.

"Looks like he was on a predetermined mission to take a life," John Aguiar figured.

Anna Aguiar played a role once she heard that her husband had been shot.

He'd met her originally at a club in South Jersey, while out with friends. As John says, talking about his lady, "It's been quite a ten-year ride, but it feels like yesterday when we got married."

She was four months pregnant with their daughter when the shooting occurred. Following standard procedures, the department kept calling and looking for her, but there was nobody at home because Anna was at her mother's house. It worried a lot of the officers, her husband recalls, because in no time it was all over the news that a police officer had been shot.

"She heard one of the reports and though no name was mentioned, she very soon put the logic together. She's very sharp. Now she's the one who's screaming.

"She calls the desk, and Sergeant Cahill, Barbara's husband, takes the call. He had a hard time trying to calm her down, trying to figure out at the same time where she was so that he could send a car for her with a couple of officers, as they usually do on such occasions."

The sergeant also tried to persuade her that her husband had injured a shoulder in a fight and that it was another officer who had been shot. Anna Aguiar didn't buy it. Thanks to an escort from the New Jersey State Police, she wasted no time getting to St. Mary's where she had done volunteer work in the cardiac unit.

"She was a Godsend, actually. Right there on top of all the doctors and nurses making sure that they were doing the right thing by me. From her cardiac experience, she knew exactly what monitor was needed and for what purpose—very much aware that since the second shot was over my heart, there might be serious consequences. She even worked with the chief of police who arrived shortly afterward. The two of them discussed getting me heli-flighted to Newark where they have a trauma hospital."

The following morning was the start of the first day in the rest of John Aguiar's life.

"I was still in shock, obviously, but even to this day, it still seems surreal. It was strange to hear some of the stories later on. The guys would come in and tell me that on the night of the attempted murder there was an absolutely phenomenal response from the Police Department.

"Guys who had been off duty or were at home or had been to the movies all just headed straight to St. Mary's after they heard. There were dozens who had called in by morning. Some off-duty cops were also coming in to help out with the police line. Others went to Jersey City, looking for the guy. By now they had a pretty accurate picture of him; they knew exactly who it was.

"That caused a kind of disruptiveness of its own, because there were three or four more shootings in that same area that same night, which was unusual.

"Some of the guys, in a curious way, were quite relieved to hear it was me who'd been shot, not because of anything they had on me, but because everybody knew I wore my vest. Some cops don't, so there's a difference. It was never a requirement in our department, and, for the life of me, I don't know why. I think it should be mandatory; next time somebody might not be so lucky. But guys get complacent once the memory starts to fade.

"I'd made a vow to Anna—and also to my parents when Dad was still alive—that I would never go on duty without my body armor. I didn't care if it was a hundred-and-twenty degrees in the shade, I'd put it on. And you know, you sweat a bit, but at the end of the day you come home, you take a shower, and no big deal.

"I think the shooting did cause some of them to start wearing their vests. The awareness of what can happen without it persists, and that helps. Also, there've been a lot more shootings in Hoboken since then, some of them with rival street gangs from Jersey City.

"Takes only one good shot . . . and you're gone."

By the fall of 2004, when I took the ferry across the Hudson to Hoboken to interview John Aguiar—after spending half a day looking over Ground Zero—there had already been four more such shoot-outs involving police officers in John Aguiar's old unit. There have been dozens since.

[1] For those interested, the company is Techon Software (www.techonsoftware.com). Based in Hoboken, New Jersey, the company is owned by Michael and Bill Halkias and provides software as well as hardware that enables departments involving police, fire, HAZMAT, and EMS personnel to do their job more efficiently through the use of advanced technology.

CHAPTER 8

Small Town Cop/City Cop

> Law enforcement in rural America—compared to that in the cities—can be as different as football and basketball. Both have a common denominator, and that's the ball. After that, it's all different.

Take Mark Bednarz, for example. Formerly of the Effingham County Sheriff's Office in Springfield, Georgia, this officer is not your typical soldier-turned-cop. The impression one retains after meeting him for the first time is of a man as astute as they come in his assessment of the people with whom he deals.

Tough, aggressive, and occasionally reckless, he served eight years in the US Army, mostly in the 82nd Airborne, followed by twenty more as a sheriff's deputy. During this time he was shot at and wounded, stabbed, burned, and has been involved in three car accidents—any one of which might have been fatal.

These days, when Bednarz is not working as a Georgia State Public Defender Investigator, you'll find him at his home with his wife Cindy in one of the sweetest little hideaways in America.

Wilmington Island, though not one of Georgia's best-kept secrets, is a quiet, understated, semitropical backwater, a magnet for city people seeking to get away. Today their home would cost dearly, though Mark and Cindy bought theirs thirteen years ago when a handsome property an easy stroll from the water cost an amount that is laughable today.

I spent time with them on my circular route between Florida and Maine. In doing so, I discovered a little niche of my own.

I parked my motor home next to the water at Lazeretto Creek on the ocean side of Tybee Island, just north of Wassaw Sound. My nearest neighbors were the occupants of half a dozen or so shrimp boats who liked good beer and good jazz, Ella, and Errol Garner. The shrimp were running and they weren't stingy with them.

Only one road links the islands to the mainland; it passes through Savannah and that was a disappointment. Picture-postcard perfect in relics, Savannah—for all its tourist hype—has fallen into disrepair.

As a cop, none of this affected Mark Bednarz, though the most dramatic event in his life happened in Savannah when he worked there almost a quarter century before. Quiet-spoken, reserved almost, it takes a few fishing stories and a couple of ales to get him going. Then it all comes out and at the end, you're astonished he's still alive.

Aside from a stabbing and being burned, his first major car wreck took place in Smyrna, on the outskirts of Atlanta while chasing a stolen vehicle. It was a wild pursuit, across half the county. Suddenly the suspect's car came to an abrupt stop, just over a hill, out of Bednarz's view. It all took place in a flash; by the time this cop knew what was happening, he was thirty yards away and closing fast on a car stopped dead in the middle of the road.

As he will relate in his soft Tarheel accent, there was no way of avoiding that hit. "I took the full impact of the steering wheel in my chest . . . broke it . . . a bit like running into a steam roller."

It might have gone better if he'd been wearing his seat belt. The suspect escaped. Bednarz was saved by his soft body armor, which absorbed most of the impact.

Another time, while with the Effingham County Sheriff's Office, he spotted his partner Mike Bohannon in a police car hauling a particularly dangerous criminal to jail. Somehow the felon had forced open the rear door and was trying to escape. At the same time, he struggled with Bohannon, who was trying to hold him and keep his cruiser on the road. This was a really big man and, as he recalls, the police officer was losing his grip.

About a hundred yards away, Bednarz jumped into his vehicle and put his foot down.

"I drove toward Bohannon, not noticing that the road ended on the perimeter of the trailer park where all this was happening. I also didn't know that there was an eight-foot drop between his car and mine. As I launched my Ford Crown Vic in Mike's direction, I was so fixated that I wasn't aware I was in trouble until the ground disappeared out from under me.

"The car landed about forty feet away, the airbags destroying my glasses and shredding my arms. Again, I didn't have my seat belt on and once more I impacted the steering wheel with my body armor absorbing most of it."

Prior to this, while working in Savannah, Bednarz was in a bar fight with a particularly nasty piece of work who called himself The Karate Kid. That ended with this officer injured and the notorious combat expert with a broken foot. He'd tried kicking his way into Bednarz's chest through almost thirty layers of Kevlar, unsuccessfully as it transpired. As a result, Officer Bednarz was put on probation and warned by his supervisor that next time, he'd put him behind glass with a sign that read "Break Only in Case of Real Emergency." It was also a time when Mark Bednarz decided to stop marching to the beat of a different drum.

None of this prevented this cop—in his day, also a member of the SWAT team (or in local terminology, the Special Operations Team)—from making detective and getting his gold shield in the minimum two years of service.

Between normal duties and until his run-in with a drug user at the wheel of a truck, he also filled in time as a police diver, usually searching for evidence and occasionally bodies. Another of his responsibilities was to command the police boat unit.

Mark Bednarz's closest shave with annihilation came with a drug operation in Effingham County, in collaboration with the Chatham County Counter Narcotics Team. Drugs are so rife in the area that Effingham is often referred to by local enforcers as Methingham.

"It was a sting in Marlow, a small Georgia town about thirty miles north of Savannah. We had some of our officers posing as drug dealers, selling fake merchandise to users. Like all these places, there was a corner where the dealers stood and did their business. We'd pick up the bad guys hanging out there and haul them off to jail. Then, our guys would replace them.

"Once cash had changed hands, one of our cars would pick up the users down the road and make an arrest for possession.

"While this was going on, some of my people provided cover for the agents in the street, which was done more in case something went wrong. There were three more doing outside cover . . . basically a Special Operations job, with plenty of weapons for back-up.

"So, with me and two more Special Operations guys hidden about twenty yards from the sellers' location, we waited for the deal to go down. They didn't have long to wait. A Chevy Suburban drove up, complete with shutters and tinted windows, and its occupants made a purchase.

"They hadn't gone a hundred yards when they stopped and came back. The merchandise was fake, they said. They wanted their money back. From where I was waiting, I could see they weren't joking either . . . these were some mean guys." Normally, if the buyers return, the bogus sellers run to avoid any kind of confrontation.

"Two of our guys did that, but the third stayed behind, which was not what he'd been trained to do. He argued with the driver that he should have bought from him to start with because his stuff was 'real.' He didn't sell bad drugs, he told them.

"When one of the suspects got out of the Chevy, it was time for us to move in, which we did. I took up a position near the front of the vehicle, and the next thing I know, the truck is on top of me. I'm under the wheels and I see a wheel go past my face."

Mark Bednarz never did figure out how he survived. One of the wheels went over his hand and partially across his left shoulder, which needed reconstructive surgery. That little episode kept him out of commission for four months.

"You don't follow orders and you could get someone killed. We had an officer wanting to be a hero. Because he failed to follow the operational plan, the someone almost killed was me."

While Mark Bednarz has a file full of personal incidents, he hit a milestone early in his career while still with the Savannah Police Department.

"I'd been in the force for three years and my regular duties involved patrol work in a motor unit. Unless something was up, we'd work alone, which is what happened on this Friday night. Because some of the officers were on vacation and others on military leave, I was given an area in Precinct 3, Savannah's east side, which is really not the best part of town. It's guaranteed for drugs and property crimes, car break-ins, and domestic violence. In some of it you don't walk around after dark, that's if you don't want to be the victim of a street robbery. Tough neighborhood, I'd call it!

"I hardly knew my way around, so I was driving with a map in one hand and a compass in the other, trying to figure out where I was supposed to go. Then a call came in for 9 Oleander Avenue . . . I'll never forget that address."

The signal was a 28, which meant domestic. There was a drunk male in a home, and the female subject wanted him out of there. Officer Bednarz arrived just before Linda Green, his back-up officer, beating her by a minute or so.

"I rang the doorbell and was met by a large black lady. 'You need to get him out of here,' she demanded. 'His name is Sanford Moss and he's drunk.' Judging from some potted plants knocked over, spilled drinks, and furniture moved, there'd been a fight.

"I said, 'Ma'am, a man has a right to be intoxicated in his own home . . . but we're here now so we'll go and talk to him.' To which she replied, 'You'd better, because if you don't get him out of here, there's going to be a killing tonight,' which I thought peculiar. She pointed toward a bedroom at the back of the house. 'He's in there,' she gestured."

Officer Green asked whether he had a gun. "He does," the woman replied. "But he doesn't keep it loaded."

In a staggered formation—with Bednarz ahead of Green—the two officers made their way to the other end of the house, which was fairly well lit.

"We were aware that this was a touchy situation, so we didn't take unnecessary risks. I stopped at the bathroom door and indicated to my partner that she should move toward the next door, a bedroom just ahead of me. I didn't want the two of us bunching up when he came out."

Moss answered Bednarz's knock. What did they want, he called loudly from behind the closed door.

"Please come out, Mr. Moss, we want to talk to you."

"Wait a second," Moss replied. And then he said the weirdest thing. "'Wait a second, I've got my dick out.'"

Bednarz just knew they were headed for trouble. "I'm going to have to fight this guy, take him to jail, and book him. And then I'll be handling paper work until early morning. I wasn't at all happy, was my immediate thought because we were having a going-away party for one of our guys who was moving back home to Detroit."

Neither officer thought it necessary to call the dispatcher. They'd be listening anyway and the routine was to keep radio traffic to a minimum, in case something really did happen.

"So, we're in the hallway, and Linda says, 'Well, come out anyway, Mr. Moss.' The next thing the door opens, and he's standing there about an arm's length away with a blue steel revolver in his hand pointed right at me."

Moments before, Bednarz had made the mistake of leaving his cover position which was just a little to the side and might have afforded some protection if anything unexpected happened. He was now fully exposed outside the door, with Moss holding a .357 magnum and standing directly before him.

Bednarz: "You point a firearm at a police officer and you're going to get one kind of reply. He's going to shoot you. That was my immediate reaction, but he beat me to it by a zillionth of a second. If you were to watch this thing in a playback, you probably wouldn't be able to differentiate between the two shots. Only he fired once, while I hit him with two bullets in a double-tap, just as I raised my foot to push him away. He took both shots in the chest, .38 Specials, which was regulation at the time.

"His bullet hit me with a thump in the abdomen, right alongside my belly button. Though my body armor stopped it from going through, I can tell you it hurt like hell. I carried a baseball-sized welt for a month."

The shot knocked him to the floor. Winded, he toppled backward, still firing his revolver and hitting the wall behind Moss, who had again raised his gun. Just then, Linda Green stepped into the hallway from the bedroom and pumped more bullets into the man. He must have died within those final seconds.

Bednarz found himself beside the doorway with an empty revolver. Before getting on the radio, he reloaded his Smith & Wesson 67. Then, keying his radio, he told dispatch, "319 . . . signal 13." In copspeak the first numeral was his SPD patrol beat number, the second is something that no member of the force ever wants to hear: officer down.

Getting up from the floor, Bednarz checked Linda Green who, by now, was on tenterhooks. She was shook up, her lovely black face having taken on a distinctly gray pallor.

"EMS came through immediately afterward and started lines on me. Just then I'm feeling great. Sore but great, because I'm alive. So they take my vest off and—surprise!—there's blood, quite a lot of it.

"Seems the bullet caught the edge of the vest. It stopped the bullet, but the impact folded the Kevlar. While it didn't penetrate much, it took a chunk of skin out of my stomach area and that scar's still visible today.

"I see the blood, and the next moment I go into shock. They've got to haul me out of there on a stretcher, on oxygen and with an IV in each arm."

It took a while for Bednarz to be able to use his stomach muscles again. He found that for some months he couldn't sit up properly in bed or get out of a chair all that easily.

The event happened on a Friday night. Following police procedures, he talked to the department psychologist the following afternoon. Two days later Homicide and Internal Affairs cleared him. A week later the Coroner's Inquest cleared him as well.

"A clean shoot," it was listed, and he was released for full duty two weeks later.

On his first day of full duty, he assisted the US Marshal's Service in apprehending a fugitive from their list of the Fifteen Most Wanted.

One of Mark Bednarz's good friends, Captain Mark Long of nearby Richmond Hill Police Department, is also among Richard Davis' Saves. Listed as #493, he took a hit in the chest from a .32 caliber handgun just seven minutes after midnight on a clear September night in 1990. At the time he was inspecting property during a robbery.

"I was carrying a 12-gauge shotgun, and though we spotted the suspect exiting the back and fired some rounds in his direction, we never did bring him in."

Since then, Captain Long has investigated a large variety of other crimes, including more shootings. One of these was another midnight shooting, this time of a seventeen-year-old black male who robbed a truck stop using a Chinese-built SKS rifle.

"Most crimes in this part of Georgia are armed robberies, some kidnappings and rapes—more than a couple of those—and the usual incidents involving firearms and aggravated assaults around the motels and interchanges in this area," he said.

Captain Long made the point that *aggravated assault* in Georgia is what the state regards as attempted murder.

"Use any kind of weapon against another person—it could be a ballpoint pen in somebody's eye—and that's aggravated assault and serious. A shooting, by the way, if you don't kill the man, could also be aggravated assault."

Boston's Darrin Greeley, our city cop—in contrast to Georgia's country cops Mark Bednarz and Captain Mark Long—has an altogether different attitude.

Committed and more efficient than most, which is why he made deputy superintendent in the Boston Police Department shortly after I talked to him, Greeley has a more detached approach to the everyday problems that cops encounter, which some city law enforcers regard as an essential attribute if they are to survive police work in today's modern metropolis.

While he still occasionally chases felons and makes the kind of convictions expected of him, his daily routine these days also includes the potential for Islamic terrorism. It has yet to become a major problem, but it is an area of increasing concern.

In the fall of 2004, I visited the then–Sergeant Detective Darrin Greeley in his offices at the Intelligence Unit, at Boston Police Headquarters in Schroeder Plaza, off Beacon Street. To the immediate west of Government Center at Scollay Square, this is a nondescript part of town. A comparatively new building, Number One Schroeder Plaza has fine futuristic lines and is as familiar to the average Bostonian as Radio City is to New Yorkers.

We spent a couple of hours together. Greeley looked trim and smart in a well-tailored three-piece suit. We ended with lunch in the police canteen. It was the best three-buck meal on the East Coast.

Greeley has traveled some distance since he joined the force twenty years ago, having entered straight from college, where he completed a Bachelor of Science degree in criminal justice. In due course he added a master's in Criminal Justice Administration, plus more graduate work. He started his career with the requisite six months at Boston's Police Academy, in Hyde Park. That was followed by regular patrol work as a uniformed officer. Having grown up in the city, he knew most of its quirks and foibles. Possibly for this reason he was selected for plainclothes work in some of the city's more depressed areas.

"Doesn't matter whether you're in uniform or out, you have your experiences. Some are unhealthy, like chasing down people with handguns, which they can either pull or throw. Either way, they've done something for which they need to answer, so there's going to be a face-off."

Then he partnered with Thomas Gomperts, who had trained with Greeley at the police academy. Working plainclothes, they did stakeouts, surveillance, and arrests. They operated in areas where drugs were a part of the fabric of life, including Egleston Square in the Jamaica Plain neighborhood.

"There were Latino gangs like the X-Men and many others besides, some black, some white, some Hispanic, and let's face it, these were violent people with all the trappings of LA's depressed areas. The only difference is that we don't have 'no-go' areas. But these are violent people and we don't always win our little wars. However, we go wherever we like if the situation demands it," commented Greeley.

"Obviously, you work an area long enough and you learn the names and traits—and sometimes even the families—of just about everybody there. You're able to talk to these people, like, 'How's your mother doing, now that she's out of the hospital?' Or something about a brother or a cousin that's just been put away, or a father soon to be released from jail.

"This can be a hard-luck town, especially in Jamaica Plain or Roxbury. But then luck is created by the circumstances folks make for themselves, and there's a lot of good people who live there too."

Greeley's epiphany as a policeman came at a time when several Boston gangs were at war. There had been attacks—shots fired every night and numerous calls into the district. There had also been some murders.

Then came the day in the mid-1990s when, with no warning, he faced a bloody showdown with a young gangster lugging a sawed-off shotgun under his winter coat. It was Richard Davis' Save #625.

"On the big night Gomperts and I are driving in the vicinity of 87 School Street, having just answered a housebreak call when we saw one of 'our' groups in a doorway. Knew them all well . . . first name basis.

"Tom pulls the unmarked car into the curb and gets out, makes eye contact like we always do, and the reaction from those hanging about tells us that something is up. That was how we worked; we didn't have to talk to people to know there was trouble. We read their body language, which told us all we needed to know. This crowd was waiting for some kind of action, something to happen. I followed him toward the entrance to a hallway where the small crowd had gathered.

"Then, to my left, I saw a man named Hector Morales, and because I didn't want anybody walking behind me, I stopped. He came past me and I greeted him.

"'Hey, Hector, what's up?" I asked, my eyes casually checking around the building, all the time watching my partner. I looked right at the young man and he turned around. About then things started to go into slow motion."

The way Greeley describes it, since it was late November and cold, just after Thanksgiving, Hector Morales wore a heavy coat. He stopped in his tracks, turned toward the detective, and pulled out a Mossburg 12-gauge pump shotgun with a pistol grip and fired. Morales was so close to Greeley that the cluster of bird shot was probably no bigger than a golf ball. Aimed at his head as he ducked toward the left, the blast went by his shoulder within an inch or two of his right ear.

"I didn't even think when I pulled out my 9mm Glock. Tom heard the shots from inside the hallway and stuck his head out to check. At that point Morales swung around and shot him in the head."

Obviously satisfied that he'd immobilized one of his adversaries, the young felon turned back toward Greeley and this policeman dodged a second shotgun blast by getting down low behind his vehicle. Morales charged toward his target.

"By this time he'd blown out two of the car windows and splattered glass all over me. I fired several times and saw he'd been hit. But it wasn't having the effect I'd hoped for because he just kept coming."

Officer Tom Gomperts staggered to his feet. Blood streamed down his face from a serious head wound. Barely able to see, he fired two rounds in the general direction of Morales and again collapsed.

Greeley: "He was hurt and it was obvious even from where I was that it was bad. I kept firing, to the point where I had to load another magazine, my last. By then I must have hit him about six times. I remember thinking, Why the fuck isn't he going down? I'd also taken a hit from Morales' third round, partially deflected off the trunk of the car and into my hand . . . you can still see the scars." The deputy superintendent lifted his arm and showed a slightly deformed hand.

Altogether Morales was able to get away four shots: three at Greeley and one at his partner, who took a single hit, up high. It was a close thing, he says today, since the perp was about to lock the fifth round when he hit him in the arm, breaking it.

"The battle was over. Conclusively!" Describing the event from his desk on the third floor of One Schroeder Plaza years later, Greeley was emphatic. "I won . . . right then that's all that mattered . . . I beat Morales at his own game and I'm alive. He's dead. Not only that, he had the advantage of surprise. He was going to kill us both if he could."

Once it was done with, and before the first back-up units arrived, Greeley sat down on the curbside next to his attacker, having first pulled his gun from him.

"Just the two of us. I asked him, why? He didn't answer me. Couldn't. Just rolled his head and nodded and made some moaning sounds . . . It was the end for him."

Hector Morales had always been a riddle, to his acquaintances, to his family, and to the police. Though still in his teens, he'd had numerous run-ins with the law. Living in a Jamaica Plains multiple-unit tenement complex, he kind of stuck to his own as he'd begun to mature. Having attended school in Boston, he spoke fairly adequate English, or at least enough to get along. The way the police pieced it together afterward, his life—just about his every action—centered on gangs and violence.

Greeley: "We found out afterward that he was going to get into a shoot-out with another neighborhood kid, a member of an opposing gang. So he'd bought the gun, and, from what we'd gathered, the other guy, also armed, was waiting for him when we arrived.

"It was a challenge, I suppose you could call it. Best man wins, sort of thing. We discovered later that those other kids standing around in the hallway when we arrived also had guns. But we scared them and they ran off, some into the building, others to the roof of the adjacent building."

Greeley met with Will Morales, the dead man's brother, in 1998. Also a gang member, who had been in jail at the time of the shootings, he came out of prison intending to settle the matter.

"When we met for the first time, we spoke about Hector, about the event. We broke some bread, as they say. The older man understood that it was one of those things that happen when you draw a gun on a cop . . . told me that obviously, he'd wanted revenge, but then he realized that it was Hector's fault. Said that if he killed me it would be an ongoing cycle, with me married by then and with children."

Will Morales, said Greeley, continued to be an outstanding member of the community. "He has a family and has worked in the Egleston Square YMCA and earned community awards helping our youth . . . saw the light and, like some criminals, he matured out of the gang and drug culture. I'm proud that he's today a valued member of society . . . Turned himself completely around. We actually did community work in that section of the city for a while. Good man."

Though Darrin Greeley was unmarried at the time of his confrontation, he took the plunge not long afterward. His wife has since given him five children.

Officer Thomas Gomperts, though shot in the face and head, came out well enough after treatment. He was fortunate that none of the pellets went into his eyes, though he did retire under stress in 1996.

While the department reacted solidly for the two cops—both of whom had come within a whisker of being killed by a brash young teenager—the public's reaction was not the same.

In a roar of protest, many elements within the city came out in support of the dead youngster. There were threats on the lives of the two officers: for a time they needed twenty-four-hour protection.

"The issue was diffused once we'd laid our side of the story on the table and some of the protestors were allowed to see the evidence. We told them to go and visit Thomas in the hospital, see his condition and how he'd been wounded by this 'innocent youngster.'"

The culprit here, said Greeley, was the media. Unabashedly hostile newspaper articles appeared, which judged Hector Morales to have been murdered by the police.

The *Boston Herald* covered the story in December 1990 with the following report:

> Residents of the neighborhood who claimed to have witnessed the gun battle . . . said police continued firing—possibly as many as 15 rounds—after Morales fell to the ground and began pleading for his life.
>
> The shotgun sounded twice then all you heard was the bop, bop, bop from the 9 millimeter automatic handguns used by police, said one neighborhood youth. He was on the ground telling them don't do it, don't do it. It's for my mother. Then they shot him again.

The person quoted by the *Herald* was later found to have been in New York City on the night of the shooting. He traveled to Boston the day after, claiming to be a witness.

As Deputy Superintendent Greeley states, this was another lie proven to be false during the course of the investigation, and it needn't have happened.

"When that sort of thing is being put out by the supposedly neutral media, what do you do? You can protest, of course. The commissioner can go and see the editor and he might even get them to print a retraction. But even if they agree, it's usually half-a-column on page eight, which can never compensate for the kind of sensationalistic trash that made headlines before.

"Obviously, it caused some serious damage. More important, it stays in the minds of people," suggested Greeley. "If they had taken the trouble to do their homework, they'd have found a very different story from the one they printed."

Looking back, Greeley estimates that the shootout lasted fifteen seconds. There were twenty-two rounds fired in all, four by Morales, two by Gomperts, and seventeen in 9mm caliber by his partner. Deputy Superintendent Greeley started carrying a firearm with a heavier caliber shortly afterward. These days he has a .40 caliber Glock.

Both men were awarded the highest honor the Boston Police Department bestows, the Schroeder Medal, named after two brothers who died in the line of duty. One was shot dead in a bank robbery in the city and the other in a shoot-out, not dissimilar to the one that Greeley and Gomperts found themselves in three decades later. The difference, essentially, was soft, concealable body armor.

Two decades ago, Boston had among the highest big-city homicide rates in the country, but since then, things have improved. Boston had 41 homicides from January to May 2005. This compares well with the 152 murders in 1990.

In those first five months of 2005, Baltimore had 145. New Orleans did marginally better with 130. Washington, D.C. lists 87 homicides in this period.

While conditions in Boston have improved, there have been a few stumbles along the way. In October 2003, residents were shocked when the city had its first triple murders in more than ten years. Three young men sitting in a van parked next to a housing project were gunned down. That the killings were gang-related was not the issue; the mindless brutality of the event was.

According to Boston's newly appointed Deputy Superintendent Greeley, while shootings and violence in the city had increased, so, to its credit, had the recovery of firearms and arrests involving firearms. This was a positive sign, he added, "and a long way from the kind of lawlessness that Boston experienced fifteen years ago when it had one of its highest homicide rates ever."

How did Boston achieve this success? There were many reasons. Greeley explained that, in part, success was due to the decentralization of police units, from headquarters back to district commands; community partnerships together with the clergy; becoming more involved with youth, which, as a consequence, had a direct bearing on the role of gangs.

"Also, demographics decreased, and more violent criminals were put into prison," he observed.

"But now more gang members and violent criminals are being released, the majority of whom return to their old haunts. Demographics have also increased, and so, as we have seen, has the juvenile population.

"Which means that we need to reenergize our community partners to help us fight crime together with many of the underlying reasons why it occurs in the first place. This includes poverty, parenting issues, drug and alcohol abuse, child abuse, domestic violence. and so on."

Surveys recently completed indicate that homicides are on the increase in most, if not all, of America's two-dozen largest cities. Many of these involve teenagers and are distinctly gang related. Indeed, in the years between 1999 and 2006, gang killings rose 50 percent across the country. In the same period, other types of homicides actually declined.

The New York Times assigned Fox Butterfield to the subject, and he found a few surprises, including the fact that in 2004, more than twenty juveniles were killed in Washington, D.C.—up from about half that a year before. Underscoring the gang conundrum, Washington's overall homicide rate was the lowest for twenty years. Gang killings and turf and drug wars between rival groups were held responsible.

This becomes a much more serious matter when it is realized that the number of young people murdered in American cities every day of the year is several times higher than United States casualties in both Iraq and Afghanistan. Because these killings are domestic, the media hasn't said much about them—except when the *Times* assigns the story to one of its senior writers.

Butterfield found that the reason for increased violence among gangs was three-fold. First, it was clear that the number of youths in the streets (as borne out by comments made by Darrin Greeley) was increasing. In Boston, the juvenile population was up 20 percent in five years.

Second, there had been cutbacks in after-school programs, the very adhesive that in the past had kept juvenile groups if not interested in extra-curricular activities, then at least otherwise occupied in those critical hours before their parents or guardians got home.

This omission is myopic and self-defeating. Not everyone scores from doing things like music, sports, and hobbies after school. Clearly, many youngsters do.

Generations of Americans discovered often unknown and undreamt-of talents in those few hours of after-hour activity.

Last, echoing the words of Detective John White, a spokesman for the Denver Police Department, because of budget problems, staffing cutbacks had had the effect of an inadequate police presence in many areas where there should have been more, not fewer, badges visible.

CHAPTER 9

Massad Ayoob: Self-Defense Maestro

If you don't know the works of Massad Ayoob and the kind of research he has put into the everyday use of firearms by law enforcement in the United States and abroad, then you need to do a little additional reading. Especially if your life depends on the weapon you carry. This man is one of the best informed, most erudite authorities on handguns this country has produced.

A third-generation American—his Syrian grandfather arrived in New York City from the Middle East in 1898—Massad Ayoob has been a sworn, part-time police officer for more than thirty years. He spent eight years as a patrolman, two as a sergeant, six as a lieutenant, and, until now, more than fifteen years as a police captain. He has also been a police departmental firearms instructor and has held the chair of the Firearms Committee for the American Society of Law Enforcement Trainers since that body was founded in 1987.

A well-known author, his articles appear frequently in *Law and Order*, as well as other publications. He is currently handgun editor of *Guns* magazine, law enforcement editor of *American Handgunner*, associate editor of *Combat Handguns*, and associate editor for *Guns & Weapons for Law Enforcement*. He is author of a dozen books, the best known being *In the Gravest Extreme*, referred to by some as *the* authoritative text on the use of deadly force.

Massad Ayoob has worn body armor since its inception, both on duty and off. He was one of the first supporters of Richard Davis' invention, from the time the company opened its doors in Central Lake, Michigan. There came a time when his life was saved by one of Richard's vests.

Involved in a head-on collision in his wife's Cadillac, he took a powerful hit that caused his head to slam the windshield. Concurrently, his chest was thrust into the steering wheel, buckling it in that critical moment of impact. Aside from serious bruises on the upper part of his torso, he took head injuries, "that stopped short of any serious brain edema but did leave me with six months of a bitch of a condition that the doctors like to call 'post-concussion.'" He also lost some hearing in the crash.

With a résumé that any police officer in America would be proud of, it is ironic that Massad Ayoob was not wearing a seat belt.

After the accident he remembers calling Diane Kucharek, Richard Davis' secretary, and leaving this message: "Tell him, with all the conversations we've had over the years, I'm making the one call I never thought I'd make. Today I owe him my life."

Massad Ayoob was Save #682, which we will deal with in some detail later, since he survived a situation in which he should have been killed.

Even before that fateful event he had spent years studying everything to do with body armor, its potential, and the effects it had on the system when wearing it over extended periods—and, thus, its shortcomings. He has also taken a great interest in the role that Kevlar and Twaron have played in hundreds of shootings, together with the psychology of those who wear protection as opposed to those who don't.

Ayoob's conclusions are both insightful and interesting.

As a policeman, almost all his observations are based on professional experience, which is to be expected when you've been involved in the business of guns and weapons training for almost all your adult life. At the same time, he has had a lot of personal experience. He can list about thirty encounters in actual confrontations that involved the use of firearms.

These have included armed encounters, weapons arrests, and the taking of armed suspects at gunpoint (or when they were reasonably believed to have weapons on them, or nearby). In a half dozen cases, he'd already decided it might be time to pull the trigger, when, to the surprise of everybody present, "They dropped their shit."

Justifiably proud of his ability to project authority when necessary, he is also happy to admit he has never actually fired a shot at a human being, ". . . and with some luck, it's going to stay that way."

An original thinker, Massad Ayoob has his own views on most aspects of the business. He doesn't hesitate to differ with conventional wisdom, evidenced in the following two examples.

"Something that I found wrong early on is the myth that if you wear body armor, the blunt trauma from a heavy bullet like a .45 ACP (or any one of the magnums) will crush and kill you. There are still people out there, to their discredit, who talk like that. I have always dispelled that kind of trash by offering practical examples of the opposite. Let's face it, Rich Davis has saved a thousand lives with his own company's vests and that should be testimony enough, but you still get the occasional no-brainer.

"Another bit of crap you hear is that if you wear body armor, you'll think you're Superman and end up doing things you otherwise wouldn't. In fact," he says, "the converse is true.

"I have an endless number of examples which show that officers who wear vests are reminded constantly that, 'What I am doing is dangerous and I need to be careful out there.' I have yet to encounter a true case of the so-called Superman Syndrome. It's a fallacy, nothing more!"

What he discovered instead, was that among many police officers who had been struck by bullets, there was an immediate awareness, literally, of "a second chance." In other words, the message imparted by the brain is that, "While they might have been hit, or even hurt, but been saved by their vests, they'd been given another chance to get out of the mess in which they'd found themselves."

He recalls the mid-1970s shooting of Dave Davies of Evansville, Indiana, which is listed as Save #23 and is also the first that involved a policeman shot with a .45 automatic. Officer Davies came within seconds of apprehending his subject without a shot being fired, when suddenly the suspect wrestled free, pulled out his concealed pistol, and pumped a shot into Davies' body. The slug caught Davies at the edge of his body armor and was deflected, causing a superficial wound that wasn't serious.

"Davies admitted afterward that the vest gave him a certain psychological advantage the moment he was hit. I spoke to him on the phone later, asking him to explain what that advantage was, and he answered, 'What went through my mind just then was that you've shot my vest, you fucker. Now it's my turn.'"

Davies went on to fire six shots at his attacker with his police issue .357 magnum and killed him. "Got him five out of six," he says proudly.

Much of what Ayoob researched in the early days involved what are commonly termed *Saturday Night Specials*: smaller calibers, like the .25, .32, and .38 Special.

"I found that about half the cops taking hits from these smaller firearms sat there stunned while their attackers turned and fled. In contrast, every single person that I spoke to who was hit by bigger handguns, like the .45 or a magnum, during that same period either killed, crippled, or captured their assailants.

"It seemed at first to be counterintuitive, until you realized that the much greater impact tended to trigger the awareness of a more severe threat, and as a result, a more rapidly initiated rage response. In so doing it generates a basic reaction that is both innate and atavistic, the need to destroy the person who has just tried to murder you."

According to Ayoob, these sentiments are echoed by another prominent researcher who studies shootings and the effect that experience has on people. He cites Jeff Chudwin, chief of police in Olympia Fields, Illinois, who is acknowledged as one of the leaders in survival training in America—and somebody who also believes that wearing concealable body armor instills caution, not recklessness.

Ayoob continues: "The blunt trauma thing is hugely overrated. In fact, going by our research, the sensation of impact seemed to be keyed every bit as much to the mental state of the officer at the time of the shooting as it was to the caliber of weapon.

"I would talk to a guy who was hit by a .22, and he would say that it was like being hit by a sledgehammer, whereas others would admit to having hardly felt the impact.

"Then you scratch some more, and you find that the officer has just finished searching a building for felons. This is like a plunge from Condition Red to Condition White, which can be precipitous.

"It's like, 'Wheeeyuu . . .' Everything is suddenly relaxed and he has dropped his guard, put his gun in its holster, and suddenly, out of nowhere, *Blam!* He's hit. Small caliber or not, this is something he is utterly unprepared for. It comes as a tremendous shock.

"You talk to Skip Beijen of the New York State Police. He was shot right over the sternum with a 158gr .357 full magnum load from his partner's gun. And at a range of only a couple of feet . . .

"He told me it felt like a big strong man was holding his finger stiff and poking him in the chest with it. Of course Skip—having taken the shot in his vest—was able to retaliate. He immediately returned fire, ending the problem. The suspect must have realized that any kind of counteroffensive could only result in disaster and he just screamed, dropped the gun, and gave up."

Elaborating, he explained that the difference was that Beijen and his partner were in the process of pulling over a suspicious vehicle with stolen TV sets. So obviously, his level of alertness was way up. Also, the body alarm reaction was operative and strong, hovering somewhere between Condition Orange and Condition Red.

The way he'd figured it, Condition Orange could be equated to an unspecified alert where the body alarm reaction is kicking in and there is hyper-vigilance, and accelerated reflexes. "You sort of end up having an extra set of eyes in your head . . . all the time you're listening, you're gathering intelligence. You're in an extreme condition of ultra-alert.

“Suddenly he hears his partner scream, ‘Skip, he’s got my gun.’ Just talking to him about the event afterward, I could feel the adrenaline dump that must have instantly hit him. He must have been in a full-blown state of flight-or-fight when the bullet hit him. And with that epinephrine dump comes the norepinephrine release, the body’s equivalent of opium, the latter killing pain and enhancing endurance.”

An interesting comment here is that in studies done in conjunction with Israeli wound surgeons, acknowledged as among the best in the world, it has been hypothesized that the norepinephrine we release in our flight-or-fight state is roughly equal to about five field syrettes of morphine in pain-killing ability. What’s more, the effect is immediate.

“So certainly, in Skip Beijen’s case, the sensation related to the actual impact of being shot was clearly not correlative to the power of that particular heavy-duty round. He took a bullet and kept going, finishing the encounter, which was very different from someone who might have been caught flat-footed.” Part of it, of course, he adds, “is *where* the bullet strikes.” But, as he goes on to say, “I’ve found that equally, the effect on the emotional state of the individual has a significant role to play in those critical after-action moments.”

Ayoob relates the condition to something to which any hunter with good experience will be able to relate. “You shoot a deer in the heart when it’s minding its own business and eating an apple in the orchard or drinking at a stream and it drops in its tracks. But shoot the same deer in the heart when it is running ahead of the hounds and it’ll go maybe two hundred yards before it collapses. It’s a direct biological analog.”

On a different tack, when discussing the best overall firearm, Massad was cautious—if only, as he declared, “because there is no ‘all-purpose’ protective weapon.

“Each circumstance is different. Each condition in which a person might find himself constantly varies, from whether it is night or day, or perhaps something that has come as a total surprise. So too with calibers, and since most officers are carrying one firearm, or two at the most, and they’re stuck with those calibers, they have to do the best they can under *any* circumstances.

“You could have a shoot-out with a bunch of crooks hiding behind their vehicle, and let’s face it, that happens often enough. Then you’d like to have a heavy caliber, a long gun perhaps, in something like .308 caliber that can blast its way through vehicle doors or a car’s seat padding.

“Similarly, it’s difficult to take a man out from the other side of a truck.

“Or if it’s a back-up weapon that we’re talking about, then you’d opt for something compact and discreet like a baby Glock. You need a firearm that can be strapped to an ankle or discreetly worn on the body where it's not obvious. If it is tucked into your belt, you don't want the bulge to be prominent, which, I suppose, is what 'back-up' is all about."

For the ordinary city dweller needing protection, he recommends double-action revolvers in possibly .38 or .357 magnum caliber, which, he maintains, are better suited to the untrained enthusiast. And for a variety of reasons.

"First, revolvers are relatively simple to operate in terms of administrative handling. Revolvers are less complicated than autos. There is also less opportunity for something to go wrong, which, in an accident can end up with somebody getting wounded, or worse.

"Put another way, if you asked me what kind of car I should buy, I might recommend the Corvette Stingray because of rack and pinion steering, the power, the responsive handling. Also, with those wheels you might be able to drive yourself out of emergencies more efficiently than in a regular car, which might not have the nimbleness or the power to emerge from an emergency. But give that same powerful roadster to a sixteen-year-old and he could end up bending it around a tree the first time he goes through a hairpin curve."

In that analogy, Ayoob explained, the revolver was the ordinary Ford Crown Victoria and the Corvette the auto pistol. "It has a higher performance ratio, is more versatile, which suggests that there is more that you can do with it. But it also has more sensitive controls, which could mean trouble to inexperienced hands."

He emphasizes several aspects whenever he lectures on firearms. These include greater magazine capacity, which in case of the Glock means greater volume of fire.

The Glock-22 holds fifteen rounds in the magazine plus one up the spout (compared to the Browning Hi-Power with thirteen-plus-one). There is also the ability to reload faster with autos, though there are some specialists who, with speed loaders, can ditch empty cases and replace with loaded rounds in less than a second.

This is one of the reasons, he declared, why he wouldn't suggest a novice starting his shooting career with a Glock, in, for instance, .40 caliber.

Another reason is that, unlike the Colt .45 ACP, the Glock has no built-in safety mechanism. You need a finger on the trigger to get a shot off, which is why there have been Glock accidental discharges.

Ayoob makes the interesting point that in developing the Glock pistol—just like the Heckler and Koch P7, as well as a few other excellent firearms—its originators tried to create an idiot-proof gun for idiots. Instead, he maintains, we ended up with an excellent weapon for professional shooters. To which he presciently added with the kind of humor that only Massad Ayoob can muster,

"There should not be something like an 'idiot-proof' gun because idiots should not have guns!"

There is some controversy within shooting circles about the advantages of having all those rounds in the magazine of your handgun, the argument being that if you haven't got your man after shooting off six or seven rounds, you're not likely to hit him at all.

The great Jeff Cooper—the eternal 1911-A1 Colt .45 protagonist—was always of the opinion that autos, like the Browning P-35 Hi-Power with its large magazines, were specifically designed for people who planned to miss a lot.

Why then, the question is often asked, not emulate Dirty Harry and field a .44 magnum?

"Too much power, too much recoil, and too much chance that it will shoot through the bad guy and hit a good guy," retorts Ayoob.

"And what about my .45 ACP?" I asked Ayoob. As a correspondent in several Third World conflicts, I was all but weaned on the sidearm that American forces carried through two world wars as well as in Korea and Vietnam, but which has now been superseded by the caliber preferred by all the NATO states, the 9mm Parabellum. In fact, I attended a Jeff Cooper shooting clinic on one of his regular visits to South Africa.

Ayoob: "There is nothing wrong with the .45 ACP. Absolutely nothing," he answered defensively. "The two occasions that I had the responsibility of picking one gun to issue to specific police departments, it was the .45 Auto."

At the same time, he is not a fan of lesser calibers like .32 and .25. Instead, he suggests, you need what the late, great Robert Ruark called "using enough gun"—though he adds, the .32 was the caliber that killed Archduke Ferdinand and led to World War I. It was Hitler's gun of choice when he committed suicide.

"The same with the diminutive .22. Most folk who know firearms call it puny, but remember, there are more people who die from being shot by a .22 than any other single handgun, particularly in suicides. It is also the favorite weapon of the Mossad, the Israeli secret service. They've been using it to ice their unsuspecting victims from up close just about forever."

On the .38 Special and its potential as a firearm, Ayoob made the valid point that this gun was the "Peacemaker" of the twentieth century, as one expert referred to it. Adequate to some, too underpowered for others, it was the standard firearm in American law enforcement for half a century.

"Then they built the .357 magnum, which was originally intended to take the *proof* out of bulletproof vests."

He is equally outspoken about the 9mm Para. "It is the twentieth century's most popular military handgun cartridge [and] has killed countless thousands of human beings in a succession of conflicts that span decades. With military ammo it has consistently proved to be an adequate in wounding individuals, though with the right rounds, the 9mm does the job. Also, it is an excellent murder weapon, but at the same time, is lousy in defense unless it is loaded with the best hollow-points."

If he had to choose the ideal .45 ACP cartridge, I asked him, what would it be? He was unequivocal.

"My department has a custom load from Black Hills Ammunition, and that's the 230gr Gold Dot bullet loaded to 880 feet per second, which is sub-sonic. But I'm comfortable with all the high-tech loads with the more modern designs like Federal Hydra Shok, or Remington Golden Saber. Others in this range include Winchester SXT, CCI Gold Dot, and PMC Starfire."

The 9mm Para cartridge loaded for sub-sonic use, he feels, did not turn out to be as effective a man-stopper as some had hoped, and most police departments looked for other options—either a lighter, faster 9mm bullet or more powerful calibers.

For those unfamiliar with some of the terms, he explains that any box of cartridges marked *Plus P*, or more commonly +P, means more powder and, as a consequence, added performance.

For example, in a .45, the 185gr bullet would have a muzzle velocity of something around 935 ft/sec in a standard load. In Plus P it would accelerate to about 1,150 ft/sec. A relatively new development out of Mexico is the Aguila 'IQ' that deploys an ultralight bullet and reaches a velocity of about 1,800 ft/sec. Unfortunately, this is a very hard bullet of about 117 grains.

The same goes for the 9mm Parabellum: the standard 115gr bullet commonly reaches a speed of 1,150 ft/sec. It will be enhanced to somewhere between 1,300 and 1,350 ft/sec in a Plus P configuration. In that caliber, Winchester 127 grain Ranger +P+ and Speer Gold Dot 124 grain +P seemed to have earned the best reputation in police shootings.

When I met Massad Ayoob in New Hampshire, he was carrying a Glock .40 and using it in a series of instructional programs that he conducted annually in New England. Why that choice, I asked?

"Because in the United States of America right now, the Glock .40 caliber, together with the 9mm auto, is not only the most popular and widely issued firearm used by law enforcement agencies but also the favorite among those enthusiasts involved in international combat competitions."

As he explained, world champion combat shooters have been earning their spurs with Glocks firing .40 caliber bullets for some years now.

"But I'm not stuck on any one gun, or even a single caliber. This is a Glock, yes. But last week I was carrying a baby Glock, and another time I might carry a Beretta, or a SIG. And at least once a year I teach with a revolver, just to keep my hand in with the different handguns."

Certainly, Massad Ayoob knows what he is talking about. At the time of our conversation he was the New Hampshire State Champion with the IDPA stock service revolver and the New England Regional Champion; he held about a dozen past state championship titles, three or four regional championships, and two minor national titles.

He has taken his children down that long and interesting road as well. His oldest daughter Cathbin—which means *kitten daughter* in Arabic—won the highest women's shooting honors at the National Tactical Invitational shoot at Jeff Cooper's Gunsite Ranch, now at Harrisburg, Pennsylvania. That was in 1996, when she was nineteen years old.

She not only beat a number of the top woman shooters in the country, but, most notably, most of the SWAT cops who were present at the competition.

The development of the .40 caliber makes for an interesting aside. It was something Richard Davis commented on when there were a number of FBI special agents present—one of whom came to him afterward and said his talk was the first time he'd heard anybody in the industry get it right. It goes something like this.

In the late 1970s and early 1980s, the government agency responsible for maintaining body armor standards in the United States, the National Institute of Justice (NIJ), did their own study of handgun ammunition. As Davis said, "They were going to set all those ballistic specialists, trauma doctors, gun magazines, writers, handgun loaders, police, the FBI, street combat veterans, and the rest to rights once and for all."

So the NIJ created what they termed the *Relative Incapacitation Index* or RII, which ended up as something of an aberration where anything related to firearms logic was concerned.

"In their wisdom they determined that 9mm (9x19) hollow-point was six times better than a .45 ACP full-metal-jacketed bullet, which any rookie who has spent a few days on the range will tell you is bunkum."

They also claimed, said Davis, for reasons best known to themselves, "that a .380 ACP (9x17) hollow-point was three times as good as the legendary .45 ACP. It was obvious that they never allowed themselves to be tested to a debate on the issue with Jeff Cooper. That old warrior would have taken about ninety seconds to destroy those absurd notions."

These same people, "then went on to create the NIJ body armor standard, based on faulty, if not spurious, imaginary data. They set an arbitrary standard of requiring vests that are much heavier and stiffer than they need to be. Thus, when you have something that is constrictive (which also means uncomfortable when you're sitting in a patrol car for an eight-hour stretch) you end up with more cops not wearing their body armor when they should be, and, axiomatically, more dead police."

What happened next was worthy of a chapter of its own. Apparently, somebody at the FBI believed the standards proclaimed by the NIJ and issued 9mm pistols with hollow-point ammo as well as thick, stiff, waterproof body armor.

"That was followed not long afterward by what is known today as the Miami Shoot-Out, in which the FBI had the blood of six of its agents, either dead or wounded, in the streets when their 9mm hollow-points didn't give one-stop shots. In that clammy heat, their uncomfortable vests were left unused, in the trunks of their cars.

"Now, the FBI aren't dummies. More important, this high-profile federal authority didn't need to be told twice that something didn't work. Consequently, there was quite a powerful lobby within Quantico that wanted to revert to the trusty old .45 ACP. But just then the US military-industrial complex was promoting equipment 'commonality' with NATO.

"That meant that the United States Army was changing from its excellent but unique .45 ACP to the NATO standard 9mm. The US military bought Beretta 9mm pistols and Italy bought F-16 fighter planes, which, looking back, was not a bad deal for the Americans."

With the FBI needing one kind of weapon and the US military another, Quantico realized that they were faced with a dilemma. Questions would certainly be asked in Washington why the FBI was trading its 9mms for .45s when the Pentagon was doing the opposite. "Hey, why don't you just trade guns?" one wag was heard to ask.

The FBI then decided to go to something between the 9mm and the 11.43mm (.45 ACP) and that was the 10mm. It made good sense all round.

While the 10mm is a fine anti-personnel round, the FBI soon found that some of their agents, especially those smaller in stature than the rest, had a hard time controlling the weapon. So they did the next best thing and reduced the gun's power from a 200gr bullet going at between 1,100 to 1,200 feet per second down to an 180gr bullet with a muzzle velocity of only 980 ft/sec, which is about two-thirds the power of a standard 10mm. They also fractionally reduced the size of the gun, shortened the cartridge, and called it the .40 Smith & Wesson.

• • •

Massad Ayoob regards the development of the hollow-point bullet as remarkable, especially in its application in today's law enforcement.

"The hollow-point is essentially safer for all concerned. It is designed to mushroom and stay in the offender's body. So it's less likely to go straight through him and strike a bystander.

"Historically, it is also a much more effective man-stopper, caliber-for-caliber. You are more likely to have to shoot him once, or perhaps twice, and not riddle him with so many bullets that it is guaranteed that he's going to die." The ball round, in contrast, he states, was almost designed to ricochet.

The jacketed hollow-point, because it rotates, has a sort of cookie-cutter effect when it hits the body. It will—except at the most acute oblique angle—tend to bury itself into what it hits instead of ricocheting away from it, "which is why virtually all American police agencies are now using hollow-points . . . There are safety reasons, and it is also a more effective stopper."

On a lighter note, he can be acerbic when it comes to relating tales about his traveling around the United States in the post-9/11 era. Having a rather distinctive Arab name raises a lot of eyebrows, and to some it is irrelevant that the family has now been in the United States for more than a century, especially since Ayoob is more American than pecan pie. Matters are often compounded because most of his trips involve his taking along a selection of firearms for training and demonstration purposes.

"As soon as these people see my name their pupils start to dilate. Then I'm ushered into another room for what is euphemistically termed 'additional random security.' These days, it happens fairly regularly.

"I told one of these guys who was being snotty about it that my people were killing bad Arabs when your people were dressed in skins and huddling in caves in Norway. This turns out *not* to be the right thing to say to airport security.

"A testimonial to the concealability of Richard's products was that after September 11, while wearing level 2A Ultima body armor when boarding planes, I was patted down about sixty times and only three people figured out that I was wearing a vest.

"The funniest was while I was going through McCarran Airport in Las Vegas after a Shot Show—that was three or four months after 9/11—and I got profiled three times in a row: once at check-in, once at security, and once again at the gate.

"At the gate the guy was patting me down. I couldn't place the accent, but as he goes over the torso, he breezes along and asks, 'What's this?'

"I say, 'Well, that's body armor.'

"He replies, 'You mean a bulletproof vest?'

"I answer, yeah. To which he replies, 'You stay right here,' with which he goes off to speak to somebody about my status."

Another time, a sergeant in camo and a beret frisked Ayoob. As he recalls, it was pretty clear that this was the first time the soldier had been asked to do anything except stand around and look reassuring.

"He comes up to me and asks what the hell I'm doing wearing a bulletproof vest.

"I look him in the eye and say, 'Same reason for which you're here at the airport.' The man's eyes start to do this little lateral squiggle, which sort of tells you that his computer is scrambled.

"Finally he blurts out, 'I'm calling the cops,' to which I added, 'I think you should.'"

Massad Ayoob was driving his wife's car when he had his not-so-little nudge with death. At the time he was wearing a light, quilted Second Chance Monarch in a deep cover carrier under a flannel shirt.

Driving down a secondary road in Bow, New Hampshire, he was probably moving along at the limit of about forty-five miles per hour.

"As I approached a T-intersection, I saw this Chevy Cavalier coming up to the stop sign. It was strange, because having been driving since I was a ten-year-old, you just know . . . you learn to pick things up.

"What immediately struck me, just then, was the somewhat obtuse movement of the young female driver's head. You recognize the look that doesn't see, and I'm heading right at her, or she at me, depending on what happened in those next vital moments.

"My foot is already off the accelerator, already starting to move across to the brake when I realize that if she pulls out, I'm not going to be able to stop.

"I hit the horn. Hard! Still, she pulled out right in front of me and I don't know if it was the horn vectoring in on her or what, but I saw her look up to her left. At that point she saw me coming and she and the car just froze like the proverbial deer in the headlights."

Ayoob admits to having been in two car wrecks in his life. Both times he was saved from death because he'd followed the advice of Tom McCahill, an old sage.

"Tom had the ideal job, as automotive editor and gun editor for one of those all-purpose mechanical magazines back in the 1950s. I can't remember if it was *Mechanics Illustrated* or what, but the bottom line was that he'd been testing a 1958 Fiat on a test track in Detroit. The car had gone out of control and into the worst kind of roll. It was one of those end-over-end experiences that can be deadly.

"Of course, there being no seat belts or roll bars in the car at the time—they were only to come in later years—he did the one thing that he said saved his life: he dove down under the dashboard figuring that firewall area would provide the greatest protection. I saw pictures of the car afterward, and it looked like a crumpled cigarette pack. We were all amazed that anyone could survive an accident of that magnitude. McCahill walked away from it with only cuts and bruises."

That event left a marked impression on Ayoob. Were it ever to happen to him, and an accident was imminent, he decided that he too would dive down to his right.

"That kind of action had saved my life once at sixteen and again at twenty-five. But just then, with that car immediately in front of me and approaching fast, I'd actually started that downward movement when I realized there was no way to drive out of this.

"I'd managed a glance at that girl's face and would have guessed that she was about nineteen or twenty, no more. I had a daughter that age, and all I could think about just then was that my impact would have crushed her like a bug. Remember, I was driving something big, with a gross vehicle weight of five thousand pounds. So instead of going down, I stayed up to do what I could to minimize the impact.

"In that last split second, I swung my wheel hard left and hit the front end of her car, literally removing that section of the Chevy Cavalier. Obviously, the effect on my wife's Cadillac wasn't too brilliant but at the end of it, the girl had a bit of red rash on her shoulder from the seat belt locking up. Otherwise, she was unhurt.

"At that final instant of impact, because I'd been so stupid not to fasten my own seat belt, I was thrown forward and everything began to go into slow motion. It's called the tachypsychia effect and a lot of people who have been in accidents talk about it. Suddenly you see things moving terribly slowly.

"Next thing, as I hit the steering wheel, there was an impact across my chest that felt like I was slugged by a baseball bat at full swing. A fraction of a second later, something like a blunt machete hit me across the head, and blotted out any awareness of a blow to my chest. I'd struck the windshield with my forehead."

Surprisingly, Ayoob did not lose consciousness. As he recalls, it was a pretty good concussion but he had the presence of mind to put the gears into park and turn off the ignition because he'd sniffed gasoline. It's something to remember if you get into a wreck, he cautions.

"First thing I did was wiggle my toes to make sure the central nervous system was still connected. Judging from the pain in my head, I figured immediately that I'd suffered a fractured skull. More important still, I felt around, but there was no blood. I hawked and spat on my hands and there was no blood there either. So I figured, okay, no serious chest injury.

"At this point the young lady is out of her car, running up to my window, sobbing hysterically and screaming 'I'm sorry; it's all my fault . . . I'm sorry . . . it's my fault.'

"I heard myself speak in a corner of my mind starting to say, "*You stupid* . . . I'm looking at her and she looked even younger. She turned out to be sixteen years old and had her driver's license for three months. I asked her, 'Miss, are you alright?' She's nodding her head. 'Yeah,' she answers and I tell her that she needs to call home.

"It couldn't have been much more than seconds later before a man with a cell phone pulled up and told me that he'd called 911." He also asked if anyone was hurt, Ayoob told him to call an ambulance. "Tell them they've got a case of closed head trauma," he suggested.

"Then I step out of the car and find that everything's still sort of working and I immediately revert to being a cop. There was a camera in my wife's car so I took some photographs of the scene, always a good precaution before everything is moved . . . just force of habit.

"The ambulance gets there. The paramedic is fumbling trying to find a flashlight, and I handed him mine. He checks the pupils and says 'Sir, your right pupil is not reacting to light, do you know what that means?' And I said, 'Yeah, I'm afraid I do.' And he replies with, 'Then you know we have to go. It's the hospital for you.' I replied something about us not wasting any time.

"Until that moment, I'd mentioned only my head. Then I remembered the baseball bat across my chest. But I'm also aware that while my head feels like crap, there's no pain in the chest. I tell the medic, anyway.

"I'm sitting there thinking oh shit! And just like every cop that I've debriefed after being shot in the vest, they open up my shirt, look down, and find nothing. No damage. Nor could I feel anything. I even took a deep breath: no thoracic damage whatever."

Having been taken by ambulance to the hospital, which he discovered had unarmed security, Massad Ayoob wasn't pleased to find that a convict from the state prison—together with an armed corrections officer to watch over him—had also just arrived. "Worse, he's one bed over from me, in the ER. I think, oh great, I need this, with a couple of guns on me if I pass out.

"I summoned one of the nurses, flashed the badge, whispered to her that I was armed and that I was a police officer. I needed to secure my weapons, I told her. So she brings in the unarmed security guy and he turns white when he hears my story.

"'What am I supposed to do?' he asks, totally flummoxed. I suggested that he take them. 'Do you have a locker?' I asked. He said, 'Yeah, but I'm not allowed to touch them; I'm not trained on that.'

"'Where's your locker?' I asked, and he pointed out back somewhere. So I managed to get up, my head barely nodding, walk with him about two hallways down, go to the lockers, take out both my firearms—one from my belt and the other from my ankle holster—and slide them into the storage space. And just as I start to put the key in my pocket, the security guard tells me, 'I'll take that key.'

"I said, 'Like Hell you will.' I put it in my pocket, walked back into the ER, and lay down. After a couple hours my pupil started to react to light, but X-rays still needed to be taken, which came out negative for fracture. No indication of any serious brain edema."

Basically it was a four-month recovery for the police captain, overcoming a post-concussion syndrome.

He describes it these days as feeling like someone was blowing up a balloon inside his head. He also lost about 10 percent of his hearing, in the right ear.

"Other than that, I'm not any more brain damaged than I was before. The doctor told me that I was plain stupid for not wearing my seatbelt, a lesson that I subsequently took very seriously to heart. I might add that I immediately became *the* most religious wearer of seat belts.

"Without question," he said, "my hit on the steering wheel would have impacted my ribs and killed me if I hadn't been wearing body armor. Even worse, without the vest, as the chest caved in, my head would have been propelled forward that much more powerfully in the impact. It would probably have been an open skull fracture with some of my gray matter on the safety glass.

"I might not even have survived the ride to the hospital."

Jim Morris, who spent quite a few months editing this book, remembers a Massad Ayoob–related event that stuck in his memory. As he recalls, while at *Eagle Magazine* in New York, he used to edit pieces by Lyle Miller of Oklahoma City, someone he describes as a dynamite writer and a most practical thinker.

As Morris tells it, a guy offered to make an estimate to mow Lyle's girlfriend's yard. Only she noticed that there was much more checking out the back of the house, rather than the yard. So she called Lyle and asked for his advice. More of a writer than a gun nut, Lyle had never handled firearms before. So he went out and bought a .357 magnum, a box of shells, together with Massad Ayoob's book on home defense. He also boarded up the back door and windows.

Lyle was sitting in the kitchen reading Ayoob's book—the loaded weapon on the kitchen table before him—when the guy tried to break in. Lyle got off a couple of rounds and hit the intruder once—and the cops found him later, passed out in his car under an overpass.

After the trial the judge called Lyle and his attorney into chambers and said, "Young man, because of your poor marksmanship this scumbag will be on the street in four years. I want you to get in some range time."

According to Morris, they look at things a bit differently in Oklahoma.

CHAPTER 10

The Shooting of a Constable

It was a classic episode that lasted weeks: three young people on a rampage across Canada. Events were punctuated by car thefts, muggings, drug dealings, shootouts involving police chase cars, the attempted murder of a cop on their trail, a bush pursuit, and in the final denouement, a double suicide. The only difference was that the cop was wearing concealable body armor.

Three individuals were involved in the case that was subsequently to become known as *Regina* [the Crown] *v. Alfred Bradley Cardinal.* Charges were leveled at a native Canadian, the only survivor of a three-week-long "Bonnie and Clyde" rampage that stretched from Calgary, Alberta, to the remote logging town of Timmins, Northern Ontario. The two deceased were the brother of the accused, John Gordon Cardinal, and John's lover Donna Yvette Lachance.

Alfred Cardinal, twenty-seven—called Freddie by his family—was convicted of aggravated assault and of uttering threats in September 1990 and had been serving time at the Grierson Correction Center near Calgary, Alberta. A newspaper report after his arrest stated that he walked away with only days left to complete his sentence. Previously he had been convicted of forgery and theft and had several breaking-and-entering (BE) charges against him. A month later, his brother Gordon Cardinal was jailed at the same institution.

This was not Gordon Cardinal's first brush with the law. He had been convicted several times on charges that ranged from theft, robbery, possession of property obtained by crime, and a number of BEs to the obstruction of a police officer.

According to the time line provided by the system, Gordon Cardinal, twenty-eight and classified "nonwhite" in court documents, escaped from custody on May 23, 1991. A month later, Gordon took up with a white woman, twenty-four-year-old Donna Yvette Lachance. At the time of her death she was heading toward Timmins, where she'd told the others her father lived.

Like the rest of the gang, her rap sheet told most of the story. A warrant had been issued by the Edmonton Police for Lachance's arrest on unrelated charges on June 23, 1991, which was about the time she formed a relationship with Gordon Cardinal. Within a week the younger Cardinal—Alfred—walked away from his sentence.

The trio's lawless escapade started almost immediately with the theft of a car in Alberta on June 25, 1991. Shortly thereafter, a series of armed robberies took place, the majority of them at liquor stores. Their hauls must have been good because the group tended to live in mid-level motels, and when they were discovered by the police, there were almost a thousand dollars scattered about the bodies.

The modus operandi in each robbery was identical. The trio would park their (stolen) car on a side street, and then the brothers would don balaclava hoods and enter the target business. A sawed-off, pump-action 12-gauge shotgun (which they fondly referred to as "Johnny") was used to relieve the occupants of cash and valuables. Lachance was tasked with driving the getaway vehicle, a black Dodge Lancer.

The gang was subsequently linked to a spate of robberies that took place in a lengthy west–east line across Canada and included Medicine Hat, Thunder Bay, Sudbury, and elsewhere. Most occurred after the three runaways had picked up two hitchhikers heading east on a highway in Alberta.

While an OPB was put out nationwide on the gang, they managed to elude the law for almost two weeks, even though one set of license plates they had stolen was black and of a type used only by commercial vehicles. Their first police chase began shortly before midnight on July 6. Earlier that day, the trio had hit The Beer Store in Sudbury, Ontario.

Heading north toward Timmins on Highway 144, Ontario provincial constable Michael Halvorson spotted the stolen vehicle. With details provided at an earlier robbery by a bystander, he knew that the gang was in a black Dodge. Also circulated were the first three digits of the plates: the numbers 365. It was then that Halvorson discovered that there were five people in the car. The two hitchhikers were apparently still riding along.

His attempts to stop them ignored, Halvorson gave chase over a distance of about fifteen miles, with speeds approaching a hundred miles an hour. At one point, he was able to pull his cruiser alongside the fleeing vehicle and positively identify the driver as the Lachance woman.

The robbers finally pulled into a ditch just north of Mattagami Lake Road and abandoned the vehicle. All three ran off into the bush on foot, and the two hitchhikers were taken into custody for questioning.

• • •

Character studies of the three individuals involved in this spree are illuminating. The brothers' backgrounds were not dissimilar to that of their moll, Donna Lachance, with both sets of parents being alcoholics.

As with their three other brothers, the Cardinals were Alberta born, and their folks separated before they were ten. The father, Alfred senior, moved to the United States where he eventually died. He maintained no contact with his family once he'd left the house.

The mother, Helene Brouno, also had no further involvement in the raising of her kids. The result was that the boys were taken in by their grandparents Gus and Mary Joy Cardinal, who lived at the Elizabeth settlement at Grand Centre, Alberta, an Indian reserve area.

Lydia Cardinal, an aunt interviewed by the police after the events depicted here, said that as a child Gordon received very little affection. He was constantly in trouble, she intimated to the authorities. She also made the point that of the two brothers, Gordon was the loudest and the most violent. He shared a commonality with Freddie in that they were both vituperative "police haters." She also told the authorities that the elder of the two was "the type of personality who would take his own life and had once declared that he would 'kill anybody who tried to arrest me.'"

On his last visit to the Elizabeth settlement, Gordon Cardinal told his friends that the next time the police tried to take him in, it would be in a box.

Other relatives spoke of Gordon Cardinal's predilection for violence. He would rarely spend time in a bar without getting into at least one fight, not that he sported the best kind of physique for fisticuffs: he was five feet, eight inches and weighed a hundred and forty pounds, though the grapevine had it that he was handy with a knife.

In contrast, Alfred (Freddie) Bradley Cardinal was the more quiet spoken and reflective of the two, though no less violent after a few drinks. Three inches taller than Gordon, he weighed in at a hundred and fifty pounds. The record books would describe him as underweight.

Unlike his peripatetic brother Gordon, Alfred stayed on at the Elizabeth settlement and lived with common-law wife Gloria Desjarlais. They then moved to Edmonton, where he "fell from a parkade" and got a head injury. The couple eventually split, with Desjarlais stating that Alfred was an alcoholic and constantly on drugs. She mentioned, too, that he became violent whenever he was around Gordon. On being sentenced to prison time, Alfred Cardinal threatened he would kill Gloria Desjarlais when he got out of jail.

In contrast to her partners, who were of Indian stock, Donna Lachance was not only white but was also the antithesis to much that her men represented.

More erudite and quiet spoken than the males, she could be a moderating influence. At one point, after the Cardinals had threatened to kill Jim and Vickie Killeen and their son—who had the misfortune to intercept the trio in their (stolen) canoe as they tried to escape after robbing the Killeens' home on Kenogamissi Lake—Donna was instrumental in getting Gordon Cardinal to lower his weapon. Before the two groups parted, Lachance even persuaded her boyfriend to apologize for what she termed was his "overhasty" action and pay $5.00 for cigarettes cadged from the Killeens.

If the Cardinal brothers had a difficult childhood, Donna Yvette Lachance's early years represented the kind of disaster that people make movies about. One of a dozen siblings (six brothers and five sisters) she was born in Timmins, whence the trio was headed. Her parents had divorced when she was about ten.

From an early age Lachance was placed in the custody of the Children's Aid Society, but by then, by her own admission, she had already been sexually abused. Court records state that "her father physically abused her." Sad but true, the expression "trailer trash" might have been coined for this family.

Interestingly, while she was moved from one foster home to another, she eventually found something permanent at about age nine in Iroquois Falls. She admits to having been on drugs since she was eight. At the same time, according to one of her minders, she was achieving marks in excess of 90 percent at school during her early years. Unquestionably, this was a bright young thing. She was also a product of the circumstances in which she was plunged.

Four years later, Donna Lachance was moved to a group home in Rouyn, Québec, where she told investigators about earlier crimes and that she had already begun to sniff gas, which would make her suicidal. Things went quickly downhill when, at the age of fourteen, she ran away.

Streetwise at an early age, tough despite her apparent frailty, and a seasoned drug user, the youthful Lachance had her first major conviction for peddling narcotics at age nineteen. Police records show her to be of average height and at a hundred and fifteen pounds, underweight, probably due to excessive drug use. By the time she got involved with the two Indians, her condition had deteriorated markedly. By then she had lost most of her teeth.

After their run-in with the gang on Kenogamissi Lake, Jim Killeen gave the police a description of Donna Lachance. Asked to describe her, Killeen talked about "a young woman with light, sandy brown hair, shoulder length . . . she was skinny."

Her hair, the statement reads, was flat and parted down the middle. "Her eyes were slits, long and thin, like squinting . . . and sunk in and black underneath. She had on a white T-shirt with an orange bikini top [together with] mauve jogging pants. She had no front teeth . . . and was yelling at [Gordon Chance] to calm him down."

Elsewhere he described the Lachance woman as "dirty" with a high-pitched voice . . . and also very excited. "She had no nails. Her hands were bony, with short fingers and she wore no rings."

Vickie Killeen, Jim's wife, saw a different person altogether, one who was not unlike herself and roughly the same height.

"She had big eyes and they were light . . . and a rounded face, more than [a long one]. Definitely Anglo, not dark, with sandy or light hair, parted in the middle and swept back on both sides, like [you manage it with] a hair blower and it looked clean. She had shallow cheek bones, small and feminine . . . an attractive person. Curvy lips with a full bottom lip and straight teeth, not big or pushed out.

"This may sound crazy, but she had a Toronto accent, a little through her nose and good enunciation.

"She was calm, right on top of things. Actually she seemed like she had admirable qualities about her. I couldn't be pissed off at her . . . she sort of let us go, and I thought that was nice."

The Killeens also reported on Gordon Cardinal, the woman's partner:

"He had on a black cap," read the statement, . . . "his hair quite long, bushy, and curly . . . layered approximately to his shoulders. He was missing teeth as well. His voice was deep . . . very well understood . . . I didn't notice an accent."

"I remember that [the two men] had tattoos on both their arms . . . but they weren't professionally done. [The elder brother] had skin that was pitted, like he'd had bad acne . . . and long weathered hands—long torso, long arms, and long fingers. I would have put him in his early thirties . . ."

Donna Lachance's life had been a catastrophe from the start, yet not without enterprise. At fourteen she'd already hitchhiked to Winnipeg, where she worked at a fishing lodge until she was sixteen. By then she was also pregnant with her first child.

Declared independent through the courts, she returned to Ontario where Christopher Lee Lachance was born. She left the child's biological father because he was an alcoholic and physically abusive toward her, although he was not abusive toward the infant. Christopher remained with his dad because the father was apparently attentive to the boy's needs.

From then on Lachance's career devolved into a succession of drug-oriented adversities, including another child. She was caught trafficking narcotics, did jail time, and was then released to stay at the YMCA under what were termed "very specific living conditions." But then she obviously blew that as well because they asked her to leave. At that point, she moved in with her friend Barbara Ward.

Court records state that Donna Lachance had been smoking hash and marijuana since the age of eight. She was introduced to cocaine at the Rouyn Group Home and continued with pills and acid. The only time she let up was during brief periods between the ages of ten and twelve and when she was pregnant with her daughter Karissa, who was born when Lachance was eighteen.

It was an existence hallmarked by tragedy and the apparent lack of anybody who cared. The fact that she had the most reprehensible parents remained seminal to her every action during her short life. During one conversation, when Donna had called her mother, the daughter was peremptorily told to "fuck off." Had circumstances been a little more favorable, Donna might very well have made something useful of her life.

Many of her acquaintances agreed that there were times when she could be both kindly and resourceful, though by then she was also furiously into drugs. Once source indicated that Donna Lachance was using the stuff on a scale that would probably have killed a less-resilient person, which was one of the reasons she was drawn to the Cardinals: they had dope in abundance and they weren't shy to share it.

In a letter from jail to his brother Clifford, Alfred Cardinal wrote kindly about her:

> . . . Donna was something special, a lovely looking girl. She was the best girl I ever did meet . . . solid in every way [and] just the girl Gordon was looking for. I think you would have liked her. Right off, I did in every ways. She was a good fighter [and] backed us in every tight spot we were in. I had to laugh when we got chased by that first copper with his dog . . . Donna started screaming because she couldn't go on . . . she looked so funny standing there saying help don't leave me please don't leave me . . . the fear in her eyes [and] scared to death figuring the dog was going to eat her up. I had to run back and grab her hand and drag her through the bush . . . but that dog sure did look scary . . .

The manhunt in densely forested country near Timmins was launched on July 7, 1991, the morning after Donna Lachance had run the black Dodge into the ditch. They had left their vehicle in a hurry and were able to grab only a few items. The rest was seized and taken to Timmins for examination. There was nothing among any of it to indicate who the owners were. The identity of all three remained a mystery for some time longer.

The area in which the gang had disappeared was an isolated region, both for the hunted and their hunters. Since the authorities had the advantage of mobility, the consensus was that the trio would be grabbed in short order: a few hours' work, perhaps a day. But that never happened, and the two men and their woman would remain on the run for days.

A temporary headquarters was established for the South Porcupine and the Gogama Detachment areas along Highway 144, with an eighteen-wheeler mobile command unit ordered north from Toronto and parked strategically along the highway. With its huge Ontario Provincial Police crest prominently displayed against the all-white paint job, it would remain there until the hunt was officially ended.

Meantime, two helicopters were detached from their units and flown to Timmins, all of it part of the ongoing chase that was now headed by OPP superintendent Doug Cobean.

As the word spread among the locals that there were criminals who were armed and dangerous and on the loose in the area, sightings came in from all over, the majority of them false. One source reported that the three fugitives were on a bus heading west toward Chapleau, a medium-sized town on the verge of the Chapleau Wildlife Reserve. The bus was stopped and searched but nothing was found.

A day later the search extended toward Kenogamissi Lake after gunshots were heard in the Cache area at the northern end of this elongated body of water that was easily seventy miles long. That was followed by a local resident who reported seeing three people—two of them Indians—heading south down the lake in a brown canoe that he recognized belonged to one of his neighbors.

Two officers were assigned to marine duties. By sunset they had found the boat. It had indeed been stolen and was abandoned near an improvised campsite that had been used by the gang. That led to a helicopter search being initiated in the adjacent area.

Shortly before midnight on the same night, Dan Glass, another temporary resident, reported that his cabin on the east side of Lake Kenogamissi had been burgled. Some of his firearms might have been stolen, he told the police, though he wasn't sure because once he'd established from his driveway that there had been a break-in, he'd left the area immediately for fear of running into the marauders.

Tuesday, July 9, was much of the same, the only difference being that the first of the canine units had arrived from Sudbury and was immediately put onto the trail. Local command was told that unspecified Tactics and Rescue Units (TRU) were also headed that way.

Within a day the search area was expanded along the entire lakeshore, with local police used to ferry detachments across the water. By now there were about a hundred law enforcement personnel involved in the hunt.

It is interesting that only on the following day—the fourth day of the chase—were the suspects identified, and then only tentatively. Until that time the authorities had no idea with whom they were dealing, except that the gang comprised two men and a woman and they had an unspecified number of firearms.

One of the first requests that came through to the local headquarters of the Ontario Provincial Police at Sault Ste. Marie was for its canine handler to immediately head north to Timmins. Instructions were specific: he was to bring along his hound and join the chase.

Within an hour of being ordered to do so—even though it was a rest day—Provincial Constable Jan Nickle was headed out on the long six-hour drive north. In the back of his four-by-four police cruiser was Magnum, a German shepherd that had only recently been trained but was already showing promise as an excellent tracker.

Nickle arrived at Kenogamissi Lake at about the same time as the first TRU group got there, and they went straight to work: Nickle and his dog would head the group with several TRU members following. John Latouf, a strong, reliable, and experience man of the bush, was designated point. His job was to follow directly behind Nickle and together with the TRU contingent look after the safety of the lead man from the flanks and rear.

Ferried across the lake by boat, they marched straight into the bush along a stipulated track and after about ten minutes were met by a squad of uniformed members in a state of high alert. The fugitives, they said, were a short distance ahead, perhaps a couple of hundred yards farther along the track: they'd heard noises that were human and one of the men said he'd spotted someone ahead carrying a duffel bag. It could only have been the Cardinal brothers and Lachance, was the conclusion.

Jan Nickle takes up the story: "From what I could make out, the suspects were in the tree line ahead, somewhere between the road and the river. We were aware that the group was armed and moved silently throughout, the idea being to surprise them if we could.

"Throughout I kept Magnum on a leash so that I had total control over his movements. It would be my prerogative to release him if I thought it appropriate, though I had already decided that because of weapons, that would be the last of my options.

"At that point, still maintaining group silence, I made the decision to wait for my tactical team to arrive for backup: they were generally better trained and equipped for this kind of operation and would be ideal for back-up.

"Meantime I called headquarters and asked that the helicopter provide us with spotting ability. Once the chopper arrived, we would have to move because they would then be aware we were on to them.

"We could hear the helicopter coming, and we set out in the general direction of the noise. Perhaps a couple of hundred yards on, we saw ahead what appeared to be someone propped up against a tree. There were arms on both sides of the trunk. A closer, cautious inspection revealed a sleeping bag with a coat wrapped round it. It had been set up as a dummy and to make it appear that there was a person there. The attempt to slow us worked because it meant that we'd have to search that area, even cursorily.

"Minutes later we were tracking north again. The tracks were fresh and Magnum moved fast. We crossed a sand road and the dog just went straight on without stopping.

"At that point, I was called back by the others. We were going the wrong way, they said, pointing at the tracks. They were going in the opposite direction. That wasn't what Magnum was telling me, I argued. A closer examination of the tracks showed that the trio had taken to walking backwards along the sand track in an attempt to befuddle us.

"The tracks we were on to took us down a bit of an incline into an area where the heavy overgrowth gave way to lighter Labrador teak, black spruce, and which was significantly less dense than elsewhere. This was good, I thought: it would give the chopper an opportunity of possibly making a sighting. At this point some of the men started to lag. Several were checking secondary tracks for a presence while a few of the others spread out to cover a greater area.

"At that point I came on a yellow duffel bag that we later identified having been stolen from another campsite. It was evident that they were trying to repeat the decoy ruse, and I must have disturbed them because it was incomplete. Just as I got there I saw the back of somebody that I recognized as the girl disappearing into the bush ahead of me, perhaps forty or fifty yards away. That was the first time I hollered for the group to stop. If they didn't, I warned, I'd let the dog go. But because they were armed, I had little inclination for doing that: we'd lost dogs in the past because of overhasty action.

"Also, I knew that I couldn't shoot at them, or even fire in their general direction. Always a delicate issue, you have to have just cause to use a firearm in a chase: there has to be a real threat to my life or to the lives of others around me. In any event, I didn't see any weapon and she was running away from me, so the threat was diminished.

"I wasted no time in following up, but by now the terrain had changed again. It had suddenly become very heavy bush country with a lot of blow-downs and windfalls. Magnum was right on them at that point, which was what I reported and what the chopper relayed back to HQ on the main road.

"Though we'd been on the trail for about forty minutes, we were starting to feel the heat. Though it was still early, it was already a very hot midsummer day with no wind to talk of and, of course, water was sparse. It wasn't easy on any of us, the dog included. I knew, too, that we were getting closer because Magnum had suddenly become quite anxious. The group was just ahead.

"I entered a little clearing about sixty yards across and again I spotted the woman on the far side. This time she was close enough for me to make out that she was wearing a blue and white sweatshirt. She was looking over her right shoulder toward me. A second later she was gone again.

"I followed the trio up a small elevation along an animal trail. At the top I got a glimpse of her striped sweatshirt again. Magnum was suddenly frantic, diving into the bush alongside the track, and I knew that we were close.

"Just then something to my right caught my attention. As I turned toward a clump of birch trees, I could make out very clearly in that foliage about eight or ten feet away the barrel of a shotgun being lowered at me.

"Which was when things start to happen very slowly in my mind, and then everything seemed to happen simultaneously.

"The gun was still not level when I moved sideways to get at the pistol on my belt. At the same time I shouted 'No!' as loud as I could. I started firing, but he'd already let rip. The 12-gauge blast caught me directly on the right side of my chest, and being buckshot, it had the intended effect.

"In the reconstruction afterward, which, of necessity, was quite detailed for court presentation, what became immediately clear was that had I not moved my body sideways a couple of inches to draw my gun, he would probably have hit my arm and crippled my ability to shoot back. But that didn't happen: my torso took the bulk of it, which is why it was painful. All I remember was being thrust backward and unceremoniously dumped on my butt by the force of the blast.

"Once I'd been floored, I lay low with Magnum's leash still in my left hand. I pulled him closer to keep him quiet so that we could pick up any kind of movement in the bush around us. My immediate fear was that these bastards would come back and possibly surround me on either side. But when nothing happened after a minute or two, I got onto the radio and contacted Norm Kerr, the helicopter pilot . . . told him I'd been shot and asked whether he could haul me out of there.

"It was then that I discovered that in the confrontation with one of the criminals, I'd discharged all my rounds. In the fury of the moment, I'd even managed to reload, even though I don't recall any of that. When I looked again, I had one up the spout and a full magazine in my pistol . . . kind of comforting at the time."

Nor was it all in vain. Of the eight shots fired, Gordon Cardinal took a glancing shot to the head. The police officer's 9mm bullet had penetrated his forehead and was deflected off his skull. It finally exited around the back of his neck. Any harm done was superficial. As was discovered afterward, the trio broke into another house later that evening and found a stash of liquor. They spent a raucous night celebrating victory in the mistaken belief that they'd killed a cop.

In the radio exchange that followed, in answer to a question about how badly he'd been hit, Nickle was able to tell the pilot that he was still up and moving. He also said that he'd head back to a dry swamp area that they'd traversed a short while before and meet the pilot there. As he recalls, it was the only prominent landmark in that immediate area that he recalled passing through.

"There were no coordinates that I could give him. All he knew was I had become separated from my support team. He had to find me, no easy task in an ocean of green with almost no distinctive landmarks. On top of which I was wearing green camouflage, and that made me almost invisible from the air.

"But locate me he did. He then directed the TRU squad toward me and Magnum, and I lay back and waited for them to arrive. Once they got there, they removed my web gear (which had been partly blasted off my body) as well as my shirt in a bid to assess my wounds."

Though the policeman was bleeding—all damage caused by blunt trauma—he had no open wounds. "Reckon I'm going to survive," he joked before being airlifted out of there.

Even though the pilot was instructed not to land until the area had been cleared, Norm Kerr ignored orders and went in anyway and picked up Nickle. He brought with him a fresh squad of TRU members to take up the chase.

The trip to the hospital in Timmins was not without incident. The crew onboard monitored Jan Nickle's condition because there were moments when he looked like he might pass out. That wasn't because the wound caused him distress, he likes to tell you today. It was because of the heat.

"It was hot that day and affected us all. Must have worried the trio we were after, too," is his comment. After a night in hospital under observation, Nickle was released the next day to continue with the chase.

Jan Nickle was shot on July 9. The search, which eventually covered an area of several thousand square miles, still had another ten days to go.

Two more canine units were brought in, as well as the Barrie OPP Tactics and Rescue Team and another OPP marine unit. By then the pattern was centered on the east side of the Kenogamissi and some idea of who the fugitives actually were had filtered through, though nothing was positive yet.

The following day the hunt moved toward Mattagimi Lake, with cottagers throughout the region being advised to stay out of the area. That night the trio broke into the Tatachikapika Lodge about fifteen miles north of Gogama and, at gunpoint, held up the occupants. Having bound the victims, they set about ransacking the building for cash, food, and liquor. It was again the influence of the Lachance woman that prevailed and nobody was harmed, even though the captives said that the two men were "highly agitated."

In a statement afterward to the police, Jean Welton, part-owner of the Tatachikapika Lodge and wife of Gary said she was awakened after midnight by one of their employees, who asked that she be taken to hospital in Timmins because of an asthma attack. Gary took the asthmatic woman, which left the wife and her adult son, Wayne, alone at the lodge.

At about four in the morning, Jean woke to find Wayne being held with a gun to his head and a woman standing over the bed. She was ordered to get up and hand over the keys to the cash register in the kitchen. While walking down the stairs, she noticed that the phones had been ripped out.

Mother and son, together with Lynn Therrien, another woman at the lodge, were secured to chairs, their hands and feet bound. Having taken the clothes they needed, the gang gagged all three hostages with nylons, took one of the cars out back—a cream-colored Jeep Wrangler—and drove off. Dawn was just breaking.

It took minutes for the three victims to free themselves, reconnect a phone, and call Timmins. It emerged afterward that the fugitive trio had considered taking one of them as hostage to be used for bartering should they be stopped.

Interestingly, they also spoke a good deal about Nickle, referring to him as "the cop who got shot." The gist of the conversation centered on the certainty that they'd actually killed Jan Nickle. They asked their victims if they had heard anything about it on the radio. They hadn't.

Jean Welton: "They just yelled at each other, and it was basically the girl [telling] the guys what to do and what she was doing. She said we need clothes and shoes. Then they left."

The Jeep had been on Highway 144 for ten or fifteen minutes when the alarm went out that Tatachikapika had been hit by the gang. An all-unit report was dispatched from headquarters, and both helicopters were sent up to patrol the length of the road north and south of the lodge. A short while later, Sergeant Paul, one of the pilots, reported seeing a Jeep matching the description moving at speed southward toward Sudbury.

The first roadblock they were likely to encounter had been established at Gogama, but since the fugitives had already tried to kill one police officer, there was concern about the safety of the element manning it. But before that happened, three police cruisers traveling at more than a hundred miles an hour caught up with the slower, fleeing vehicle.

Provincial constable Gordon Vandergrinten, at the time serving as a canine handler for No. 15 District Headquarters in South Porcupine, was at the wheel of his cruiser when the first reports came through. He immediately got into the chase. An excerpt from his statement reads:

"I was alone in my vehicle, the third in the chase . . . as I approached the suspect I could see flames coming from what appeared to be the end of a barrel. [They] were shooting toward the following cruisers very rapidly at a distance of [about] a hundred and fifty [yards]."

Vandergrinten couldn't see who was shooting at them, but from blast and muzzle flashes, there was no mistaking that shots were being fired at the cruisers. At that stage the first police car in line—with PC Kendall at the wheel—used his .223 carbine to return fire.

"I could hear from some of the radio transmissions that PC Kendall was hitting the suspect vehicle . . . and after one particularly heavy salvo, I smelt a strong odor of gasoline . . . I surmised that it came from the Wrangler."

The chase went on for approximately fifteen minutes with one of the police cars taking sixteen hits. Its windscreen was completely shot out. The helicopter following reported a huge amount of fire coming from the Wrangler and even managed to record some of it on the choppper's surveillance camera, which was later used as evidence.

Shortly afterward, the jeep pulled off the highway onto a dirt road and headed into the bush before stopping over a short rise.

Because it appeared to the pilot that the fugitives were prepared to fight, he advised the three patrol cars to wait for the TRU group to catch up and continue the chase.

When the searchers finally reached the abandoned jeep, there were traces of blood on a seat. (Six days later, after the bodies of Gordon Cardinal and Donna Lachance were discovered in the bush several miles away, it was found that the older brother had taken a hit in the lower back, with the bullet exiting his buttock.) A doctor with the team suggested that while Cardinal would be relatively okay as long as he kept on the move, the moment he stopped to rest, any further effort would become excruciating. Also, since the bullet had penetrated his intestines, it was only a question of time before septicemia set in: in that heat it could happen in as little as six or eight hours.

Later the same day, Alfred Cardinal, having become separated from the other two, was arrested by a follow-up team while he was hiding in a culvert. Shots were fired, though not by Cardinal. (Since his partners-in-crime were nearby, they must have surmised he'd been killed.) The other two committed suicide a few hours later; their bodies were discovered about fifty yards from Highway 144 six days later by a search team from Thunder Bay.

Scattered around the badly decomposed bodies the police found some of the stolen money, almost fittingly as a tribute to futility. Donna Lachance inscribed her final message to posterity on the back of a cigarette pack, using a burnt stick for a pen.

She was going to be with her lover, she wrote, and was going to where she would live happily ever after.

After a lengthy investigation, Alfred Cardinal stood trial in Timmins. He got five years for aiding and abetting in a murder attempt on a police officer.

CHAPTER 11

One Different Choice Would Have Changed Everything

One of the problems facing someone who has taken a hit in the face from a 12-gauge shotgun is that there is blood everywhere. The victims are often temporarily blinded, if not from pellets in their eye socket, then from blood oozing into the eyes. Darren Bristow absorbed more than a hundred shotgun pellets from a felon who tried to kill him in Tulsa, Oklahoma, on the night of October 13, 2002. Though partially blinded, he still managed to defend himself and haul a frightened citizen to safety.

Tulsa cop Darren Bristow is not the kind of guy you'd normally mess with. He's big, he's tough, and he's smart. He also knows a thing or two about combat, armed or unarmed.

While being guided to where gunfire had been heard by a complainant, Officer Bristow was shot three times by a man wielding a 12-gauge shotgun. In the confusion that followed, he not only managed to protect the informant but was able to return fire and drive his attacker back into the house. Wounded or not, he still snatched his guide out of the field of fire to safety.

Officer Bristow's comments about the incident were, "I shouldn't even have been there . . . it wasn't my call. But I took it anyway."

There were several decisions on Bristow's part—any one of which, had he decided otherwise, would have resulted in his not being in this shoot-out. As Bristow explained, his story began several nights before the attack.

"My wife's birthday is on October 11. In the year 2002, that fell on a Thursday. The shooting took place two days later, on the following Saturday. Because

Cindy teaches school, we decided we'd have dinner on the Friday night. Then with some of my buddies and their families, that Saturday we'd watch the big football game at home. We'd have the game on TV, burn some meat, tell a few tall stories, drink a few beers, and enjoy the occasion. This was *the* big game, between longtime rivals Texas and Oklahoma. Later that evening, since I was on duty, I'd leave home for the midnight shift, so it all slotted in."

Since joining the Tulsa Police Department (TPD) Darren Bristow had always worked with two fellow officers, Steve Stoltz and J.J. Peters. With time the trio had become good buddies, both on and off the job. Quite often they'd get their wives and families together and perhaps go off to a game or to dinner in town.

"In fact, I'm the godfather to one of Steve's sons. So it wasn't all that surprising that the entire Peters and Stoltz clans were there that day. All three of us worked the same shift, so when I went off to the station, so did they."

Officer Bristow felt no different when he got ready for duty that evening. As usual he slipped on his body armor, though he remembers reflecting at the time that this was some kind of job where he had to wear protection at work.

"I'd thought about it often enough in the past, though I'd never seriously second-guessed my decision to become a cop. It was just that there were times when it seemed like an odd job to have, especially since there was always the possibility of some nut getting a notion in his skull that he needed to kill or seriously injure somebody. And let's face it, that's as much a reality of being in law enforcement these days as having to do your taxes.

"The big difference, of course, is that you do a lot more tax returns than there are people trying to kill you, or at least that's what I'd like to believe. Still, while most times it doesn't happen, you're aware that it can. So is your wife. And the kids, as they get older . . . It sort of comes with the package.

"What I do know is that to be a good cop, you have to love the job . . . There is simply no other way."

On that early Sunday morning, all three officers were designated to work parts of south Tulsa, an area of shopping malls, businesses, and restaurants. It was a given that things tended to slow perceptibly after midnight, with very few calls coming in—not in that part of town, anyway.

Then, about an hour into the shift, after Officers Peters and Stoltz had made an arrest, and while they were taking their prisoners to jail downtown, a call came through that somebody was firing a shotgun in a residential neighborhood. The incident was reported from David Squad in the northeast part of town.

According to Officer Bristow, it was all routine. "There are always reports of shots being fired. Because I knew the area pretty well, I decided I was probably closer than another car that offered to take it. He was on the far side of the city and I could get there sooner. This was the first decision I made that was to have some pretty stupendous long-term consequences.

"I had also just finished backing another officer on a fight call and he offered the arrest to me. I turned it down, and this decision too—had it been the other way—would have prevented me from getting myself shot that night.

"So I drove up there, circled a park in the area that I knew, but didn't hear anything. I even wound down my window to listen, not that I expected to hear gunfire in this quiet neighborhood at two in the morning.

"Just as I was heading out again, and about to radio in that the trip had been a lemon, I turned eastbound on 4th Street. Suddenly I saw a guy running out of his house, frantically waving his hands. This was unusual because I didn't have my overheads on. He'd been waiting for a car; he was the guy who'd initially called the precinct."

Officer Bristow stopped his cruiser, got out, and was told by a middle-aged man who identified himself as John that there was somebody in the house behind who had been letting off gunshots. He was clearly upset. "They're shooting right next to my backyard," he told the policeman in an excited voice.

"Because this had now developed into a real callout scene, I got back on the radio and told dispatch where I was and what had taken place. I was going in, I said. At the same time, I reached into the cruiser and grabbed my shotgun from its rack. Loaded with Double-0 buck, this was something I'd never done before . . . never gotten my shotgun out on a call. And that was my third fateful decision.

"I recall walking toward the back of John's house and him showing me a small waist-high chain-link gate that led into his neighbor's garden at the rear. That's the way in, he said pointing, but he'd never used it. In fact, he'd hardly ever communicated with the guy; said he had no need to.

"Meantime I was reporting back all the time by radio. I described the house to my left. I said I saw a light, though it was partly obscured by a row of trees. On my right, partly in shadow, was a large trampoline standing in the middle of the yard and in between, a light-colored dog running around apparently excited by the gunfire. John, meanwhile, warned that whoever had fired the shots was in the house. 'He's right inside,' he said in his high-pitched voice, and I became a little more concerned, which was when I moved a few paces ahead. I thought that if somebody were to come out with a weapon, it would be important that he see me first and not John, who was unarmed.

"All the while I was communicating with other cars that were arriving in the area. But they were having difficulty in identifying the house. Remember, I was in the backyard, not the front of the place. The fact that much of the area was in darkness didn't help either.

"All this, and keeping up a conversation with John, must have taken about five minutes, which was when I began to think that if this guy does come out shooting, I wouldn't really have anywhere to take cover. It would also place John in a perilous situation, which was when I spoke to Sgt. Gary Otterstrum and expressed my concern.

"As he was my supervisor, I was able to ask him to send through some kind of back-up before I closed in on the house. He affirmed, by which time the first of the patrol cars had stopped in front of the building. One of the new arrivals said he could see somebody inside lighting a cigarette.

"First reports, following routine checks that we usually run when this sort of thing happens, were coming in about the occupant. He had an Hispanic last name, but there was little more information, no rap sheet, and no warrants. John told me that from the little contact he'd had with the guy, he spoke very good English.

"I was beginning to think the episode was going to turn into one of those all-night things. The suspect wasn't going to come out willingly and we were going to have to wait for the Special Operations Team to come and talk to him."

Bristow heard a noise coming from the house, by which time John had moved forward again. "I looked back and raised my flashlight and immediately I saw a man about twenty yards away. He was walking right toward me with a long gun in his right hand.

"At that point I had no way of telling whether he was carrying a carbine or a shotgun. It was a firearm, that much was clear, and he was holding it muzzle down at an angle of about forty-five degrees from the perpendicular. Jeez, I thought, *this is serious!*"

Without thinking, Officer Bristow yelled: "Police! Get on the ground. Now!" John hit the dirt and curled up in a fetal position a few feet ahead of the policeman.

"That's when the suspect fired his first shot and there was a sharp impact as something hit my left arm and side. It felt a bit like gravel being sprayed hard on me but it was also very hot. I reacted immediately and returned fire. Just a single blast from my shotgun.

"I hadn't yet registered that this bastard also had a shotgun. Nor that some of the pellets had hit the hand that was holding my flashlight, which I dropped. Then it registered: this guy shot me! I guess I was more surprised than shocked.

In fact, as we found out afterward, his gun was loaded with birdshot, which was fortunate. Anything bigger and I probably wouldn't be talking to you now."

Still more shots followed in quick succession. As Officer Bristow explained, "He let rip, I retaliated—after which we repeated the process. It became a volley of shooting . . ."

Though he didn't go unscathed from this exchange of fire, Bristow's immediate concern just then was for his guide who lay a short distance ahead of him. In fact, he was in a position almost directly in the line of fire, right between himself and the attacker.

"I had to get ahead of him, was the thought that raced through my mind. At least I had a vest on. John had no protection if anybody were to take a dip at us. So I jumped forward a few paces and placed myself between the two, which must have surprised my assailant because he fired again. I was also able to retaliate with my shotgun, though I had no way of telling whether my aim was good or not."

At this point Officer Bristow—having taken two more hits in the leg and in his chest—was having difficulty raising his shotgun, though he managed to get two more shots off. "I was thinking that if I didn't start hitting him, he was almost certainly going to kill the two of us." More shots were exchanged, but when the policeman pulled his trigger again, all he heard was a click. His weapon was empty.

As Officer Bristow turned his torso toward the right, in a bid to use his uninjured hand to get at his pistol, his attacker raised his shotgun once more time and fired. This time the cop was struck in his face and shoulder, though his body armor absorbed much of the blast.

"I'd managed to get my pistol out, a Glock .40 caliber, but suddenly my vision was blurred and there was a lot of warm stuff running down my face and into my eyes. I hadn't yet realized that it was blood oozing from dozens of pellet holes in my face and skull, and you know how head wounds bleed . . . there's no stopping it.

"I tried to look up, and that's when I noticed that my glasses, though still on my face, were at a crooked angle. So I ripped them off and they fell to the ground.

"Wiping my face I heard another shot, but felt nothing. I raised my pistol and fired three rounds in the direction of the perp."

Officer Bristow recalls that suddenly everything went quiet, almost as if the shooter had decided to call a halt. It was eerie, not a sound. For a moment or two he thought his attacker might be reloading, though he couldn't be sure. Because so much blood was streaming down his face he could see very little.

"I couldn't miss John lying on the ground next to me, though. He wore a white T-shirt and his hands covered his head. Because he was motionless, I thought that perhaps he'd also taken a hit and been killed. Then he moved, which was when I grabbed him.

"I reached down with my good hand, wrapped it around the nape of his T-shirt, and yanked him to his feet. 'Let's get the hell out of here, Sir!,' I said quietly.

The other man needed no further urging.

"Once on his feet again, he was back in his own yard in a blink and I, too, was moving backward, trying to keep the back of the house under observation through my blurred vision and, as I realize now, not being too successful. I couldn't see the guy who had tried to kill me, and when I got to the little gate, it was John that grabbed me and hauled me backward. He was now helping me, and it really was a real help, bit like leading the blind."

Looking back, Officer Bristow estimates the entire confrontation couldn't have lasted more than a minute. Yet, he told a lecture meeting afterward that there were so many things happening, it could just as easily have been an hour. The mind does that to a person at critical moments, he recalls.

The next phase of the incident started immediately with Officer Bristow using his radio to tell the others that shots had been fired and that he'd been hit.

"I listened to the tape afterward, and you could hear me yelling, but only some of it could be understood. I was clearly distressed, as I suppose I should have been.

"John continued to help me make my way back to the road and my cruiser. At one point we passed one of his neighbors, a woman. I must have looked grim because she took one look at me and shrieked 'Oh my God!' At that point I thought perhaps things were a lot worse than I believed. I must have presented a pretty grim picture because she kept on repeating, 'Oh my God! Oh my God!' Then she ran off and that was when I asked myself what the hell was she seeing? Was I that badly wounded?

"You have to give her credit, though. Moments later she was back. Towel in hand, she used it to start wiping down my face. In no time at all it was blood-soaked.

"Then Brian Booth, another of my buddies—the same Brian who rides his Harley-Davidson to work—ran past me, shotgun in hand. He was headed for the attacker's back garden along with several other officers. That worried me and I shouted that they should watch out because there were no lights and they were going to be ambushed. I also yelled that I'd dropped my shotgun. It was empty, I hollered, just in case anybody picked it up and thought they could use it. I followed that up with the same message on my radio.

"Officer Scotty Allison arrived moments later. He got me back on my feet and we slowly started walking toward the far side of my patrol car, doing so for very good reason. The sounds coming from the perp's garden sounded like a war zone. There was some serious shooting going on there. I later found out that three other officers were hit in that exchange, though none seriously.

"I was glad to be out of it though because by now my wounds were starting to hurt."

Fortunately, Bristow took no hits in his eyes. That was a consequence of another fateful decision he'd made some weeks earlier.

"I'd been to the optician to get a new pair of glasses. That was when he asked me whether I'd prefer polycarbonate lenses, which would cost an extra twenty dollars. I'd never done that before, because, let's face it, that's extra money. But when he explained that it might be a good idea because while the polycarbonate wouldn't deflect any larger round, it would certainly be effective against something like a .22 bullet or most kinds of flying debris.

"And that's what basically happened. When I took that blast to the face, my glasses absorbed much of the impact from pellets that would otherwise have blown my eyes out of their sockets. I went back to that optician afterward for a new pair and took the old ones to show him. That's when he told me I'd be blind today except for them. Pretty good investment, that twenty dollars . . ."

"Once I was in the cruiser, just before they rushed me to the hospital, I decided to take stock of my condition. I was still bleeding, but not nearly as profusely as before. At least I could see, which was when I started to count my fingers and check whether I'd lost any. I also closed one eye at a time to establish whether I still had vision in both. I did.

"I knew somebody had called for an ambulance, but the word was that they were being held back until the area had been cleared of the shooter; it is customary procedure under that kind of circumstance, but just then it didn't help me much.

"Then a fire truck came up and parked between our car and the house. They offered to take me, but I thought, hell no, I ain't going to no hospital in the back of a fire truck! Or perhaps that was because I was in a bit of a state of shock. At that point I started thinking about possibly bleeding to death, which was when Officer Tonya Bull pulled up in her cruiser and I promptly jumped into her passenger seat. She screamed when she turned to look at me.

"Go! Get me to the hospital!" I ordered. "St. Francis Hospital, and make it quick!" She didn't argue. In fact she pulled out of there so fast I had to ask her to cool it a little. I'd survived the shoot-out and I didn't want to die in a wreck. Then, because she didn't know the area and there were a lot of dead end streets, I had to guide her out of it."

Aware that his wife Cindy had not yet been alerted, Officer Bristow used the ride into town to call his colleague Steve Stoltz to find out where he and J.J. were at. They replied that they were both en route to the scene and were moving it "as fast as this machine will go, my man!" J.J. quipped. They'd heard the news about the shoot-out—as had every cop in town who was still awake. In fact, they'd been following events on the radio: it shook them to hear that their buddy had taken hits.

Darren Bristow's immediate concern was for one of them to get the news to Cindy. She was at home asleep, unaware of what had happened to her husband. What he didn't want was a strange cop car pulling into his driveway at two in the morning. As he said, "If she sees an officer at the door and doesn't know him, she's going to think I'm dead."

The wounded officer didn't have to explain: "Will do," Stoltz replied, and that pleased him.

Having got to the scene, both Stoltz and Peters were involved in the final shoot-out when the perp came out of the front door firing his gun at random. Stoltz was hit in the nose and Peters took a small wound in the temple above his left eye, which, as Darren Bristow sagely comments: "We cops really are a different breed. Everyone else runs from gunfire, in our work we go as fast as we can *toward* it."

At St. Francis Darren Bristow was rolled into the ER on a gurney; there was a medical team waiting. Within moments his uniform was cut away and he was hooked up to various machines.

"It's not the kind of situation that I recommend," he told me when I interviewed him two years later. "In fact, it's pretty damn awful. There wasn't a face there that I recognized.

"Then I remembered that Kristina, Steve's wife, worked at St. Francis. I remembered her telling me earlier that she was on night duty in the pediatric ward so I asked someone to go and get her, and they did. After a few minutes I spotted Kristina standing at the doorway. She waved and I lifted a hand. It was one helluva feeling, a friend there, batting for you . . . strange really, because we'd all been watching the game only a few hours before.

A little while later, Steve and J.J. were brought to the ER to have their injuries looked at. The three men were together again, though none of them thought it would be anything like this.

At that point Officer Derrick Osmond walked into the ER. He bent down over the gurney and whispered into Bristow's ear. The man who had tried to murder him had been shot and killed by officers.

"Best news I ever heard . . ."

CHAPTER 12

Friendly Fire

Not all shootings are by criminals. Quite a few casualties are self-inflicted. It is also true that police statistics show that only about one in five shots fired operationally by police officers hit anywhere on the intended target.

In the language of the shooting fraternity, mistakenly firing one's weapon is termed an accidental discharge, or AD. Though the majority of shots fired accidentally are harmless, there have been some horrific accidental shootings. All firearms have the potential to take a life, or—as experienced has demonstrated—lives. In short, guns are designed to kill.

Do a Google search under *accidental shootings* and you will find more than six hundred thousand entries listed, the majority of them linked to people who might have been killed or wounded while handling or playing with firearms. Among these is former Israeli Prime Minister Ariel Sharon's son Gur. He was accidentally shot while playing with his father's rifle. In short, it can happen to anybody. Even our otherwise intelligent vice president.

Historically, accidental discharges are as much a part of conflict as are deaths from enemy action. Stonewall Jackson, for instance, was accidentally killed by his own men. He was struck by three smooth-bore musket balls, fired by troops of the 18th North Carolina Infantry Regiment. So too with Boer War General de la Rey, shot while in the car of his friend and colleague General Christiaan Beyers. That happened in the early days of World War I when the South Africans, just emerged from their own civil war, threw in their lot with the British, their former enemy, to fight Germany.

More recently, US Army Ranger Pat Tillman, formerly with the Arizona Cardinals, died from an accidental shooting in Afghanistan. To some, a cloud still hovers over that tragedy, which, at the time of this writing has not been adequately explained either to the US public or to Tillman's family, which happens often enough in what the pundits like to call the fog of war.

Quite a few police officers who have been accidentally wounded have died. Some were killed outright by what soldiers like to call friendly fire. By all accounts this problem is even worse in the military.

The situation is serious enough for the British Army to take a stronger line and refer to ADs as CDs, Criminal Discharges. Those responsible for such acts are tried by courts-martial. It doesn't matter whether the gun went off while being cleaned or possibly when it was dropped; if circumstances warrant, the offense could lead to a prison term and, conceivably, to the individual responsible being drummed out of the military.

The United States has yet to adopt such a policy, though the families of those who have died as a consequence of negligent action might wish otherwise.

Take Deputy Rodney Rought of the Kalamazoo County Sheriff's Department, Michigan, listed at Davis' Save #647.

On July 29, 1994, while working as an undercover member of the Southwest Enforcement Team (SWET) he was mistakenly shot four times by his group leader, a Michigan State Police lieutenant.

Rought was in a prone position, crawling back to his group when .223 friendly rifle fire hit him in the right arm, left hip, and lower back. The fourth round came from a Michigan State Police–issued short-barreled Heckler & Koch HK-53 in .223 caliber and caught him in the chest. Fortunately Officer Rought was protected by his two-week-old Second Chance Level II body armor. He was also lucky that the angle at which the bullet struck the Kevlar caused the bullet to stop in the vest.

Richard Davis comments on this case: "H&K makes extremely fine and dependable rifles. My 'end of the world' weapon is an HK-91 .308. But when I heard the company had sold the short-barreled .223 Model-53 to my home state police, I half jokingly admonished the H&K sales manager when I saw him later at the International Association of Chiefs of Police Convention.

"In terms of ballistics, the only thing a .223/5.56 x 45 has going for it is its velocity. It has no significant weight or diameter. Once you produce it in the short-barrel version, you trade velocity for nothing but excessive muzzle blast and a modest amount of portability.

"The H&K sales manager became instantly defensive. He stated that he had virtually begged to have eighteen-inch barrels fitted to the Michigan State Police order instead of the less than twelve inches which they finally used and which, ultimately, proved to have inadequate stopping power.

"Fortunately, in the instance of Officer Rought, it was a case of compensating errors. As I remember hearing the story from him, the first two shots hit his soft body armor in the stomach area. Center-fire rifles are not supposed to stop, or hardly even slow down, on any kind of soft body armor during a close-range perpendicular hit, said Davis.

"In this event, however, I feel that the shorter barrel handicapped the little .223 speed merchant enough that the first two shots just barely entered the policeman's body. Nor did the bullet jackets rupture or mushroom.

"I was told that shot number three severely injured his arm, and that the final bullet hit a one-inch-diameter tree branch and then struck Rought directly on the heart. It was stopped cold because the tree limb slowed and mushroomed the .223.

"As an epilogue to the case—and I am unable to confirm this—I was told that whereas an officer normally would have a very difficult time suing his own department for being at the wrong end of an accidental discharge (because police officers sign waivers when they accept employment), this case was different. Officer Rought was shot by a member of *another* department.

"The story goes that he got himself a good attorney and a handsome settlement. A further uncorroborated aftermath is that the lieutenant with the itchy trigger finger was not charged formally, but rather, was demoted two ranks to ordinary Trooper and allowed to serve out a year or two until he became eligible for retirement at a lower pay rate.

"Even this is a happy ending, compared to being kicked off the force and being charged with manslaughter," was Davis' final comment.

Thanks to his soft body armor, none of Rought's injuries were considered life threatening. In multiple bids to speak to him, while passing through Kalamazoo several times in the fall of 2004, Rought refused to discuss the incident. This was hardly a cover-up, since the circumstances are in the public domain. But his version of events would clarify this sad episode.

There are other examples of ADs. Officer John Brooks of Indianapolis, Indiana, wondered what would happen if he were accidentally shot in his body armor. He found out while holstering his own weapon. Peculiarly—and against all odds—the .357 magnum slug lodged in the lower right edge of his body armor. According to Richard Davis, Brooks' superiors were not amused.

Officer Joseph Miller, of Elmira, New York, was accidentally shot in his vest during a training exercise. The bullet lodged in his vest, just alongside his heart. Miller became Save #897.

Richard Davis, who has had decades of experience in shootings, accidental or otherwise, believes many more ADs take place than are reported. From conversations with officers from several of the larger metropolitan police departments, he came to believe there is at least one accidental discharge each day in just about every big city. They go unreported, he feels, because ADs don't look good on the record of either the officer or his chief.

Too many ADs in a precinct, for instance, will raise questions about the quality of training. While it might make sense not to go public with every single AD, things are a lot different when an officer is killed or seriously wounded. It is impossible in this age of instant communications to keep such things quiet.

Range work, as any competent instructor will tell you—that essential routine process of "keeping your eye in" with your personal firearm—is a bit like physical exercise. Go slack and you quickly lose the edge. And that which might have been second nature before now loses a vital nanosecond—which could be the difference between life and death.

Many officers interviewed after a save, have credited their survival to doing what came naturally, reacting without having to think about it. Case in point is Angela Watson-Spitler, the first save in this book. Only five feet two inches tall and a bit more than a hundred pounds, this little lady officer took a hit in her ribcage from a .44 magnum.

Instinct, the fundamental survival response, took over and rescued her from a dire situation. The atavistic nature of the human psyche pushed her through; Watson-Spitler, the victim, became the killer, though her crazed attacker took his own life after she shot him several times.

Richard Davis raises some interesting points on accidental discharges. When he first began to chronicle the number of saves attributable to his body armor, he wasn't sure whether he should include ADs. Strictly speaking, these saves weren't incurred during the course of what might be termed "regular" line of duty.

But as the number of ADs increased, and proportionately, the number of saves, he gave it more thought. He realized that in sparing the life of an officer who had been accidentally shot, perhaps by his partner, or as a consequence of sloppy procedures during an arrest or a confrontation, he'd rescued not one policeman but *two*. This makes sense when you realize that, at last count, there are roughly seventeen thousand police agencies of one kind or another in the United States.

"Thus," says Davis, "when an officer accidentally kills a partner, it is one of the severest tests any police establishment can experience. Once the guilty party emerges from the departmental wringer, that officer is out of a career. And it is immediate.

"Further, as any veteran cop will endorse, just about all the old-timers know someone who left under that kind of circumstance. Many of these transgressors end up if not on skid row, then taking their own lives after years of battling with guilt, and booze. That is not only destructive, but can be illogical if it was genuinely an accident and unintentional."

George Orwell had a word for what these officers become, in his historical novel *1984*. Though used in a political context, the word *unperson*—in relation to what happens to an officer who shoots his partner—is strikingly appropriate.

There is no question that during the period under review, body armor has made a significant and long-term difference between the number of officers who might have been killed by accident and those who emerged with their lives intact. The following are only some of them:

- Dave Mowry, of Phoenix, Arizona, was involved in a car chase that ended when the suspect vehicle collided with another Department of Public Safety unit that had arrived at the scene for back-up. The officer in the other car got out after the collision and attempted to take the suspect into custody. The new arrival discharged a single shot from a .40 caliber auto that struck the suspect in the head and went on to hit Officer Mowry on the left area of his chest, just over his heart. The moral here, when firing a gun, is to check the area behind the perp before pulling the trigger. The officer could just as easily have missed the suspect and hit Mowry in the head.
- Detective Kris Smith of Union City, Georgia, had just fired for qualification on the range. He reloaded his Glock 23, in .40 caliber, with Winchester SXT ammo and then decided to clean his gun. During unloading, it went off, the bullet striking Smith in the lower, left abdomen. Luckily he was wearing his department-issued body armor and suffered only a bruise and abrasions.
- In another cleaning accident Officer Jay Longley of Clovis, New Mexico, was sitting alongside a policeman with a .45 ACP pistol. A slug ricocheted off the floor and into Longley's body armor, just below the left armpit. Deputy Chief Mondragon told Richard Davis afterward that if he hadn't been wearing his vest, he'd have been a dead man.
- Sergeant Thomas Fern of Beloit, Wisconsin, was an attendee at a SWAT training session in Oshkosh. Fern had asked a question about a shooting technique. As the instructor moved toward the group, he raised his gun and pulled the trigger of a 9mm Sig. Fern says he "saw and felt the blast,"

which hit him center chest, blowing out a portion of the zipper on his body armor. Lucky man.

- An unusual AD happened in Westland, Michigan, when David Hochstein and his partner went in pursuit of a speeding vehicle. The suspect turned into a dead end and came to rest in front of a barricade. As the two policemen approached on foot, Hochstein's partner drew his gun just as the suspect threw the car into reverse and drove forward around the barrier and down a steep embankment. Descending the incline, Hochstein's partner began to slide in the mud, hitting the car's trunk and rolling over the car onto the hood when he accidentally discharged his 9mm. He hit his partner on the end of his body armor. Curiously, we know Hochstein's name but nowhere does that of his careless partner appear.

- Virginia Beach was the scene of another training accident. Detective Duane Hart was at the firing range with members of the VBPD special investigative unit, when, for no apparent reason, he zipped out the ballistic panels of his Second Chance Investigator jacket and placed them on his torso for what he termed "additional protection." Hart was standing outside the right side entrance of a cardboard structure that depicted hallways and a three-room interior. A search team of SIU personnel entered the building and within minutes, a single 9mm bullet struck Hart. It hit him in the right upper back after passing through one of the "walls" of the structure.

- Even more fortunate was Kent Lamont, a ballistic weapons expert who was demonstrating a CETME 5.56mm belt-fed machine-gun at Knob Creek, Kentucky, when the extractor broke. He opened the bolt and reached for the shell in the chamber. But as he did so, the shell "cooked off" and sent the .372 diameter casing back dead center into Lamont's chest, which fortunately was protected by one of Richard Davis' vests. The velocity of the exiting case was somewhere about 800 ft/sec, which would be equivalent to being hit by a .38 Special wadcutter. The body armor had earlier been "temporarily borrowed" from Richard Davis, whom Lamont bumped into as he staggered backward in surprise.

- There is little detail about how Herman Reichold was struck by a 124gr 9mm hollow-point bullet accidentally fired by a fellow officer in North Prairie, Wisconsin. It hit the officer right center of his chest. According to the attending physician, he would not have survived the hit had he not been wearing body armor.

- One of the earlier Second Chance Saves involved US Marine Sergeant Steve Lawrence. On the firing range at Parris Island, South Carolina, he took a hit from an M-16 in his Model-Y Second Chance vest. The distance from muzzle to vest was about eighteen inches and the angle about thirty degrees. The AD from a prone-positioned recruit caused the slug to enter from left to right, blowing off the NCO's uniform buttons while being deflected by Kevlar. Off to the stockade went the shooter, while a medic examined the sergeant. He'd suffered only a hairline crack in his sternum.

Other "accidents" also happen, including an officer taking a hit from his own firearm (which might have been forcibly removed from his control), or from that of his partner.

In this regard, there have been a series of unusual saves. Take William Moss, who was working as a uniformed security guard at a Holiday Inn in San Bernardino, California. Moss used pepper spray to break up a fight in the hotel lounge, when, en masse, the brawlers turned on him. They beat and kicked him mercilessly, even after he'd been floored. Then they took his gun and shot him. The bullet was stopped by his soft body armor (about half an inch from the top), after which he was taken to a hospital and released. There is no record of what happened to those responsible for this fracas.

Moss told Davis afterward that he *almost* hadn't worn the vest that night, because it was a Sunday. "Those nights are supposed to be pretty uneventful," he stated. He was mistaken and subsequently entered the record books as Save #852.

Then there was Deputy Gary Herbst of Stark County, in North Dakota's Sioux country. Herbst was aiding in the apprehension of a felon who was handcuffed and being dragged through a narrow hallway. As they passed each other, the criminal was able to grab the officer's .40 caliber handgun. He squeezed off a round that struck his own leg, glanced off the wedding band on his other hand, and slammed into Herbst's K-30 plate on his body armor. Then the gun jammed. The upshot was that instead of going to prison for a short time, the felon got an extended term for attempted murder.

As Richard Davis commented tartly afterward, and with some with acrimony: "another stupid crime committed by a stupid person."

Noteworthy here is the accidental shooting of Timothy Stansbury, a nineteen-year-old Brooklyn teenager who was shot dead by a policeman in 2004.

An article in the *Village Voice* in February of that year by Erik Baard explained that ongoing research into the circumstances of such tragedies has shown that it is possible that human neurological wiring might lead to accidental killings of this nature. Baard put this hypothesis forward.

In Stansbury's case, he explained, the shooting took place on the roof of one of the Louis Armstrong Houses in Bedford-Stuyvesant. This complex has been a haunt of drug dealers, criminals, and rapists for a long time. Stansbury and two of his friends were bounding up the badly lit stairwell, intending to cross between buildings to a birthday party and using the linked roofs as a skyway.

Concurrently, as Baard explains, New York police officer Neri and his partner Jason Hallik were on the edge of fright in the post-midnight darkness and cold. Like many law enforcers, they walked "vertical patrol," leaving the street and climbing to the upper stories, with guns drawn.

The accident happened when both Stansbury and Neri reached the same door, but on opposite sides. No one can say who actually opened the door, but, in doing so, a psychological chain reaction appears to have been set off resulting in Neri unintentionally firing his weapon. The bullet killed Stansbury.

Says Baard, "Scientists are intensely studying the amygdala, a pair of almond-shaped neuron clusters inside the brain to understand its role in post-traumatic stress disorder. The amygdala encodes memory with emotional weight. It also alerts us to sensory information that we associate with danger.

"It's the jittery small mammal inside us, always awaiting loud noises, sudden movements, and glints of teeth. The more we expect a threat, the more excitable it becomes."

He goes on to detail mankind's three responses to a scare, which, he says, are the same for any animal: fight, flee, or most commonly, freeze. "But we expect cops to be a different breed," he states.

Alexis Artwohl, a retired police psychologist and consultant to law enforcement agencies, had her own interpretation of events. "We try to train the freeze response out of police because if they freeze, they could be killed," she said. She added that, "We also don't pay cops to run away."

Baard quotes Roger M. Enoka, chair of the Department of Integrative Physiology at the University of Colorado. He thinks that "it is important to distinguish between discharges that are accidental and those that are unintentional."

He elaborates on an accidental discharge, which he says, "occurs when a weapon is not being handled correctly. In contrast, an *unintentional* discharge occurs when a physiological response causes the trigger to be depressed while the gun is being handled in an appropriate manner."

* * *

Davis is extremely vocal about how some of these issues are solved by wearing concealable body armor. It is a form of support, he says. Some cops find it comforting to wear something that might someday save their lives.

"I'm always telling those ultra-liberal, money-controlling politicians that a cop's vest sometimes makes an officer not so afraid for his own life that he can take that extra second or two to identify the target and *not* shoot the six-foot-tall twelve-year-old who is in the wrong place at the wrong time with a toy gun . . ."

CHAPTER 13

Nutty Professor With an Intent to Kill

> A Carnegie Mellon University professor has been charged with attempted murder in a Sunday night shootout with Mt. Lebanon police officers who had come to his home to investigate reports of a domestic dispute. Edward G. Constant, 59, an associate professor of history who was wounded in the melée, was arraigned by District Justice Charles McLaughlin yesterday at Mercy Hospital. In addition to attempted murder, Constant was charged with four counts of aggravated assault, criminal conspiracy and simple assault . . . Constant's wife, Susan, 47, who police said shielded her husband as he fired his gun, was charged with conspiracy to commit attempted murder, conspiracy to commit aggravated assault, recklessly endangering another person and obstructing the administration of justice.
>
> **—from a report by Frank Reevese**

During the thirty months and thirty thousand miles that it took to research and write this tome, I was hosted by many law enforcement agencies. With a little advance warning, often from Richard Davis himself, there were few police departments where I was unwelcome. Among the most pleasant was the Mount Lebanon Police Department (MLPD).

I'd always make contact with a departmental spokesperson beforehand. I'd be given a run-down at the station, meet the people who mattered, and, quite often, go on patrol with a unit. More often than not, that would allow me—as well as those who traveled with me, such as my son Luke and Jim Mitchell, an American national presently living in Africa—to see things from up close.

Jim, an avid reader and book editor, was fascinated by the American legal process. He became even more engrossed after we spent time with the cops in an upmarket bedroom suburb of Pittsburgh, Pennsylvania.

The first time we went out with Danny Rieg, then a sixteen-year veteran and one of the more illustrious characters in the MLPD, we were thrust into an ongoing drama almost from the moment we opened the doors of his patrol car. But let me backtrack a little.

We got to Mount Lebanon, in Pittsburgh's South Hills region, on August 17, 2004, following the tail end of Hurricane Ivan. The region had just received the highest recorded rainfall ever. Wherever we went, small streams had turned into violent torrents of water that swept away everything. In some places, entire areas were flooded.

That first morning, driving on the outskirts of town, we spotted a fire engine covered in water almost to the top of the cab. That didn't stop the driver going ahead anyway and making higher ground a short distance farther on.

We'd hardly set out on phase two of our patrol when an emergency call came through on the cruiser's radio. Two kids, both thirteen years old, had been playing in a parking lot. One of the youngsters had apparently been too close to the river and was swept downstream by a surge of water that suddenly overwhelmed the bank he stood on. His buddy jumped into the maelstrom after him. It was a desperate gesture, a brave attempt to save his friend.

All we heard then was that "Matt and John are gone . . . they're in the river." At least we had their names.

The alarm went out immediately. In a few sparse moments it seemed as though the entire Pittsburgh area was mobilized. It took us about two minutes to reach the scene. In the crazy process of getting there, we were forced to drive several times against the flow of traffic, and sometimes—with lights flashing—on the wrong side of the road. When we arrived, six other patrol cars had already pulled up. Moments later a police helicopter hovered above as well.

The police stopped all traffic in the area, and there were people running all over the place looking for the two boys. A woman, probably one of the mothers, stood on a bridge spanning the raging flow immediately ahead of us. She clasped her hands to her head, absolutely distraught, and she wept unashamedly.

On a hunch, Danny took his car a few hundred yards downstream. There this giant torrent disappeared in a gaping hole under the highway. Built for drainage, the inlet was never designed for this huge volume of water.

We left the car and saw that everything that floated was being sucked into it. There were fair-sized trees, shrubs, chunks of lumber, even a plastic forty-gallon container disappeared into that black hole, a lot of it trapped inside. If the boys had gotten that far downstream and were dragged into that black culvert, there was no way they would come out the other side.

Worse, as other police units started their search of the riverbank, we saw that both sides were completely overgrown. It had been a good summer, with every patch of earth in the area green and verdant, right to the water's edge. The undergrowth was so thick there were places where you couldn't see the water. No one could hear anything above the roar. Trying to find the boys by calling out, or listening for their shouts, wasn't going to work.

Another boy walked by, also about thirteen or fourteen years old. "Those are my friends," he said. "I was there when it happened." Tearfully, he ran off downstream to look for his buddies. We didn't try to stop him, because by then there were officers everywhere.

Everything going on around us was being relayed by radio. Another helicopter joined the search. It reported that the riverbank was too overgrown to see anything lodged there, even if the boys had been able to cling to something. One officer reported seeing some clothing next to the torrent but that turned out to be discarded linen. The minutes ticked by.

"I can see something!" came a sudden cry on the patrol car's intercom. An officer identified himself and in the first flush of excitement, shouted hoarsely into the mike. We could barely make out what he said.

"I see . . ." His voice broke off or became garbled. We heard him mention something about a boy. More incoherent shouting followed. At which point one of the officers in charge ordered him to relax and not shout. Once he'd settled down, we were able to hear his report. He'd found one of the boys holding on to a branch and had brought him to safety. There was elation in his voice. Shortly afterward, they found the other little guy.

The recovery of the two kids was a small miracle. No one passing, even close to the torrent, could have seen them. We certainly couldn't hear their calls, though they told the police afterward that they never stopped shouting. In fact, they were both quite hoarse for all the effort.

What had happened was that two cops, Officers James Zeiler and Pete Sutek, decided to search down in the water. They lowered themselves waist deep into the stream, clinging hard to the overhang so as not to be swept away. Then, quite suddenly, they spotted John. And it was John who told them that Matt was clinging to a branch a dozen yards downstream. The rest of us had missed them because that section of the river was also totally obscured by growth. One of the engineers who arrived later said that if they had lost their grip, it would have taken the kids only another forty seconds to disappear down the culvert.

Then came another chilling call. Someone reported there had been a third youngster. He was now unaccounted for.

His name was Anthony, the radio told us. The only other detail they gave was that he was about the same age as the others, and a little more thickset. Danny reported back that a kid matching that description had walked passed our cruiser going south toward the drainage culvert some minutes before. That youngster was thickset, he told control.

A minute or two later, we saw the same boy walking toward us. He was wet through, bedraggled, and his body language indicated that all was lost. He was crying for Matt and John. We told him that they were safe.

"And what's your name, son?" asked Danny.

"Anthony," said the young man, wiping his eyes.

Mount Lebanon Police Department has great community relations. Almost everybody we encountered during the course of normal patrols nodded, waved, or shouted a greeting.

Over time the department had built an enviable relationship with the community. Officer Danny Rieg observed the process from up close because his father had been with the MLPD for thirty-two years. He retired as a lieutenant, and, like his son, was known to everybody in town. With another officer, Jim Howell, Lt. William Rieg established the first Crime Prevention Unit in the area, one of the reasons why the MLPD became as service-oriented as it is today.

"The department encourages as much interaction between the community and the police force as possible," said Rieg, Jr. "As part of policy, it advocates officers interacting with local folks and the system works well. Also, people seem to prefer it that way. We work for *them*. We protect their interests." One feature of this policy is the encouragement of block parties throughout the town whenever the occasion warrants.

"On Labor Day, for instance, we'll have eighteen or twenty streets blocked off so the kids can run around and play in safety without their folks having to worry about traffic. They'll set up trampolines and rock climbs on the streets, have a few drinks, prepare their meals, and all that. It often all happens right in the road in front of their homes.

"Anybody can have a block party, for any reason they choose: birthdays, anniversaries, bar mitzvahs, whatever. They just tell us beforehand and we arrange for Public Works to get the information, and they drop off the barricades at whatever time it's asked for, from eleven in the morning to ten at night."

Other, more serious innovations include joint operations with other law enforcement jurisdictions in the area.

"We have two other South Hills police departments—Dormont, Castle Shannon, and, of course, ourselves—using the same radio frequencies. They share borders with us and we're able to call them whenever we have a need to, and, of course, they us." It's a sort of 911 conglomerate, he explained. Further, mobile data transmission computers in their cars (MTDs) can patch into about thirty other Pennsylvania police departments.

"That helps a lot when we're involved in a chase, or there's an APB for somebody really dangerous."

That too happened recently. A thirty-four-year-old criminal, Richard Baumhammers, committed five murders and other nonfatal shootings before he was apprehended. Danny Rieg's SWAT team was in on the manhunt. The man was apparently a psychiatric nut case. Court documents and testimony came to light during his trial that indicated a long history of association with both racist and anti-Semitic groups.

"He abhorred people who weren't what he regarded as 'true blue Americans'—Asians and Jewish people especially. One time, in a bar across town, he spoke to a lady who had come to the States from Germany. When he discovered she was Jewish, he hit her. Knocked her right off her stool and onto the floor. Asked why he'd reacted that way, he told the cops that she had no right to speak to him because she was Jewish. Then, not long afterward, he went out and murdered five people."

Richard Baumhammers fatally shot Anita Gordon, his Jewish neighbor, before driving to a grocery store in nearby Scott Township. There he killed Anil Thakur, an Indian, and then shot and paralyzed Sandip Patel, another Indian. He followed that by going to a Chinese restaurant in Robinson Township where he killed Ji-Ye Sun, a native of China. Then came the murder of Thao Pham, a refugee who left Vietnam in 1979. After all that he drove into Beaver County where he shot Garry Lee, who was black. Finally he was apprehended after being spotted and stopped by police.

"It was an interesting case for us because we had just started SWAT. It was actually the very first call-out we had. We'd been training for months for exactly that kind of scenario and most of us were at home when the call came through.

"It was close. Once he'd started his rampage, there were reports coming through all the time. His mug shot appeared on TV and people were constantly calling the cops. He'd be seen simultaneously in downtown Pittsburgh and minutes later a hundred miles away. And you have to act on all those reports . . . all pretty confusing, especially when you're so close to something like this. That was when the Joint Operations setup worked like it was intended to.

"Officers were positioned at various strategic points and it was one of those who eventually spotted him driving by. After being pulled over, Baumhammers offered no resistance. He got out of his car and put his hands up.

"He tried to plead insanity. But that didn't stop him from becoming the two-hundred-and-forty-sixth person on Pennsylvania's death row after an Allegheny County jury passed down a death sentence in May 2000. Baumhammers was awaiting the outcome of his appeal while we were in Mount Lebanon.

For this—and other reasons—the Mount Lebanon community has been generous to their police force. A local security company, for instance, donated an International 4700 armored car to the department for use in any emergency, including acts of terrorism.

That prompted Chief Tom Ogden and Deputy Chief Gene Roach to call for old discarded Kevlar body armor vests. Quite a number came in, and these were used to line the inside of the vehicle for additional reinforcement in the event of someone using larger-caliber or explosive-type weapons. Officer Rieg made the point that this was a significant morale factor.

Someone else gave the department a very substantial grant to build a full-size gym at headquarters. Once complete, it was better than some commercial gymnasiums in town. The equipment is all top-notch, and during our visit, it was constantly in use by unit members.

The facility plays a useful role in keeping Mount Lebanon's ten SWAT members in fighting trim.

Danny Rieg was in his sixteenth year of service when we met. He originally became a cop on the eighth day of the eighth month in 1988. In the interim, he became not only the unit's firearms training officer but also one of the founding members of SWAT.

None of that prevented either Rieg or Jeff Kite, his partner, from becoming the target of a local academic who used a Smith & Wesson .44 Magnum to almost blow him away. The event took place on Memorial Day 2002, and it also made him Richard Davis' Save #865.

"I was working the late-afternoon-to-midnight shift," Officer Reig recalled. "That was from four in the afternoon 'til midnight, and we got this anonymous call for a domestic in the last hour. The address was 105 Piper Drive, which surprised us because that's an upscale district, nice homes, large gardens, that sort of thing. I don't think I'd ever been called to Piper Drive before, though obviously I knew where it was.

"I told dispatch that since the matter was labeled urgent, I'd handle it. I gave them my call sign, Six-Yankee-One. Without switching on my lights or siren, I sped across town a little faster than normal and pulled up in a quiet street, right on the border between Mount Lebanon and Bethel Park. There were lots of trees, which seemed to shroud any streetlights and made it eerie. It was also very dark.

"By the time I arrived, Jeff Kite, one of my buddies, was already at the front door. He was having difficulty conducting a conversation with the owner of the house. In fact, it had become more of a yelling match than a discussion. Jeff was being thoroughly abused and ordered to get himself and his 'fucking' car out of the area.

"Being a two-year rookie, Kite didn't have much to say when the man behind the screen door told him that police had no legitimate reason for being there. There was obviously a lot of anger in his voice, and the first thing I observed on arrival was that he'd been drinking. He was really letting go. Then, he turned both his attention and his venom in my direction, which worried me.

"This was not a very big man. He was in his late fifties, about five feet ten, but overweight. What struck me most was that he was scruffy and unshaven. It didn't go with the house.

"In any other circumstance but in his home, he'd probably be regarded as a little unhinged; he was that vituperative. By now, between curses, he'd identified himself as a professor, adding that his name was Edward Constant, if the department wished to check at Carnegie Mellon.

"So I'm on the front porch. It's not a large area but has a railing around it and a garden six or eight feet below, which stretched all the way to the road. Jeff is standing off to my left and now this guy starts calling us Nazi bastards. That came as a shock. I motioned to my partner that we'd have to do something to establish whether there was anybody else in the house and whether they were okay. This guy had lost it.

"Between tirades, he protested that only he and his wife were at home, and that she was fine, adding that we'd better believe him or else . . ."

The rant went on for a minute or two, with the suspect refusing to budge on his question of rights and whether the police were even justified in demanding to see anybody else in the house. Our presence was a violation of the Constitution, he told us, adding that he should know, because he taught history, which we thought a bit odd considering that he'd equated the United States with Hitler's Germany.

The police were on his premises illegally, he shouted in language that by now had turned ugly. In the few brief moments of respite, usually when he paused to take a breath, Officer Rieg tried to tell him that he really did want to see his wife and that neither he nor his partner were leaving until they had done so. That led to more ranting.

Danny Rieg admitted later that while he remained insistent throughout, his own actions were conditioned to some extent by a murder that had taken place in the precinct earlier in the year. It was the same sort of thing, people reporting a domestic on 911. The cops arrived, found nothing, and left. Then somebody else phoned to say that a man had just walked through the lobby and that he was covered in blood. After breaking into the apartment, the authorities found a woman lying on the floor. She was dead; her throat had been cut.

She'd apparently dumped her boyfriend. He, in turn, couldn't live without her so he chose to murder her. Then he went back to Ohio where he shot himself.

"So, we'd gotten into a situation which was hardly similar, but at the same time was something we just couldn't ignore. The prior situation was fresh in our minds and anyway, the man was acting irrationally. Something had to give and it wasn't going to be the law."

Something did. Constant slammed shut his main door and bolted it, leaving the two officers standing outside on the porch.

"I looked at Kite and shrugged. This couldn't go on, I told him. Then I started banging on the door again. About twenty seconds later it was opened by a woman dressed in a pink bathrobe. She was later identified as Susan Constant, the obnoxious one's wife.

"Right off the bat she starts to get belligerent as well, shouting insults, telling us to get off her porch. Now I'm really taken aback and I tell her that we're there for her, and that some of her neighbors called. Though the front door is only open a crack, I used the opportunity to shove my foot into the opening so that she couldn't close it on us again.

"As soon as I did that, Edward Constant rushes up behind the woman and now he's furious with her for opening the door. He pointed at my foot and warned me that he'd take whatever action was necessary to get us away from there. At which point he started calling us Nazis again.

"Both his attitude and his temper were getting worse. The time had come to call for back-up and I used the radio on my belt. Though I had the set in my hand and had keyed the mike, Constant gave me no opportunity to tell dispatch what was going down. It was an endless flurry of insults and diatribes.

"They got the message, though. Pat O'Donnell, one of our most experienced, came through during a brief pause and told me that more cars were on their way."

At this point Constant gripped his wife around her neck. He was pulling her backward, away from the door. The next thing he violently threw her to the ground, right in front of the cops.

"I looked at Jeff, and then at the man. 'We're going to arrest you, sir!' I told him. Already I'd pulled out my pepper spray in anticipation of any violence that might follow. 'You did that right in front of us and we're going to take you in for assault,' I added.

"What surprised both of us then was that a moment later the woman jumped up off the floor, like one of those dolls that you punch and go down and pops up again. Then she started with a new string of abuses. She abused us, cops in general, as well as what she termed the 'fascist' government. In fact, she insulted just about everything she could think of. She was small and wiry and this time she came forward and got her hands on me, trying to push me backward, at the same time, telling me to fuck off her property. Wow, things were really humming and it was all happening quickly.

"All of a sudden her husband disappears and we're left alone at the front door with his screaming wife. The thought goes through my mind that that's not the kind of thing normal people do. What did he have in mind, I asked myself."

The two officers took a step backward to try to bring some stability to a situation that by now was clearly out of hand. A moment later Constant pushed his wife aside and appeared before the two cops. He couldn't have been more than four or five feet from them when Rieg heard a loud explosion and felt a hammer blow in the chest. The impact flung him involuntarily backward over the railing onto the grass below.

"I remember lying there, face down, with my legs touching the concrete pathway, thinking, What the fuck has just happened? I knew I'd been shot, but had no idea how or, for that matter, where on the body I'd taken a hit—though there was pain to holler about in my chest, just below my left nipple. Meantime, I hear Jeff's voice on the radio shouting, 'Officer down.'

"Momentarily I pulled myself together. As I turned my head to look up, toward the porch, I could see that Constant was still there and I tell myself that I've got to get away from this position. I'm too exposed. More shots followed as I started to roll away, including one that hit the ground just where my head had been a moment before. I saw it cut a furrow in the grass right alongside my face."

At that point, Officer Rieg summoned all his strength. He got to his feet and about all he remembers is running toward his cruiser and, at the same time, hauling his .40 caliber Sig Sauer pistol from its holster.

"Now I'm in the dark and Constant, my attacker, is back-lit from behind. I yelled at him to drop his weapon. He didn't listen and fired again, and that's when I emptied my magazine in his direction and he went down.

"I fired twelve shots altogether, and hit him in the groin. There was one, maybe two entry wounds, and it certainly stopped anything else from happening. Even the doctors were uncertain how many times I'd hit him, because the wound was mangled . . . caused a lot of damage. Also, we didn't recover all the bullets afterward."

Because Susan Constant stayed alongside her husband throughout the shootout and had put herself in a critical position—directly between Officer Kite and the shooter—Rieg's partner wasn't able to get off a single shot. If he had done so, he told the MLPD departmental inquiry afterward, he would almost certainly have hit the wife. Her actions were subsequently interpreted as "recklessly endangering another person and obstructing the administration of justice."

By the time Susan Constant was hauled off to the station, she was aware that her husband had shot a policeman. She'd seen two ambulances arrive, one of which removed her wounded husband. Questioned soon afterward about the incident, and still confrontational, she asked about Rieg's condition. When the interviewing detective told her that he'd been taken to the hospital, she spat out: "He deserves all he got . . . I hope he dies!"

Danny Rieg went to the trauma center with a dinner plate–sized bruise on his chest. Edward Constant, meanwhile, was only a few paces away, in the same hospital and wailing loudly about his own predicament. He cried like a wounded cat, Officer Rieg remembers.

"It was annoying, actually. He had a lot to say to the doctors as well. Then more cops arrived and they charged him right there in the ward. At the hearing, he was initially denied bail. His lawyers fought that all the way to the Superior Court and he was eventually given a half-million-dollar bail. But at the same time he had to surrender his passport and take a drug that would make him ill if he drank alcohol.

"And the next thing we know he's involved in a road rage incident that sends his vehicle headlong into a school bus. That little show of his put seven children in the hospital.

"What happened was that he'd had a difference with another driver on the road. The two cars had just come off Pittsburgh's Liberty Bridge when it happened. As soon as they left one of the tunnels, Constant tried to pass the driver he'd earlier insulted, and he did so on the wrong side of the road. A lot of people almost got killed because of his mindless stupidity."

In the process, the nutty professor with the mean streak broke his back. He cracked a vertebra and acquired a host of other problems, including prostate. By then he'd been returned to jail because the road rage incident was deemed criminal. In court his lawyers tried to use his ailments as a reason why he shouldn't serve time for his assault on the Mount Lebanon officers.

"Well, the prosecutor and the judge didn't go for that. Most people agree, even those who were not involved, that he couldn't go around shooting cops and then demand special treatment.

"Even his neighbors concurred. We had a lot of offers to testify in the shooting but they only used the word of one willing soul who came forward. She told the court how the Constants would carry on and drink and scream and call the kids in the neighborhood names. She was afraid of them, she told the judge. In fact, while all this was going on, the neighbors even petitioned the court not to let Edward Constant out of jail. They wrote something along the lines of: Please don't let him out of jail. We're afraid if he did that to a policeman, God knows what else he can do."

The Nutty Professor, as they refer to him in the precinct, got fourteen-and-a-half to twenty-nine years. He must serve the minimum of fourteen-plus before he becomes eligible for parole.

The last word on Edward Constant came from Danny Rieg. "I just heard that his attorney is filing a petition to try to get him out of jail because of health problems: he's in a maximum-security state penitentiary in Pennsylvania somewhere. If I know the judges, he won't get out. Having tried to kill a cop, he will almost certainly spend the full term behind bars, which he deserves.

"I wonder if he will ever get so far as to accept or even admit his responsibility in what could have been something fatal?"

For her part, Susan Constant, never having been arrested before, avoided prison time. She was finally allowed to go into a program called Accelerated Rehabilitative Disposition, or ARD. Meant largely for people who hadn't made crime their lifestyle, it's a first-time thing.

If she is arrested again, the original crimes are likely to count against her, so there is a distinct incentive for her to stay clean.

For all the goodwill in Pittsburgh's South Hills, it can still be a dangerous place. While preparing this chapter, a Pennsylvania State Trooper stopped a car late one night on what was supposed to be a routine traffic stop. The occupants jumped out and overpowered him and then killed him with his own gun.

Danny Rieg says it happened very quickly. He was dead before we could get there to back him up. "Also, many of the details are not clear as to why he was murdered. The suspects were rounded up within days and are all behind bars now . . . It was a great piece of investigation . . . really good police work.

"His funeral the next week was something to see. Tear-jerking for many, especially me. Thousands of us, and what a police procession it was. It was a great shame, because he left behind a couple of teenagers."

Then another local police officer, Pete Sutek, was in a cataclysmic accident that almost killed him. As with Danny Rieg, his body armor saved him, though under totally different circumstances.

On patrol one night he was making a turn. A drunk driver heading in the opposite direction smashed into Sutek's cruiser in the middle of the road. The police car was totaled, and according to the chief, it didn't look like anyone could have possibly lived through it. But he did.

What happened was that, with the force of impact, the patrol car's MDT computer and its bracket impacted his body. His ballistic vest prevented his being killed or seriously injured. Officer Sutek walked away with only minor injuries.

Rieg said, "Most people don't know it, but those vests are good for many things."

Danny Rieg comments on an episode that dominated his life and his career for so long: "I have been having many lingering issues since the incident. We had that State Trooper shot and killed on duty just a few miles from my district at the end of last year, and that, among a lot of other things, colored my perception.

"My fears after I returned to duty, of maybe over-reacting or under-reacting, had become too much for me, even though I received the Medal of Valor from my chief, of which I am very proud. At the same time, I simply cannot afford to place my fellow officers, the public, or even myself in danger of civil and criminal liability.

"I consequently made the recent decision, or rather, should I say, the shooting made it for me, to leave the department on early retirement. My knowledge and experience as a police officer are immeasurable and this is really not the way I wanted to end my career. But I also know that it is the right way, for my sake and the sake of my family. My wife Doris, my kids—Brittany who is nine, and seven-year-old Billy, who we named after my dad—are solidly behind me in this decision. They're the best family anyone can ask for. I am a very lucky person.

"I think I told you my slogan, given to me by my SWAT instructor: 'When your life is on the line, it's too late to learn a new skill.'

"My father taught me the same thing, and I keep that with me all the time."

> Former Mount Lebanon Police Officer Dan Rieg was honored with the Order of the Purple Heart in October 2003. The Military Order of the Purple Heart was founded in 1958 for military personnel who had been awarded the Purple Heart, an award established by George Washington during the American Revolution for soldiers killed or wounded in combat. Since September 11, 2001 when more than four hundred emergency service personnel died in New York, the order has recognized police officers and firefighters who were wounded in the line of battle.
>
> —Vince Guerrieri, *Pittsburgh Tribune Review*

CHAPTER 14

Grappling with Violence in New England

Among the thankless, sometimes hopeless tasks expected of the police is providing protection to residents in public housing. Whether it's South Central Los Angeles or New England's Providence, the cops are often confronted with unprovoked abuse, distrust, and drug-incited violence. It makes for a dangerous environment in which to earn your pay. At the same time, commented an officer working in one of the "projects," it's a job that needs to be done. "There are people living out there who need our help . . ."

Every big American city has its "war zones" where battle lines are imaginary boundaries between those who obey the law and those who don't.

These are not tiny inconsequential pockets of cultural resistance or indifference. They're great sprawling neighborhoods where many of the residents are not only youthfully rambunctious, but also in a state of rebellion against all forms of authority—especially the police.

Some of these places are almost cities within cities. Philadelphia has its Southwest Philly. There is Watts in Los Angeles, immortalized in the fiery 1986 riots. Chicago's Caprini Green is simply Hell on Earth. The same is true of 12th Street in Detroit. Let matters slip in any of these places, say those who maintain order there, and it would only take hours for anarchy to replace the veneer of order.

New York City used to head the list for lawlessness, at least until Mayor Rudolph Giuliani imposed his will. Still, conditions in America's biggest city remain critical in quite a few areas.

South Bronx, east of the Hudson River, for example, is a huge, sprawling conurbation whose unofficial credo centers almost solely on survival. For a long time the place was a synonym for slum, and many people say nothing has changed. We saw some of it in the film *Fort Apache, the Bronx*, in which Precinct Four Two's station house was the fort. Precinct Four One had originally been nicknamed Fort Apache, but it was later referred to as Little House on the Prairie because so much there had been burned down.

Most Americans ignore the reality of inner-city rot and crime. There are those who refuse to accept that such places exist. But they do. "They're culturally quaint," the apologists say, and they are likely to blame the "indifference" of current administrations for the aberrations there. But don't ask these armchair critics to visit the place. Denial, as they say, is not just a river in Egypt.

The downside of the American Dream is right in your face, if, of course, you'd care to look. As one New York cop warned after I'd asked directions (and mentioned that I'd like to take a look around), "You take great care if that's where you're going. And if that's a gold bracelet your wife is wearing, I suggest she take it off before you get off the subway."

One of the most perspicacious reports on this kind of work is contained in a book written by Connie Fletcher almost twenty years ago, titled *What Cops Know*.[1] Her take on the dangers is both succinct and disturbing because Ms. Fletcher pulls no punches. On "project" work, she comments:

> If you work the projects, you have to be on your toes. You have to constantly, constantly be on your guard. Constantly. I don't care if things look rosy, you have to be careful. Because the one time you let your guard down, that's when things will happen.
>
> Any time you go in the buildings in the projects, when you get out of the car, you always look up—to see if anybody's in the windows. So you don't get bottles dropped—if they fire a saltshaker at you, and they're up ten floors, if it hits you in the head it will kill you.
>
> If there are two of you, when you get out of the squad, one guy will always watch the windows; the other guy will eyeball the lobby.
>
> You eyeball the lobby first, to make sure nobody's about to open fire on you. If the lobby looks clear, then you look in the hallway to see who's in it or what's in it. You run up and down the stairways—we call working in the projects "running up and down stairs"—because you never want to take the elevator.
>
> They're stuck, mostly, and they get stuck real quick if the police are in them.

• • •

New England is not immune. While the crimes in Providence might be more mundane than those in the housing projects in New York's Claremont Village, this city with a police force about five hundred strong still makes the news—as it did in the spring of 2005 when a sixteen-year-old was arrested in Miami, Florida, for killing Barry Ferrell at a bus stop outside a Providence apartment complex.

Keith LaFazia, a still-youthful, thirty-five-year-old Providence police officer, knows all about the city's public housing units. He and a small team of cops—his Target Team—help to keep order in Hartford Park, the biggest of the lot and also one of the most depressed economic zones in New England. He says that covering an area of twenty-seven square miles (which also includes scattered houses owned by the Housing Authority) can sometimes be horrendous. It more than once almost cost him his life.

A consistent problem, says LaFazia and his partners, is that apart from basic patrol duties, drug arrests, firearm problems, together with homicides, the location of the unit's police station is in the heart of what people have compared to some housing projects in New York City.

"A few years ago," he says, "I was on desk duty in our substation. A robbery actually took place about a hundred yards from our office. We went out and the next thing I know the suspect is coming straight at me with a Colt .45. I took him into custody after what I'd prefer to call 'a bit of an altercation.'

"Then we had a drive-by shooting, once again outside our office building, while two other officers and I were inside. So you can imagine, as a police officer, your senses are on high alert at all times."

The Hartford Police Station, a compact autonomous sub-station with television monitors and electronic systems to keep the officers abreast of activity throughout the complex, is on the ground floor of a large multi-storied apartment building. When Luke and I visited the place in our motor home, the cops on duty were able to watch our approach on their monitors from some distance out and give us all the directions we needed to make base.

"Consequently, while we have additional support systems," as this thirteen-year veteran of the Providence Police Department tells it, "each of us needs a double set of eyes to check not only what is going on around us, but what might come down on our heads from above." For security, the unit now has chain-link fences on the outside walks.

"We've had some pretty big things hurled down from of the apartments upstairs, sometimes twelve floors above, including television sets and refrigerators," says this always-sanguine cop. "Often the stuff that comes down is detritus 'of the human variety,'" is what he tells you, and then smiles.

"We're in a public housing area and our unit is responsible for keeping the entire community safe, or as secure as we can manage. We also handle all public assistance talks to new tenants concerning their welfare. In fact, we're required to handle *everything* linked to the housing authority, HUD, or public housing." He admits too that while the majority of the residents at Hartford Park are genuinely happy that there is a strong security presence, there are obviously some who aren't. In that category is a proportion of the younger generation, he explains.[2]

"Part of what we do is what we call *community-oriented policing*, or, in police-speak, CPO. The CPO units no long exist; they were a bit like a reserve," he explains, "but they set the ground rules for the system that we now implement."

Porky O'Rourke, the unit supervisor, has been on this mostly underpaid job for twenty-two years, though he's now a full-time police officer. His partner of more than two decades is Jack Costa, whom the men call Mamma Jack. "They're always helping us through our paperwork or life issues. These two guys actually laid out the parameters for us young bucks in efficiently policing the projects," says LaFazia.

Without Porky—like Porky Pig, he used to stutter, which is how he got the name, one of the cops told me—he feels his unit might have had it much tougher. Still, Porky O'Rourke hasn't come out unscathed. In numerous run-ins with criminals he's been beaten and battered, and he lost an eye in a shoot-out. But, as LaFazia says, this hasn't prevented him from being one of the most valued men on the force.

While LaFazia was still at school, his father—who had served as a police officer in Johnston, a small town adjacent to Snake Den State Park on Interstate-295—told him "to find a job that I'd love to do and make a living out of it. So it's natural that I followed in his footsteps."

Entering the station at Hartford Park for the first time, you get a sense of siege, of urgency.

The entrance to this otherwise unglamorous and functional operational center is dimly lit. The interior—glum, but well kept—presents an immediate impression of being at the start of a succession of security warrens, very much as Beirut's Christian Falangists organized their defenses along Lebanon's Green Line. This is not an inexact analogy, as there is very much a low-key conflict going on in the environs.

The people living there are threatened, in one way or another, every day of the year. Some have been hurt, others killed. There were moments while there that I felt the only thing missing from this battlefront scenario was the thump of mortars or 122 rockets overhead. Instead there was rap. Lots of it. And fast, souped-up hot rods. Also, Beirut's police force didn't wear the dark-blue uniforms known in the trade as LAPD blues, just like those that LaFazia and his guys had on.

He explained that within the complex there were roughly two thousand two hundred housing units. Multiply that by four, five, or in some cases, even six, he reckoned, and you had a rough idea of how many residents there might be. It was more than ten thousand and the place contained a lawless element that was sometimes difficult to control. A lot of time was spent picking up people who had no business being there in the first place.

"Shots fired" was always being reported. Murder was a constant, which is why the number of police working there had been increased by a third in the preceding year. As one of the officers commented, "Too many crimes, too few of us."

These days, he told me, "Our biggest problems are drugs and guns. Or guns and drugs, take your pick. The two go together, like heroin and crack, and the gang members who do this stuff. Many of 'em live right here in these housing complexes . . . pretty violent bunch. Not tough, just violent."

LaFazia explained that there were transient druggies and gang members moving into the Providence area from other states, and, as he suggests, "There are parts of Providence that are getting really bad."

Ethnically, he says, it is a diverse mix. "We have a lot of Hispanics. Also quite a large expatriate Italian community, folk like me, though I'm third-generation American. The really bad guys are in gangs like the Bloods, Crips, MS-13, and half a dozen more with the names you'll find in all the big cities. There's even a Hells Angels chapter on Messer Street."

Many Asians living in Rhode Island have their own mobs, even some triads, he said. The South and Central Americans are there as well. There are Latins on one side of the street and Orientals on the other. In all, he reckoned, there were about fifty of these groups, each one battling for dominance and turf in a city with a population that is about a million.

LaFazia: "Just about everything that happens comes out of the housing projects. Mainly, we've got people here without much money. Others might be scamming, you know, they got full-time jobs, they're driving their Escalades, they're drug dealers. But they live in the projects with their brand-new BMWs."

And when one section of the community throws money around, he suggests, "There are others who want some of it."

As to homicide, Officer LaFazia says that Providence is about neck and neck with Boston. But the past year, he thought, had been "a slow year for us." By the end of August 2004, Boston had had forty-six murders while Providence was yet to reach thirty.

"For a long time we were the second murder capital of New England, though we beat Boston a few years ago. Thing is, Providence is small and everybody sort of looks past it.

"We had a deputy police chief before who came from New York City, and he was always baffled by the number of arrests, murders, and major crimes in such a small, pretty place. There were so many crimes that we actually compared favorably—or unfavorably, depending on how you phrase it—with his old home ground. Said we were like a precinct in the Big Apple. That was how he viewed it."

The last officer who was killed in the line of duty, LaFazia said, was Detective Sergeant James Allen.

LaFazia: "James was one of the best men you could meet, an outstanding policeman with a memory like a computer. He could remember everybody, and in a moment, recall events that had taken place years before, often in the most intricate detail.

"He was killed on April 17, 2005, right here in our own station at 325 Washington Street. He was questioning a dirtbag who had stabbed an eighty-four-year-old lady in the back as he tried to rob her . . . and this fucking piece of shit shot James in the head.

"Then the killer jumped out of the third floor window and tried to flee. We got him and he'll stand trial.

"Then barely a month later, in May 2005, while responding to a call from a place we've nicknamed Chad Bronx—another housing area in the north of the city, about five miles away—one of my old classmates was in the process of training a rookie officer who was sitting in the passenger seat. They were in their cruiser waiting to take a witness back to her house when some garbage walks up and fires his gun at the trainee officer, only inches away from his face. Luckily the bullet hit the car door. The perp was using a .25 caliber auto, loaded with .22 ammo.

"So, while the first shot went off, all you heard when he pulled the trigger again was click . . . click . . . click. The semi-auto piece that the criminal had was a crappy Saturday Night Special that wouldn't feed. And what's worth mentioning here is that our young guy had been on the job only about two days.

"He returned fire, got out of the cruiser, and ran that evil bastard down. Without any assistance, he then arrested him. We need more of his kind around . . . He can give me back-up any day.

"Then, three days ago a Cranston officer tried to stop a suspicious person who just kept walking away from him, having ignored his orders to stop. As he made to grab the guy, the suspect turns around and shoots six shots at the cop. It was a 9mm semi-auto and they were about seven or eight feet apart. The thing is, he missed with them all. The officer got three shots away but it was raining quite hard and the criminal took off. Never did find out if he was hit or not. So, you see, we have a lot of our own stuff to deal with here in lovely Providence, Rhode Island."

Fortunately, said Officer LaFazia, the wearing of body armor on duty is mandatory in the city. It has saved quite a few lives over the years. His as well.

There was a time when law and order in Providence was almost a joke. Mendacity, some of the old-timers will tell you, was its second name.

Yet Providence, Rhode Island, has a charm that is all its own. It is one of those cities that conjures images of order and industry, along one of the most beautiful coastlines in New England. Travel northeast out of Connecticut, on Interstate-95, past Pawcatuck, down Hope Valley, through the outskirts of Nooseneck, and inevitably, all roads lead to Providence.

Once regarded as among the most promising dozen or so waterfront cities on the Eastern Seaboard, things stayed like that until the Mob moved in after World War I and began to take over many facets of local government. Even after the FBI had displaced this underworld hierarchy, things remained unsettled. One columnist noted at the time that the gangsters of that period seemed to have introduced a banality of evil from which the city was still trying to resuscitate itself, but then, that is probably the story of all cities where the Mob has played a role.

These days, while Providence has a share of the tourist industry, mostly from beyond New England, the majority of visitors don't linger. They move on to Boston, Nantucket, New Hampshire, and beyond.

For all that, the city reflects a charm that is quiet and dignified. Its appeal is enhanced by Brown University, the Museum of Natural History, and Cormack Planetarium. There is also the Russian Submarine Museum, all of it topped-off annually by the Festival Ballet Providence, as well as groups like the Trinity Repertory Company and the All-Children's Theater Ensemble.

Providence has a very distinct suburban charm, which could be why it attracted the Mob in the first place.

While Organized Crime played a role there, for much of that time, New York City crime families oversaw things. Before that, the *capos* came from Boston, which took a real hold during the reign of Raymond Patriarca in the mid-1950s.

Even earlier, during Prohibition, Providence made a name for itself as one of the biggest liquor smuggling centers in the region. Small boats and aircraft from Canada, and from points as distant as the Bahamas, would come in and unload—sometimes with cops keeping an eye on proceedings and getting paid a cut. From Providence, the booze would be shipped out to other East Coast destinations and parts of the Midwest.

Officer LaFazia's own save was like something out of a Mad Max film. As he recounts events surrounding what he calls his "little episode," it was about a half-hour or so before they were due to clock out that evening at eleven. Which makes one wonder why so many saves have taken place in that last fateful sixty minutes of a shift . . .

"Just the four of us were in the station. There was Teddy Bogda, his partner Darren, as well as my old partner Greg Sion, all of us sitting in the office doing paperwork. At the same time we were following Maxwell Dorley who'd radioed in a short while before that he was behind a stolen car.

"There had been a murder on the East Side at about the same time that Max was broadcasting details about his own chase, and, as I see it now, that started a chain of events that changed my life forever. All we knew from the reports coming in was that the first officer on scene stated that there was a subject shot in the head.

"She'd put out a brief description, and as luck would have it, we thought that Maxwell's stolen car was the suspect. As with any murder, we're especially interested, though just then we weren't altogether sure whether it was this particular car or another that had been involved.

"As the chase developed, we could see that they were headed in this direction, right toward the projects here at Hartford. The next thing, they're driving right up toward the office. We're really on it by the time their car drives past the chain-link fence that separates the parking lot from our building and can see that it's the two youngsters that Max had been chasing.

"There's Maxwell Dorley—a black cop, one of the best in the business, and now working with us housing units—right behind. We'd already run across from our offices by the time their car pulls up in a horseshoe parking area across the way. All four of us go for the vehicle, which we see is a new model Honda Accord. By now Maxwell has arrived, and he's pulled up close behind the suspect vehicle, illuminating it with his headlights. He's also got his overheads and take-downs on, so everything was pretty well lit.

"A moment later both doors of the suspect car open. We see two juveniles inside, about to step out and possibly make a run for it. We're bracing ourselves for a foot chase. But it is February 8, 2000, and there's snow and ice everywhere. Obviously, this isn't going to be easy. Also, since these guys were acting so erratically, I wasn't sure whether they were on drugs or what. They certainly weren't doing anything logical."

The driver of the suspect vehicle then did the unexpected. Both he and his buddy jumped back into the car and slammed their doors shut. Even with all the ice on the road, he jammed his car into gear, put his foot on the gas, and tried to get away. The only problem was that Officer LaFazia was directly in his path.

"The next I know he's coming straight at me, almost like in a video game. Shocked, I weaved sideways. He followed, doing his best to hit me. When I veered left, he did too, tires spinning on the ice. Several times I slipped and fell on the slippery surface, got up, and tried to get away again. Though all this took place in a few seconds, I could see that he was gaining on me.

"Finally, just as he was closing in, I slipped and thought this must be it. I remember falling on the ice. Just as the car was about to ride over my head, I managed to get up, put my hands on his hood, and jump. If I hadn't acted at that precise moment, he would have hit me and probably dragged my body down the street."

But LaFazia's efforts didn't have the required effect. He hit the windshield of the pursuing vehicle, and then bounced off. That was about all he can remember, though he was told afterward that if his head was two inches higher, his neck might have been broken.

"I know my partner was shouting at me to use my gun and told me afterward that I managed to get off two shots. I also recall getting thrown to the ground, hitting Darren as I landed hard, and dropping him as well. Then, vividly, I saw his shoes as I lay there and thought, "Wow! Shiny shoes." Meanwhile, before he'd been taken down by LaFazia's flying frame, Darren had also been shooting at the suspects.

"As for the two shots I fired, I still don't know whether or not I hit the driver. Probably not, because altogether there were thirteen shots fired by us, of which only one hit him, in the arm."

Meanwhile the teenage driver went after LaFazia's partner, Greg, who at one point had rushed up alongside the getaway vehicle. Then, he slipped and twisted his ankle. Trying to do his thing in the police car behind, Maxwell couldn't get around fast enough on the icy track in his rear-wheel-drive cruiser.

In a final bid to escape, the young driver gunned his car hard and headed toward the adjacent road. At this point one of the shots fired by a cop must have hit his arm because though it was estimated that he was doing about thirty-five miles per hour, he went straight into a telephone pole.

"He hit it so hard the back of the car actually lifted off the ground and the vehicle finally came to rest at an angle of about forty-five degrees." The impact was violent enough to hurl the passenger forward and embed his teeth into the dashboard, with the driver taking a hit from the steering wheel in his chest.

"And even then they tried to make a run for it. Though they hurriedly got out of the car, my partners certainly weren't going to let them go free. With me dead, they thought, this was one score they were going to settle. Everybody that could went after them and while it took a little time, both young perps were arrested."

Court records show that the then-juvenile driver was Victor Pagan, a name that LaFazia says he just cannot forget. Though Pagan already had a criminal record, he got the astonishingly lenient sentence of six months in a detention center, from which he escaped after seven or eight weeks. Recognized by one of the project cops in the street afterward, he was rearrested and put into a more secure institution.

On the night in question, both he and the perp, a scrawny five-and-a-half-foot wimp with orange hair, ended up in the hospital with their injuries. The suspect's gunshot injury was a straight-in-and-out flesh wound that needed to be cleaned out and a few stitches put in before he was taken into custody.

LaFazia's were more serious. He'd taken a powerful hit from the perp's car and suffered both internal injuries and bleeding. If he had not been wearing his body armor, he was told, he'd have been killed outright.

He also took a blow to the back of his head from where it struck the windshield and left a four-inch indentation in the safety glass. He suffered severe swelling of the brain and lost his memory for about six months. Some residual brain damage is still there because, as he puts it, "I sometimes just zone out . . . sometimes my thought processes are not there. But it'll get better with time, I hope."

LaFazia: "I ran into him again not so long ago, in Onyville. He was out of jail by then and he knew exactly who I was. Said something clever about my not walking in front of cars again. Smiled too, when he made his smart-assed comment. By the time I realized what he'd said I stopped the car, but he'd taken off through some buildings. No doubt we'll meet again, probably in court."

"If I hadn't been wearing my vest, I'd have been seriously hurt, being hit by a car doing that kind of speed. While I broke no bones, I was bruised up pretty good. I also ended up with several herniated discs on my spine."

Officer LaFazia was incensed at the way the newspapers handled the story. "Again, it was a case of a poor innocent being maltreated by an insensitive moronic police force. They tried to make a racial issue of it and suggested that we had beaten up the kid. But then, both my partners—Darren as well as Maxwell—are black, and both were involved from the start.

"Also, Maxwell had been raised in Hartford Park, and as another officer commented, he was one of those who not only survived that tiny slice of Hell, but thrived."

The two young criminals were not strangers to the criminal justice system. Where they were fortunate, said another officer, was their age. Had they been two years older, he suggested, these issues would have been handled very differently, as potential cop-killers always are. For a start, he said, they would have been treated as adults.

LaFazia has observed a disturbing trend in recent years. Kids, he said, are now committing crimes at much earlier ages than before. While editing this chapter, a fourteen-year-old Hartford Park boy was murdered by a kid who was a full year younger than the victim. "Apparently their argument was over a measly ten dollars; the kid wouldn't pay for his hair having been braided."

Yet, as Officer LaFazia, a father of two, says with concern, Providence's juvenile courts, for reasons of their own, tend to be lenient on serious crimes, including murder committed by minors.

In the interim, Officer LaFazia and his team have been involved in several more shootings. One of the felons living in the project got it into his head to buy a police car that he and his friends used to conduct their drug deals. The idea was that if they got in a chase with the cops, they'd at least be on an equal footing, or wheels, as it were. While the concept made good sense, its implementation did not.

LaFazia and his partner pulled into a notorious vacant lot during a routine patrol and heard the engine of a car parked somewhere behind, but with no lights showing.

"That's when we pulled out our flashlights and identified one of the local kids, a major crack dealer. Then, just over our heads—we'd got out of our cruisers by now—we heard a door lock, sort of metal on metal. But it could also have been something else and I yelled his name. But by then he'd taken off.

"The chase was on. The suspect's police car was about the same age as ours; some of these drug people have brand-new Mercedes for their second cars. Another cruiser soon cut him off and he and his passenger vacated and ran, so we continued on foot.

"It was down alleys and across roads, past rows of buildings. I can see the two guys ahead of me running with guns in their hands. We come around a corner and the perp has opened a door.

"The next moment he throws a pit bull at me. It was apparently his animal, come out from inside his house, and, of course, the first thing it does is lunge at my arm. So I shot it. Just like that! Killed it. I had no option because it was the dog or me. This one was one really big, bad mother.

"There was quite a standoff after that and also an exchange of gunfire. But we got them in the end; one of the bad guys was pretty seriously wounded. Took a bullet where it mattered, and he's lucky to be alive. He's still around, still causing lots and lots of trouble."

Another time, remembers LaFazia, they chased a juvenile after a robbery. They had been doing routine paperwork in their little office at the complex when they received a radio report of a hold-up.

"There was no shouting or anything else that told them the situation was unusual. But we looked up at the monitors and sure enough, there it was."

The suspect's car was heading right down the road toward their area. Again, he explained, there were the four of them and the chase team quickly split into two groups—one pair going in one direction and the other two policemen up an adjacent road.

"I take a corner and there, right in front of me and coming my way, is a kid with a .45 Colt pistol in his hand. And, though I'm supposed to be used to this kind of thing, he takes me by surprise. Totally! But it's not enough to prevent me bringing my own gun to bear and I fire a round at him. There's no way that I'm going to let anybody point a firearm at me without taking some kind of action; you'd be dead in a month if you didn't in this kind of place, and the criminals know that.

"But since we're running pretty fast, there couldn't be any kind of deliberate aim. So obviously, I missed. He gave himself up pretty soon after that and when I took the pistol from him, it was cocked . . . sure as hell, he intended using it. I just beat him to the punch . . . not too brave, these guys."

Just months later there was another shoot-out that took place within twenty yards of the Hartford Park cop station. Two guys were running around a car, one of them with a weapon, the other without. Several shots were fired before the unarmed youngster ran into his apartment, found his own gun, came out, and shot the man who who'd been after him.

"Of course we had to arrest the guy. He'd just shot someone. But he couldn't understand what all the beef was about. He'd only retaliated to protect himself, he said.

"Takes all kinds," said Officer Keith LaFazia with his ingratiating smile.

Then Officer Maxwell Dorley got hit by two cars five times in one incident, and in so doing, set a record that still stands and that absolutely nobody is going to try to better anytime soon. He also acquired the nickname Speed Bump.

It seems a man took his wife's car and she reported it stolen. The matter would have been amicably settled as a domestic issue if only he'd stopped when challenged. Instead, he took off. A car chase followed across half the city, first along Broad Street then onto Prairie Avenue.

As Dorley says, the driver is mad as hell, swerving into the police cars trying to approach him, including Dorley's. Back and forth he went, ending up in Cranston where the police opened fire and the vehicle crashed.

Dorley continues: "I immediately got out of my cruiser and started moving toward the suspect vehicle. The driver is still sitting at the wheel. He sees me. I'm watching him and he backs up a little at an angle. As I'm running forward he puts his car into gear and heads straight for me. There was no warning whatsoever, so I took a serious knock and ended going head-over-heels across the hood. So that's two hits.

"I emerge from that little scrape not badly hurt, though even while still in the air I managed to get my weapon out . . . got to my feet and started running after the car, at which point he stopped, backed up, and I then got caught between him and another police vehicle that had arrived on the scene. All I hear is the screech of tires spinning and he's coming at me again. This time I was able to jump aside and fire my gun, hitting him in the leg.

"So he takes off once more and the police car that was there all along, and had been backing up to avoid a full-on collision, now moves forward in the chase—but doesn't see me. Boom! I get struck again, this time by the patrol car, and I go down.

"And because he can't get out of the narrow confines into which he's been forced, the policeman driving the cruiser goes into reverse to try to wiggle out. So he hits me a second time. He then takes off and crashes into the vehicle that we were after all along and arrests the driver.

"So now they call me Speed Bump. But though there were no broken bones or things, it also put me in the hospital and resulted in my being off regular work for almost six months."

Officer LaFazia didn't escape all the action while on light duty. As is customary in Providence, he was allowed to choose where he would like to serve during his time off routine patrols. He opted for "home" so that he could be among his buddies at Hartford Park.

"So I'm in civilian clothes, with just my gun and Porky is outside. He's talking to his wife. Suddenly I hear a succession of shots and see Porky running, gun in hand. Then more shots. Of course we get up and run out. Just as we come around the corner we see a fairly new Toyota Tacoma truck in mid-air and upside down heading straight for our offices. Just a moment later, it flips over, right there at the main entrance.

"There were a lot of shots fired there, but you know, you let your training take over and you pretty well know what to do. Things like that happen all the time around here.

"That time, though, what we didn't know was that it was a drug customer's—or in drug world language, a *custy's* truck that was being targeted by criminal types. The vehicle had barely come to rest in the road when the rest of us were bailing out of the office to see what was going on. Another cop had already broadcast a 'shots fired' report.

"But we get out there and we can't see who was responsible. We know there are guns possibly pointed at us, perhaps from a nearby building, but can see nothing. They'd obviously ambushed the vehicle from a hidden position and if we hadn't been there, those bastards might have finished the job.

"We couldn't just leave the situation either. We were concerned that whoever was responsible would come back, since the kid who'd been driving was trapped in the cab.

"So I force open the door and get into the front. Immediately I recognize the driver as one of the kids in the area. He's lying unconscious behind the wheel. Then he stirs, opens his eyes, and says, 'Hey Keith, get me out of this.'

"Which we did, to the sound of the sirens of our cavalry arriving. It's the best sound in the world when you're in trouble, especially when they *know* you're in trouble . . ."

Officer Keith LaFazia's housing unit seems to have always been regarded as a dangerous assignment. In getting to meet with Officer LaFazia and his crew, we were "talked" toward his area by cell phone, guided street by street as we approached the station. For the last eight or ten blocks, they could follow our progress on their screens.

"But we wouldn't suggest you bring that rig here after dark," LaFazia suggested. "I'd guarantee that you'd be carjacked, or, more appropriately, RV-jacked. We'd find your motor home in the morning, somewhere around here, or perhaps in Chad Bronx, but it'd be stripped down to its essentials. You'd have nothing left but the shell."

Talk about a war zone.

Keith LaFazia's ground-breaking law enforcement work has finally been recognized by his superiors. Shortly before we went to press he was moved to a more senior position as a narcotics detective.

---

[1] *What Cops Know,* by Connie Fletcher (Villard Books, a division of Random House, New York, 1990). If there is one book that needs to be read by every aspiring police man or woman, it is this brilliant, no-holds-barred exposition of everyday cop life in one of America's big cities. Its insights alone are useful pointers to saving unsuspecting lives.

[2] Edward Conlon, a New York policeman, provides a marvelous interpretation of the problems encountered in law enforcement in New York low-cost housing estates in *Blue Blood* (Riverhead Books, New York, 2004). Joseph Wambaugh is on record as stating that "It is the most stunning memoir ever written about the cop world."

CHAPTER 15

Two-Wheelers and a Remarkable Motorcycle Save

Richard Davis has had his share of motorcycle saves. One of the first was San Francisco motorcycle officer Bob Hooper, who took a hit from a .38 Special.

As Richard Davis says, you only have to visit the United States' major cities and check the honor roll at any precinct or headquarters to see the inordinate number of motorcycle policeman who have been killed in the line of duty.

Stories about cops on bikes, he adds, are legendary—especially since the second leading cause of police deaths during the early part of the twentieth century was motorcycle accidents. From 1910 through 1939, there were a total of almost 500 officers killed in motorcycle accidents, compared to 323 who died in automobile accidents during the same period.

As law enforcement agencies relied increasingly on the automobile, motorcycle deaths during the latter half of the century declined. But they still account for more than a thousand officer fatalities during the twentieth century. This is all the more telling when one understands that there were only a few more than two thousand deaths in patrol cars and other police vehicles during the same period.

Television programs about intrepid two-wheeled police proliferated in the 1970s and after. Then, suddenly, the four-wheeled police patrol became the TV rage. What also changed was that, depending on the intensity of crime and danger in any particular area, patrol cars were usually manned by single officers. In the old motorcycle days, teams mostly went out in tandem.

Conditions on the road were no less severe in the earlier period. If anything, they were worse. Take Michael Flynn of the LAPD who was riding his bike in the slow lane about three in the morning when he met a drunk driver running a red light in a construction area. Flynn's bike hit the vehicle and he was hurled to the sidewalk.

A year of reconstructive surgery followed. Fortunately, Flynn's vest took most of the impact. His doctors told him that without it, he would have been killed.

Another DUI struck motorcycle officer Bruce Blackman of Las Vegas, Nevada. He'd stopped his bike behind a truck at a red light when another vehicle came up behind and slammed him into the tailgate of the semi. Much of the impact was absorbed by his body armor. A short while before, Dennis Kubik of Tucson, Arizona, was also rear-ended while on his patrol motorcycle. He too survived because of his vest.

John Robertson of Gainsville, Georgia, was hit head-on by a speeding car. Robertson was thrown onto the hood of the vehicle with his vest taking full blunt chest trauma before he was hurled to the asphalt. Without his vest, his doctors told him, chest and lung damage would have been terminal.

Breaking a record that nobody else would like to try for, Eugene Smith of Johnstown, Pennsylvania, went into a hundred-and-eleven-foot skid with his Harley-Davidson and struck a utility pole. His bike slid another seventy feet. Though seriously injured, his vest prevented him from being impaled.

Bike riders of a different sort attacked West Virginia State Trooper Tom Cueto with clubs and chains at an outlaw biker bar in West Virginia. The mob went to work with deadly intent and his vest took much of the impact from sharp instruments that would otherwise have killed him.

Then Officer James Burt of Ventura, California and his partner used a sledgehammer to gain entrance to a known motorcycle gang clubhouse. As the door swung open, his partner turned out of the way, exposing Burt to a blast from a .357 magnum handgun fired by a gang member. Like Cueto, Burt was lucky. His vest stopped the slug from entering his abdomen just above the navel. Having done his deed, the shooter ran out the back of the building and into the cuffs of waiting officers.

Incidents involving renegade bikers—including some who occasionally take on the law, as did a reckless felon in Raton, New Mexico—are legend.

Trooper Jeff Faison and Reserve Officer Ron Fisher were called to investigate a complaint about a biker reportedly tailgating motorists on the main drag through Albuquerque. Fisher stayed in the car while Faison handled the routine questioning of the rider. Instead of presenting his license, the suspect drew a three-inch barrel .357 magnum and drilled a hole part of the way into Faison's vest. It was an excellent shot, the authorities conceded, hitting the police officer just over the heart.

The criminal then turned to Fisher and put a slug through the cruiser door, hitting the second officer in his shoulder. Not yet done, he got off his bike and ran over to Fisher to finish him off. But by then Faison had recovered enough to draw his weapon and shoot his assailant.

Police two-wheelers are to be found in another guise. A recent news report in *Policemag.com* said that the New York Police Department had purchased three hundred Piaggio scooters that were first deployed at the 2004 Republican National Convention to re-elect George W. Bush.

Trim, fast, and lightweight, the Piaggio BV200 is already in use by the New Orleans Police Department as well as by the Spanish and Italian police forces, These twenty-plus-horsepower machines with top speeds of seventy-five miles an hour were acquired because they are ideal for a metropolis like New York. There, officers sometimes need to drive on sidewalks and maneuver adroitly through tight, heavily populated neighborhoods.

On the wrong side of the law, Canada has seen a remarkable upsurge in criminality by people using motorcycles.

Blue Line Magazine, the Canadian law enforcement publication, had several news stories about Hells Angels and other bikers who tangled with the law, in its November 2004 edition.

The publication featured a Québec biker war that had so far claimed an astonishing 170 lives, including an unspecified number of innocent bystanders. In sentencing Walter Stadnick and Donald Stockford—two former Hells Angels—to prison sentences of twenty years, court reports detailed profits from drugs of roughly $2 million *a month*. The Angels had managed to sell more than $111 million worth of cocaine and hashish in the twenty months prior to December 2000.

Elsewhere in Québec, a Banditos chapter that called itself the Rock Machine had almost fifty of its members arrested in a 2002 sweep.

In April 2006, eight Canadian *Bandido* gang members were murdered by their colleagues in Southern Ontario in what was termed by the police as "a housecleaning exercise," whatever that was supposed to imply. Five gang members were almost immediately arrested—one of them living on his property only a couple of miles away. All were charged with murder. Not too bright, committing a major crime almost on your doorstep!

The pattern of violence among these bikers continues, and it is certainly not getting any better for all the attention these crazy antics are being given.

Bicycles might be flimsier than their larger two-wheeled cousins, but accidents involving either can be deadly.

James Kang discovered that while on routine bicycle patrol in Los Angeles. He was in the middle lane turning left when he collided with a red Maxima making a right. Thrown over the hood, Kang was badly hurt with lacerations to his body. His vest absorbed the impact.

Also in LA, Officer Peter Foster was on bicycle patrol when unknown assailants, presumably on a gang-bangers' initiation hit, shot him in the back. His vest took the bullet, but he suffered more serious injuries from his fall.

While bicycles loom low on the radar of both local and international law enforcement, they are increasingly useful in combating crime.

A feature in the July 2004 *Law Enforcement Technology* highlighted the role of bikes in law enforcement work. The article said: "Contrary to the more common image of a bicycle officer handing out trading cards to small children are images of bicycles used in undercover surveillance, drug interdiction and riot control. Bicycle officers use their stealth mobility to swoop in on a drug deal or isolate an agitator in the middle of a demonstrating crowd."

The magazine goes on to explain how cyclists work well when they use the silent shadows of parking garages, stairwells, and alleyways to their advantage. Linked by radio, bikes can quietly swoop down on a crime in progress, often from three or more different directions without the criminals even being aware they were there.

"The Seattle Police Department has taken this kind of surveillance one step further with the use of cameras, positioned throughout downtown known drug areas. According to Sgt. Ashley Price, Seattle PD Bicycle Patrol, while one officer monitors the cameras, others hide in alleys." When an illegal deal goes down, they zoom in.

So too with the Ann Arbor, Michigan, PD, which uses bikes and police officers in plainclothes—usually in sports gear—to patrol the University of Michigan–Ann Arbor student housing areas in a bid to decrease the number of break-ins during holidays and weekends.

Bikes are ideal in heavily congested downtown traffic areas where the two-wheelers can compete for speed with slow-moving traffic lanes. In San Antonio, Texas, bikes are used to combat illegal cruising on weekend nights.

As one officer with the International Police Mountain Bike Association commented, "Bikes are right there, sometimes in the face of evil-doers, whether it be in cities along the California coast or in some parts of Colorado. We go where others don't, very often because they cannot."

Bicycle patrols have become an increasingly visible presence in the past decade, especially in heavily populated areas. These units are not only cost-effective; they are also efficient and serve as a meaningful supplement to traditional patrolling.

There are supply companies specializing in bicycle police needs, of which there are many, for units that spend eight or more hours in sun, rain, sleet, and snow. There are months when temperatures vary by as much as thirty degrees during the course of a normal working day. Apart from accidents there is dehydration and overexposure to the sun, which can lead to skin cancer.

There is a range of police equipment on the market, designed specifically for bicycle patrols. This includes featherweight handcuffs, smaller rechargeable lights, compact batons, hand-free communication sets with radio earpieces, and synthetic duty belts with good back support.

Helmets, gloves, and eye protection in the event of an accident should be mandatory—but oftentimes, they are not required. Most departments won't have anything but the best for their patrol cars, but this is not always the case with the officers who are arguably the most exposed.

Possibly the most unusual use bicycles can be employed for is as a defensive tool in riot control. Officers can line their bikes up, chain side facing outward, and stand beside them.

Seattle's Sgt. Price explained that if a crowd starts to rush the bikes, they have an approved tactic whereby the bikes are picked up and the officers take one step forward and order the mob to move back. The bike can also be effectively used as a barrier between an officer working alone and a potentially dangerous suspect.

Generally, bike officers are instructed to drop their bicycles ten or fifteen feet from a situation that requires attention.

Officer Brendan Allis of Waterbury, Connecticut, became a motorcycle cop because he'd always wanted to be one. He'd always ridden two-wheelers and believed that taking the bike route might be a good way to maintain interest in his chosen career. Once he'd achieved the requisite grade in the department, he applied for the motorcycle unit. After passing demanding training, he was given his shot.

Beyond the Police Academy, prospective motorcycle police spend two weeks at the State Police School at Meriden, Connecticut. By all accounts it's not an easy school.

"These were not your everyday, routine-type bike sessions," he explained. "They made us do things with motorcycles that we'd never believed possible. We learned to take them through rivers, creeks, streambeds, across open fields, sandy hillsides, and some of the most impossible mountain-type terrain imaginable. It can be pretty hard-going in those far hills.

"Also, you're not doing it with anything special. We used regular police bikes throughout. These were the department's 1,550cc Harley-Davidsons, which are big machines compared to the bikes you're likely to encounter every day on the road.

"Also, the bikes can move when they have to, as fast or faster than we'd ever need them to go." So speedy, Allis said, that he'd never yet maxed them out, which, he believed, would be somewhere in excess of a hundred and fifty miles per hour.

"At school, they get you accustomed to taking the bikes off-road, through the woods and elsewhere. That's where you're going to have to ride and learn to maneuver with competence, because sometime or another your life might depend on it. They put us through different kinds of turning techniques, small-circumference turns, like when you have a parade or there's a large crowd within touching distance, and in tiny spaces where turns might be limited. There could be a situation where there might be kids or old folks around. The same with very slow speeds, maintaining control of a bike at the pace of somebody who might just be shuffling along.

"Then there were speed exercises and we would go fifty, sometimes sixty miles an hour. They pushed us hard in that section, to just before the point where our lives might be in jeopardy. Inevitably, you're going to crash the bike sometime or other on this course . . . it's all part of the program, as is high-speed breaking, slides, and other related stuff.

"By the time we'd qualified, under instructors who were some of the best bikers in America, we really knew our stuff. Those who didn't make the grade went back to their original units. It was quality these guys were after, nothing less," Officer Allis opined.

Thirty-one years old and a pretty big guy, Officer Allis spends much of his off-duty time working out, lifting weights, and fighting in mixed martial arts tournaments. His friends say he's not someone to mess with, which could be one reason why he managed to survive two serious accidents.

He was riding a bike at the time of his second save. The immediate consequences were three major surgeries and nine months off the job, while recuperating. On his return to work his chief asked him what he'd like to do, thinking that Allis might have acquired an aversion to two-wheelers. The young officer was unequivocal: "I'd like to get back on my motorcycle, Sir." And that's exactly what he did.

Officer Allis' body armor saved his life in a vehicle accident by absorbing much of the impact, which is why Second Chance listed the event as Save #861. However, it was not the first time that he survived because of his vest.

Allis is one of those rare individuals who credits his body armor with having saved his life twice. Listed as Save #737 in Second Chance's record books, the incident that occurred on the previous occasion is no less momentous.

"I was working midnights on patrol, alone in a cruiser. That was before I went onto bikes. Got a call, must have been some time after one in the morning. Shots had been fired in a bar downtown on North Main Street. I even remember the address, 629 North Main . . . a bar called Mingle's Café . . . It's still there today . . . been the same forever, it seems.

"The place had always caused us problems, same types of calls, same kinds of fights. I was still pretty new on the job, and like most inexperienced policemen, I was eager to get into every hot call that came through.

"Dave Shehan, another officer, showed up at the same time. We looked at each other and decided that since nobody else appeared to be en route, we'd tackle it on our own. That wasn't the wisest choice since there were just the two of us and, literally, there were about a hundred of them.

"I didn't have any qualms that we couldn't do the job. Dave is an ex-Marine, real tough. So we marched in, patch-to-patch, shoulder-to-shoulder, and though it took time, we got the combatants separated. Then one of them turned on me and took a swing. We grappled on the ground until I was able to subdue him.

"To make a long story short, we finally won the fight. Got the people involved—five or six of them; took them into custody and they were hauled off to the station in the paddy wagon, which is what they still call it in Connecticut."

He and Shehan then decamped for breakfast at the local Howard Johnson's on South Main Street. While he was leaning across the table, one of the waitresses came up and said, "Brendan, your shirt is ripped."

"I replied something about a small tussle at Mingles and that I'd ended up on the floor . . . you know, people trying to kick me, and broken bottles all over the place." Didn't look like that at all, she retorted, looking closely at Officer Allis' back.

"From what she could see, she said, I'd been cut or stabbed. She reckoned it was a pretty big cut.

"But though I'd been pummeled and kicked, and was sore and bruised in a few places, I wasn't really hurt. And since it was already after six and we'd soon be heading back, I said that I'd worry about it when I got off duty, which I did."

Allis got back to the locker room, took off his body armor and to his surprise found that somebody had actually sliced right through his shirt with something very big and very sharp. The blade had gone into his Twaron vest but hadn't penetrated.

Examined in some detail afterward, the cut was at least eight inches long. Someone had made a determined effort to hurt him. If he hadn't been wearing his vest, he'd probably have been stabbed to death.

"I called the owner of Connecticut Police Supply, out of Newington, the next day and spoke to Tammy, a very nice lady who'd originally fitted us for our vests when we were new on the job. I told her about the stabbing and asked her whether the cut through the Twaron was going to affect the structural integrity of my body armor. That really caught her interest.

"When we went into some detail and the vest was examined by experts, they decided that I'd have died on that barroom floor if I hadn't been wearing body armor. The good part is that I was given a new vest by the company and also listed by them as an official save."

When I arrived in Waterbury to interview Officer Allis, I was held up by an unusually long funeral procession making its way from the church to the cemetery.

The same thing happened on the day Officer Allis was designated to ride escort from Albinis Funeral Home on Chase Parkway all the way through to the Catholic church.

"There were three bikes in the escort at the time, whereas today we would have five. One of them had left a bigger space between us than we planned, and as I was coming up the left side of the procession to get to the next intersection to block it off, a car pulled out of a driveway on my side of the road and broadsided me.

"It was a really damaging hit. The guy came at me at some speed. We found out later that he was an addict who'd just come out of a liquor store. Imagine it, he was boozing at nine in the morning.

"The impact sent me flying across two lanes of road. For much of that distance I slid along with my chest scraping the pavement. There was so much friction it wore my .40 caliber right down to the frame, with the Kevlar in my vest taking the brunt of it. The friction actually went through several layers of the stuff.

"When things like that happen, you don't always register first what's happening. It must have been some hit, because the force propelled me toward a truck coming down on the other side of the road, and that was some thirty or forty feet."

"What happened next is one of those small miracles. It was my day, very clearly.

"As I was sliding along that one, perhaps two seconds in which it all happened, all I could see was this truck heading right toward me. It seemed inevitable I'd be hit.

"I thought, Oh-uh, this damn thing's going to go right over me. And while I felt no pain—even though the impact had seriously torn my posterior crucial ligament—I knew that this could be it!

"Everything went into slow motion, like I was watching it, sort of detached from my body. Fortunately, the truck driver was pulling over to park and as I slid under his rear tire, that big mother of a vehicle stopped, his rear wheel physically touching my chest."

If the truck hadn't halted there, Allis says, the wheel and the eight or ten tons it supported would almost certainly have gone over his body. He would have been crushed.

"With the driver's eight or twelve wheels shuddering as he applied his brakes and brought his vehicle to a halt, so too was my forward momentum stopped. He'd initially seen a bit of what had taken place with my being hit, and when he got out to examine the damage, he was really pretty shook up. He thought he might have killed me."

Officer Allis doesn't remember much of what happened afterward. He recalls a person coming out of a house from across the street and saying kindly, when he tried to raise himself, "No . . . no officer, you just lie there. They're coming to help you. Any minute now." A little old lady then brought a blanket, which she lay over Allis. She told him they'd called 911.

There was not much the rest of the escort could do until help arrived. Allis was down and nobody would even venture a guess as to how badly he was injured. Judging by his totally smashed radio, they could only conclude that the prognosis would be bad. Gary Dipremio, his sergeant—who had been an instructor in the original motorcycle unit and was part of the escort group—parked his bike and waited quietly alongside the young cop for the ambulance.

By then word had reached the station and more officers responded to the scene. Many of them followed the ambulance to Waterbury hospital.

"You know, looking back afterward—and there was a lot of time to look back in the hospital, and while I was being rehabilitated and going through therapy, because I had seriously damaged my back, my knee, and my shoulder—I realized that I was blessed to be in this department.

"I spent my first six years on the job working in C Platoon, which is the midnight shift. We were chasing dealers, had bar fights, and the rest. That's when my vest saved me the first time. That's also when I discovered the brotherhood, the loyalty of the men and women you work with and what a fine bunch of people they are. There's just nothing like it.

"Later, I was praying the whole time, through the surgeries and the rehab to get myself back to where I could go on doing what I'd learned to love. I lay there for months, having absolutely no idea what I would do with my life if I couldn't go back to being a cop. Not just any old cop, but the cop that I was . . . the man that I was."

There are several postscripts to Officer Allis' story that are worth mentioning. The thirty-year-old drunk and crackhead who hit him was arrested and released on bail. His car had been impounded by police, but he broke into his ex-girlfriend's house that same night and stole hers. Last heard of, he was in jail for dealing drugs.

Allis has had reconstructive surgery on his back. The impact of the crash blew out one of his discs and they had to do both a laminectomy and a discectomy. They removed the damaged disc and fused his spine. Meanwhile, he also got married, which was a change from the usual humdrum bachelor lifestyle that he enjoyed before.

When I visited Waterbury in the summer of 2004, Officer Brendan Allis already had a fourteen-month-old son. There was a daughter due two months later. And he wasn't intending to stop there either . . .

A sidelight to the Allis saga is the way this moderate-sized Connecticut city has combated endemic drug and street crime problems. As drug use increased, so did related thefts—from cars, muggings, home burglaries, and store robberies. Much was linked to violence, which caused several homicides and numerous injuries, many of them serious.

When Allis started with the department almost a decade before, gangs were the single biggest problem faced by the Waterbury Police Department. Chief Flarity, head of the force at that time, decided that drastic developments in the community demanded drastic action.

As Allis explains, several specialized units were established within the 330-man force, the fourth largest in the state. They included a gang task force and a tactical narcotics team. Both were tasked to grapple with problems that, until then, had confounded the police and, as a consequence, were escalating.

Allis: "We had specific teams, between four- and eight-men strong, and they had the additional support of our vice and intelligence units as well as the Waterbury Detective Bureau. They went to work, swooped down, and though it took a few years, the combined effort eventually crushed these criminal elements.

"That program had already started before I joined the force, but I was able to see its impact. I eventually became part of it."

What Chief Flarity and his successor, Chief Neal O'Leary, were able to prove was that it could be done, said Allis. They took it up a notch by declaring publicly that the authorities were not going to let criminal groups get ahead of them again. What made a difference, he added, was that the teams were not only young and enthusiastic, but also well educated and well trained.

"These were dedicated people. In the end that's what mattered. What happened afterward was that several other police departments in Connecticut took notice.

"Some tried similar tactics and they worked for them as well. But all that we've been facing—and are still facing—is very much today's problem. It is unfortunately compounded by the difficult world in which my children will grow up. So, we've just got to keep at it.

"Steel pins in my body or not, I'll be one of them out there for a while yet."

CHAPTER 16

Attacker Killed with His Own Gun—by a Female Cop

Illinois State Trooper Kim Rhodes answered a distress call on Interstate-70, had a gun pulled on her, and was shot three times. She wrestled with the man in the front of seat of his car, eventually turned the gun on her attacker, and killed him. It is possibly the only time a perp, having shot a cop, had his own firearm used against him.

When you meet Kim Rhodes, a buxom, steely-haired matron with intense eyes and a professional manner, you understand why she was commander of Illinois State Police District 10. At that time she operated from the Champaign area. We met her shortly after she'd retired from the state police, at Effingham, a modest, comfortable town along Illinois' Interstate-70.

These days—after a quarter-century on the road—former Illinois State Trooper Rhodes is a part-time instructor in the federal National Highway Watch Program. But she likes to go back on the highways when the mood takes her, which is often.

Ms. Rhodes enjoyed her job, she'll tell you gravely. She liked the discipline and the demands made on her and her associates. "Like everything else," she added, "it had its moments when you wished you were elsewhere . . . It comes with the uniform."

There is an event in the life of Kim Rhodes that she speaks about often, especially to new troopers, because it happened well before she was appointed to command District 10. It was an almost-midnight confrontation on Interstate-70, following a motorist assist call that left her seriously wounded and her attacker dead. She shot her assailant while he was fighting to regain control of his firearm, a 9mm semi-auto pistol that he'd pulled after Officer Rhodes emerged from her patrol car.

In the fight that followed, Officer Rhodes was able to wrestle the gun from her attacker and turn it on him. The event is the only known time that a criminal, having shot a policewoman, was then killed by that officer with the same weapon with which the attacker had initiated his action.

The fight, she recalls, was brief. It lasted perhaps half a minute. "But those thirty seconds," she told me, "were the most violent of my life."

Totally mismatched and aware only that if she failed, she'd be dead, Officer Rhodes desperately grappled with the man while trying to counter the superior strength of her opponent. In the end, the man was killed, hit by several bullets fired by both the policewoman and her partner, Deputy Kimble.

Two of the three bullets the criminal fired at Rhodes were stopped by her concealable body armor. The third—the one that put Kim Rhodes in the hospital—entered her torso just below her kidneys. It then sped across eight inches of her lower back before lodging alongside her spine. Doctors fought to keep her alive; she'd lost a lot of blood.

In theory, this outspoken, tough, and efficient state trooper should be a paraplegic, crippled from the waist down. She is not.

It was a close call, she admits, grimacing. "I fought very hard to contain a situation that could have left both my partner and me dead." When they approached the man in his car, which was stopped innocuously alongside the highway, neither of them had any idea that the driver was bent on murder.

In the end, she recounts, everybody except the attacker succeeded in their objective. "I survived and went on doing what I've always done, though it took a while. My partner came out of it unscathed, and the attacker was hauled off to the morgue for an autopsy. But there was a price.

"I remember waking up in the ward after surgery with 125 flower arrangements around my bed. For a while I thought I was in a funeral home," she says with an infectious chuckle. Once her wounds healed, it didn't take Rhodes long to get back in uniform and on the road again.

That was not Effingham's first Interstate killing. She had lost a colleague, State Trooper Layton Davis, in roughly the same area just seven years before. Exactly as she had done, he'd made a traffic stop. There were two men from Chicago in the other car, and for no reason whatever they shot and killed the officer. The sad part is that Davis wasn't wearing his concealable body armor: the incident took place in the early days, and Illinois took a while to come around to the concept.

"A high-speed chase followed and they finally got those cop-killers after they'd crashed. They should have got the death sentence," she says. "But instead, they went to prison, which bothered a lot of us, especially since they kidnapped an eighteen-year-old college kid who survived both the chase and the accident."

Something similar happened about the same time, in Arlington, Texas, when a local woman left home one Friday morning with the words, "I'm going to get me a cop today."

Not finding one during a drive through town, she stopped at a busy intersection and waited. Officer Gene "Buddy" Evans presently came by and, seeing a "disabled" vehicle on the side of the road, he pulled up behind her and flashed his lights. She was disrupting traffic, he explained afterward, which was why she attracted his attention. He also noticed that she was sitting in the passenger seat with all the windows rolled up.

As Officer Evans went around the side of the car to find out what was wrong, she opened the window, leaned out, and placed a .38 Special bullet neatly between the second and third buttons of the approaching policeman's shirt. It was about the only thing the woman got right all day.

Returning fire, Evans shot out several of the car's windows. His assailant—suddenly shocked by a cop who was supposed to be dead and who, instead, was very much alive—dropped her weapon and exited the car. She was handcuffed and taken to the station to face charges.

Evan's vest made him Save #415. It also underscored the danger faced by police officers working the open road.

Something almost identical happened to Deputy Sheriff Tommy Frederick of Okaloosa County, Florida, not long afterward, which made for Save #442.

In that case, Frederick stopped a vehicle that displayed no tags. When he approached, the driver stepped out and, on being told to put his hands where they could be seen, the man pulled a magnum revolver from his belt and shot the officer in the chest. The hit on Deputy Frederick was powerful enough to partially deform the protective K30 plate he'd inserted in his vest.

Uncharacteristically, the slug pushed the deputy back a step or two, but the impact didn't unbalance him enough to prevent his drawing his own weapon and firing back. As Frederick called for assistance the perp fired again and then sped away.

Also in Florida not long afterward, Deputy Brent Evans of Minneola County, like Frederick, stopped a driver for a tag violation. Evans was going forward from his own patrol car to check the driver's license when the man suddenly got out of his vehicle and fired his .357 magnum. Evans was hit four times, twice in his vest and with a bullet each in his wrist and ankle.

Knocked to the ground, this versatile cop was still able to return fire at the escaping auto. He hit it with eleven of the fifteen rounds he fired in the direction of his attacker. Also significant was that Brent Evans had only started wearing his vest three weeks before.

Then there was Officer Jerry Lucas of Moore, Oklahoma, who also made what he thought was a routine traffic stop when he pulled over a suspicious vehicle shortly after three in the morning. As the driver stepped from his '85 Mazda on a lonely road, he pulled out a 9mm pistol and pumped six shots into the policeman. Three of the bullets were stopped by Lucas' Second Chance vest; the others hit his hand and the lower part of his body.

Left for dead, with his assailant having taken off on foot, Lucas was able to crawl back to his car and radio for help. A four-hour manhunt followed, and in the shoot-out that followed, the felon was hit seventeen times.

Kim Rhodes' story, in contrast, began with a call from what was initially said to be a motorist in trouble along the highway. Apparently a car had broken down and the driver needed some help. Dispatch could offer no more detail. Another officer took the call from just east of Effingham, but Trooper Rhodes said she'd take it. Her car was closer, she radioed.

"I had another officer with me, Deputy Kimble—who actually came along for the ride because we were working on a burglary ring detail. So on the face of it, everything was pretty routine. We pulled behind a black Camaro straddling the shoulder of the Interstate. It had its hood raised, and as a consequence, we surmised the obvious: that the problem was something mechanical.

"Just then, our dispatcher came through again. She warned that we should be cautious. The occupant possibly had a gun, she told us. But again, she couldn't offer any details.

"We only heard after it was all over that a truck driver had tried to help this man earlier. But he saw the gun and took off. So it was basically a CB report, something about him having the gun in a holster and waving it around on the median. At that stage, though, we didn't have any specifics. We were just told to be careful."

Details about the man only came out later.

"What we had here was a guy from New Jersey who had been living out west in Las Vegas. He was white, fairly presentable looking, and almost thirty years old. There was nothing suspicious about him.

"I addressed him after I'd exited our cruiser and asked him to step out, which he did willingly enough, and then only partially. We didn't see any gun because he'd emerged from his vehicle only far enough for us to see what he was doing with his hands. We couldn't see his right hip and that, we discovered a few moments later, was where he'd holstered his weapon."

Looking back, Trooper Rhodes realizes that from the start, the driver's "motorist in distress" gimmick was a setup. The police only uncovered his background after the man was dead. The report makes for interesting reading.

Having gotten only partway out, the man turned sideways toward Trooper Rhodes as she approached. At the same time, his head was turned toward her. As she remembers the event, he held a set of keys in one hand while the other was extended in front of him, exactly as he'd been instructed.

"Since we had our spotlights right on him and the place was lit up like daylight, there was no way we could miss any gesture or suspicious movement on his part. Obviously, having been told that the guy might have a gun, we were ultra-cautious.

"I got up fairly close to him, like an arm's length away, when he suddenly threw his keys onto the floorboard. The next moment he pulled his firearm and swung around, facing me. By now my partner was on the passenger side of the car and I couldn't do much more than yell something about a gun—which, of course, set the whole thing off.

"Then I did the only instinctive reaction possible; I made a desperate grab for his pistol, which I managed to get a bit of a grip of. At the same time I twisted my body round hard to my left so that my back was now toward him. It flashed through my mind that it might be possible to twist the gun out of his hand, bearing in mind that I had both my hands on it."

At this point he pulled back hard and managed to elevate the gun, firing three shots in quick succession at her.

In a sense, Kim Rhodes was fortunate. Two of the bullets fired within inches of her body were stopped by her concealable body armor. The one that did all the damage—the third bullet—struck the lower part of her back. It entered the part of her torso unprotected by body armor.

"Obviously, if I'd had an opportunity to do so, I'd have made an immediate grab for my own pistol. But I couldn't. I needed both hands to keep a hold on his and he was much stronger than me. If I let go, I knew, he'd shoot me again.

"By now, both of us were fighting for dominance. Somehow, through the fog of all this interaction, the two of us wrestling inside the open door of the Camaro, I was aware that if I could keep the muzzle away from my head, I might just have a chance. I just had to hold on; it was my ticket out of this disaster, even though I started to feel the effects of being shot. Bear in mind that up to that point, all this had taken place in the space of ten, perhaps twelve seconds.

"A million other images flashed through my brain. I gained some comfort from wearing a vest and the fact that he wasn't. Also, I knew that at any moment my partner would come around to my side of the vehicle. All these thoughts, cumulatively, sort of stacked the odds slightly in my favor. But then I was also aware that he had a much firmer grip on the pistol than me, and he was much bigger and stronger. We found out afterward that he was a karate expert.

"Most unsettling of all was that his man was trying to murder me. His eyes told me that. I saw it in his face . . . couldn't miss it, not for a moment. Remember, we were very close together—barely inches—for the duration."

She calculates that the entire showdown, from the moment she stopped her cruiser to shooting the man dead, lasted perhaps thirty or forty seconds. As she is able to reflect years afterward, "It went by like a flash in Purgatory."

The critical moment came when the two struggling bodies fell in through the open door of the Camaro with Rhodes on top and on the front seat.

"He fell backward and I followed and landed heavily on top of him. That was when I was able to swing my body around, my hands still clasping his gun. In those two or three confused seconds, I somehow managed to turn the muzzle of the gun toward him and when it fired, the bullet struck him in the chest. It hit him just below the heart."

Rhodes' partner, Deputy Kimble, had meanwhile raced around from the one side of the vehicle to the other. With both of them inside the car and hearing the fourth shot, he surmised that Rhodes had taken another hit, if only because her attacker was much stronger and bigger.

Kim Rhodes: "I was aware my partner had reached the car door where we were going at it. I also knew he couldn't just fire his weapon at random because we were thrashing around inside. He could easily have hit me instead of the man.

"I knew too that if he hesitated three or four seconds, that was a lot, because I saw him point the gun, first this way, then that. And so did my attacker. He couldn't miss it . . . that service pistol was right in his face . . . and in mine too." Finally reaching down into the front seat area, Deputy Kimble got to a position where he was offered a clear shot.

"The man must have known at that moment that it was coming because for a brief moment he turned his head away. The bullet that slammed into his cheek, rearranged his jaw as well as the side of his face. It was a terrible mess. But he was dead and I'd survived. Also, I was badly wounded and on my way to the hospital.

"I was told afterward by the coroner that what had actually killed him was my shot; the bullet had apparently nicked his aorta. It shattered the lower part of his heart.

. . .

After the event there was a good deal of conjecture in Illinois law enforcement circles as to the motive for the attack.

Ultimately, police elements from three states worked on the man's background, his predilections, lifestyle, and finances. There were a hundred questions about his actions which were clearly illogical.

Kim Rhodes offers two theories of her own, the first being that the man was unemployed. He was also deeply in debt and in a state of overwhelming depression. As things started to come together they discovered that he was going home to New Jersey. Having traveled all the way from Nevada on his own, he'd obviously had a lot of time to think things through.

"He'd been a blackjack dealer in Vegas for a while, and from other reports, things hadn't exactly panned out as he'd planned. We know that by the time he crossed the state line into Illinois he'd called his parents several times and asked for money. We couldn't establish whether they'd cabled any cash.

"Also, since he had a gun, there's a pretty good chance he might already have used it to rob somebody. This was a very desperate man . . . He might have been involved in a robbery that had gone wrong. It's the sort of thing that happens all the time. So when we arrived, flashing lights and all, he could just as easily have thought we'd come to get him.

"My other theory is what we today refer to as 'suicide by cop.' Back then, more than two decades ago, the term wasn't in as common usage as it is today. People want to commit suicide and they sometimes choose to go out in grand style. They haven't the nerve to end it themselves, so they'll threaten the police with a firearm and then, more likely than not, end up on a slab."

There have been some unusual "suicide by cop" confrontations. *American Police Beat* reported in October 2004 that the Iowa Supreme Court had reinstated the conviction of a Mills County man whom the authorities said had tried to get himself killed by the police. Consumed by guilt over his addiction to child pornography, he'd begun drinking and confronting the law. Several times he'd opened fire at officers in hopes of being killed in retaliation.

Not long afterward, in Orange, New Jersey, a distraught seventeen-year-old pointed a replica firearm at Patrolman Edward Commune's head from only a few feet away. Ordered to surrender the weapon, the youngster refused. When he still wouldn't take his finger off the trigger, Commune fired three rounds, hitting him in the leg.

The youth's lawyer led him through the subsequent questioning session, and at one point directly asked him, "Your intent was that the officer would, in fact, shoot you?" To which the young man answered, Yes.

One study of suicide by cop showed that this is not the most efficient method to kill oneself, since less than 20 percent of all people who are shot by the police in the United States actually die. The majority are wounded, while a small number escape without a scratch.

Kim Rhodes never met the parents of her attempted murderer when they arrived to claim his body. Nor did they communicate in any way, except through their lawyers.

They didn't waste time finding someone to file a lawsuit for wrongful death. The case lasted five years, regardless of the fact that the criminal had fired three shots into a state trooper and was killed by his own gun.

To Trooper Rhodes, this was one of the most stressful experiences of her life. As she says, it took up a lot of time and effort. "But these people obviously thought they could make money out of the state. Or perhaps that's what their lawyer told them.

"Ultimately, the case was thrown out. It was a frivolous exercise and, in the end, caused damage far beyond what was anticipated because we were just doing our job. We'd answered a routine distress call from a motorist . . . trying to help.

"It was tough . . . very tough. But we had to go through it all and do what was required of us. It's all part of putting on the uniform, the badge, the gun. You perform your duties, and you accept these impediments," said quiet-spoken Kim Rhodes with the same winning smile that Davis used for his Save #303 in many promotions for concealable body armor over the years.

How did she cope? Kim Rhodes said that throughout, she had her family right there, her mom and dad, her nine brothers and five sisters. And many police officers throughout America who sent cards, letters, and flowers in support.

"No question," she added. "When things happen, we're like one big family . . . We look after each other, which is how it should be."

CHAPTER 17

Jim Martin: Shooting from the Lip and a Massacre Avoided

Officer Jim Martin was working for the Mena, Arkansas, Police Department when he pulled over a drunk driver. In the shoot-out that followed, he was hit four times by a killer intent on murdering hundreds of innocents at a Fayetteville shopping mall little more than an hour north on Highway 71.

Former police officer Jim Martin is one of those forthright cops who likes to shoot from the lip when it comes to talking about guns.

These days, working for the Arkansas Game & Fish Commission, he covers a lot of ground through six counties, from Little Rock city limits to the Oklahoma line. All told, that's an area of roughly twenty thousand square miles. In a career that spans more than thirty years, he's had his share of run-ins with people who "carried." In fact, he considers himself fortunate to still be alive.

On owning guns, he's all for it, though he also feels that certain limitations should apply. As he says, "There's nothing wrong with owning weapons. In fact, I advocate it on farms. And for hunting and in some of those wide-open spaces that have so blessed America.

"At the same time, guns and alcohol don't mix. Neither do guns and idiots." The sad thing, he adds, is that, "You cannot legislate idiocy out of people."

Martin's philosophy about most things is homespun. But he knows he's got the measure of the problem because he's been out there for decades, been shot several times, and put a stop to what would probably have been the biggest massacre of innocents in Arkansas' history.

Before moving to Game & Fish, he was a police officer in Mena. Not a big town, it had experienced only moderate violence over the years, most of it linked to domestic disturbances or the drug trade. A sheriff's deputy was shot and killed when he was called to a family disturbance in Mena some years ago. After that, even though members of the Mena police force had become wary of "domestics," another family disturbance ended with the chief getting shot in the leg. His chief deputy ended up firing through a screen door, killing the shooter.

The biggest day in Jim Martin's life came shortly thereafter, on February 15, 1987. It was a cold, wet, and winterish Sunday with rain falling heavily all day long. Working days, he'd started early that morning in a marked police cruiser patrolling the main road into town. Just after four that afternoon, about to return to base, he did his final sweep on Highway 71 and parked at the former site of a Dairy Queen. It was a good place from which to observe the traffic.

"You could see cars coming long before they saw you and that afternoon there were a lot of vehicles on the road. Then I spotted a truck that kept crossing the center line." It was probably a '79 or '80 model Chevrolet pickup, red in color with a short and narrow bed that had a spare tire carrier behind the driver's side.

The man's driving was erratic and though Martin suspected liquor, it was department policy to give everybody the benefit of the doubt. As his chief had told them all, don't be over-hasty. It could be medication. Or the driver might be tired, which was possible since it was already almost evening. Or the man behind the wheel might be elderly and perhaps his judgment was not up to scratch.

"The traffic went by. I started the engine and got into the line because I couldn't just let it go. As some of the vehicles turned off, I kept trying to get closer to the pickup. Eventually we got to a motel about a mile down the road, and this vehicle—it had Texas plates—pulls off, which was good; it would get him off the highway. By then I was several cars behind the truck.

"But he didn't stay put. As I passed him, the darned vehicle fell in behind me. I told myself, hell, that son-of-a-bitch doesn't want me behind him. So now I'm watching him in my mirror and I go another half mile and pull over.

"I waited for the man to come by again and then slotted in behind him. At that point we were already in the center of town. Meantime I'd run the license, checked for wants and warrants to see if it was stolen or anything and it all came back negative.

"Trouble was, by now this guy's driving really bad. He'd go off across the fog line and then he'd come back on to the yellow line, go across it again and return. Worse, Highway 71 was then only a double-lane road, not four-lane divided like today. Also, I'd noticed that his speed varied between twenty-five and thirty, which was way too slow.

"We went another quarter of a mile or so when I turned on my blue lights. I saw him check me in his rearview mirror but he still didn't stop. Finally I turned on lights and siren and he's still weaving.

"I called dispatch and told them I was behind a suspected DWI that was failing to stop. We went about a mile and a half outside the city limits, still on 71, and that's when he finally pulled over. So I approached the vehicle, went up on the driver's side, where he'd lowered the window, and asked for his license. There was a strong smell of liquor.

"My very first impression was of a very big individual. He was really huge, must have weighed in at almost four hundred pounds. Tall too, well over six feet, like they grow them in Texas. I reckoned at first sight that he must be in his mid-forties.

"Told him that I needed him to step out of his vehicle. He asked why, and I said I wanted him to take a field sobriety test. He complied without objection.

"On the face of it, there was no problem, no overt actions. He was just as nice and polite as could be. No cursing. Nothing out of the way to raise my suspicions. But he couldn't do the things that I asked him and I finally told him after I'd taken his license, 'Well Mr. Massey, you're under arrest for driving while intoxicated. I'm going to have to take you to jail.'

"Howard K. Massey. And I'll never forget his face either. I can see this massive guy before me to this day.

"Because it was raining at the time, and Massey had a sliding back glass window in his rig, he asked that he be allowed to close his back window. We were a kinder, gentler agency then and most times us police officers would try to accommodate the public, so dumb-ass me, I agree.

"Together we walked back up to the truck. I watched him open the driver's door and he leaned into the vehicle and closed his sliding window. But then he did something strange. He just stayed in a leaning position with half his body in the cab and his butt outside.

"I asked him three times, 'Mr. Massey, please step away from the vehicle. You're under arrest for DWI.' Finally, after the third time, he turned around with a revolver in his hand. I could see at a glance it was a .357 magnum, pointed at my chest.

"The only thing I heard from him was, 'Fuck you!' I never even registered when the gun went off except that I saw the flash. Felt none of the impact of the bullet when it hit me either."

The next thing Officer Martin remembers was finding himself at the back of the truck behind the tailgate. Crouched down low behind Massey's truck he had in his hand his 9mm pistol, a model 59 Smith & Wesson.

"And my back was hurting. I was pretty shocked, amazed actually, to realize that he'd shot me, which would have happened when I turned, ducked, and ran. The bastard shot me in the back . . . that really made me mad!

"I then fired two quick shots at him, hitting him with both, but to no avail. Didn't seem to worry him at all, which is what happens with some big people. They just absorb bullets that would have dropped a smaller guy . . . would have dropped me for sure had I not been wearing my vest. I also got on the radio and told dispatch that shots had been fired. Using the radio with a mike at my side, I said I was in a fight with this drunk.

"Now we started our little game of cat and mouse, with him coming after me and me maneuvering gingerly around the cab to avoid taking more shots. As he moved around to get a better sight picture, I'd shuffle over to the right rear quarter panel of the pickup. That's when a round came through the bed.

"I couldn't miss that one. It was in line with my eyes: a few inches to the left and the bullet would have hit my head. Also, it was as loud as hell, a blast next to my face or so it seemed. When that round came through the bed, I saw the hole open up in the metal right before me and felt a sting across my nose."

What had happened was that the bullet expanded on hitting the truck and then disintegrated. It splattered tiny chunks of shrapnel on the other side, where Officer Martin had taken up his position. He now had blood on his face from a small nose wound.

"That's when I started firing back in earnest. I really let rip. He was sheltering behind the spare tire carrier in the left corner of the driver's side bed where the back glass and the door frame came together. For my part, I was putting rounds through the spare tire and the left quarter panel of the truck. In fact, anywhere I thought I could hit him. Now I was really determined to get him. Then Massey started moving around again, toward the tailgate and I shuffled forward toward the front."

Meantime, a gunfight on Highway 71 didn't exactly stop traffic. Officer Martin recalls seeing people drive by and actually watch him dodge Massey's bullets, like it was a side show at a country fair. They would deliberately slow down so as not to miss anything. "Now I'm concerned about shooting people as they go by," he declared in his distinctive Arkansas drawl.

"I'm also worried like hell because my 9mm pistol is not doing what it's supposed to. We worked out afterward that by then I'd shot a total of twenty-nine rounds and Massey had taken quite a few hits." Also, Officer Martin had already changed magazines once. Not only had he shattered the windshield but all the glass at the back was in smithereens.

"At the time it seemed like we were prancing around that vehicle for hours, but all this had happened in just a couple of minutes, if that. I was also starting to get desperate. My fire was on target but nothing was happening to Massey.

"I could see my hits. There were red blotches on his clothing where the slugs impacted. I knew I was doing damage. I also sensed that he must be bleeding. We'd been trained to aim for center of mass. Whereas it's all body armor today, back then it was center of mass. Moreover, we trained once a month and I was good with a pistol. But dammit, I was shooting and nothing was happening!"

At this point, Martin took another hit. As he explained it afterward, he normally carried a large set of keys on his duty belt. Only later did he discover that those keys had been deformed by a bullet strike. If they had not deflected the slug, he would probably have taken a serious hit in the lower abdomen and that could have ended it. He also took a glancing round across his right knee. Though it was more of an abrasion than a bullet wound, it ended up getting badly infected in the days ahead.

To be so plastered and shoot so well, as Massey had done, was puzzling. The consensus afterward was that this big fellow must have been an outstanding shot. Or an outstanding drunk!

"When I went back to the driver's side, we'd maneuvered our way right around the vehicle. Just then I'm at the driver's side again and he's standing toward the rear.

"At this point he walked to the passenger door and was trying to open it. He wouldn't be doing that if he didn't have a purpose. I figured he had more guns inside, more ammo. Also, I hadn't counted his shots. It's the darn last thing you think about when somebody's trying to kill you but it was pretty obvious that if he didn't already have to reload, he'd soon need to.

"Finally I told myself, the hell with this. There was nothing happening even though there was never more than eight or ten feet between us. Also, I'd been shot and he'd taken innumerable hits himself and hadn't dropped. I was a little alarmed as to why he was trying to get back in his cab.

"I was only vaguely aware of the sequence of events that followed as things progressed. Only after it was all over and I was able to go over it with investigators did it all come back to me. But right then I knew I had no option but to end this business. I had to, for the sake of my own survival.

"Looking back, I accept that it was a terrible decision. But there was no going back. I said to myself, I'm going to put two head shots into him, and with that I fired twice right here by his left ear," Martin told me, pointing toward the side of his head. And of course, this time he goes down." Martin said afterward that Massey collapsed like a huge dollop of jelly onto the road, dead. Which was when this cop called for an ambulance and back-up.

"Naturally, everybody in town has heard the shots and by now they're already on their way. Once other officers arrived we discovered another loaded pistol in the truck's locked toolbox, plus over five hundred rounds of ammunition. And the look-alike Thompson .45 semi-auto, also loaded. There were lots more rounds already loaded in its spare magazines. It's all there in my report."

According to the coroner's report the attacker had taken seventeen 9mm bullets—many in his body—and some of which would surely have destroyed a smaller man. But, Massey kept on fighting, and who knows what would have happened if he had been able to bring his pseudo-submachinegun to bear? By his trying to re-enter the cab in the final stages of the shoot-out, that seemed to be the man's intention.

Martin was hit four times. Two of the .357 magnum bullets were stopped by his body armor. The other two, including the bit of shrapnel on his nose, were glancing hits.

There was more. In the cab they found a handwritten note that indicated that the dead man was terminally ill; he had cancer. His intention, he wrote, was to go to a shopping mall in Fayetteville, and with all the guns and ammo at his disposal, kill as many people as he could.

Richard Davis' views on the issue are instructive. "I'd never say this on the air, but if your goal is to kill a large number of unarmed, and unarmored, people with a portable weapon, a semi-auto .45 Carbine is an excellent choice. It has .45 hitting power and the 16-inch barrel provides the shooter with anything from 25 to 50 percent more energy per round than a five-inch pistol barrel. Combine this with light recoil and thirty-round magazines, and you have a very deadly weapon. We'll never know how many people owe their lives to Jim Martin."

As Martin recalled, Massey seemed to accept that a police SWAT team would get him in the end, but as he boasted in his letter: "I want to go out in a blaze of glory."

If that had been allowed to happen, dozens, perhaps hundreds, of innocents might have been killed. He had both the intent and the means. Except for the tenacity of Officer Jim Martin, he might very well have done it too.

Though the complete story was never given any kind of publicity for fear of inspiring a copycat killer, Jim Martin is in the record books as one of Arkansas' heroes.

He may have prevented one of the worst massacres in modern American history.

* * *

The death of Howard K. Massey was compounded by an assortment of nebulous legal considerations that seem to delight district attorneys with time on their hands.

Instead of sending Martin off to the hospital right away to have his wounds attended to, "somebody at the top" ordered his weapon taken away, which, some thought, was the ultimate insult.

"I'd carried a firearm for twenty-six years. It's like a part of my body. It was natural for me to have it on me or with me at all times. Now I was left naked. That seriously diminished me as a person and let's face it, there's no other way of looking at it. When they took my firearm it made me feel as if they did not trust me. All they needed to do was tell me that they needed it for the crime lab for forensic comparison, which was routine. Then, even before I was attended to, my superiors asked for a statement. That was done immediately, where the shooting took place and even before I was put in an ambulance and taken to Polk County Hospital for X-rays."

Since Jim Martin went to work for the Arkansas Game & Fish Commission, it has become police departmental policy to issue an officer with a replacement weapon if his own firearm is removed after a shooting.

The bureaucratic nightmare that evolved as a consequence of the shooting, Martin strongly feels, made a sham of his stopping a potential mass murderer. The consequences of the investigation that followed, he submits, put him through a nightmare. It was also a situation with which every policeman involved in a shooting can empathize.

"Only after we were able to go through his things did I find that I'd actually killed a man with an empty gun. But, consider the circumstances; that's not intentional. There's no way I'm able to count his shots.[1] He's trying to kill me. I must suddenly be a superhero and in complete control. That's just not possible. And those assholes that put me through the grinder knew it.

"Look at it another way. Massey expended all his ammo. The way I read it, when we were battling out there, he was trying to get back into his truck where his other guns were. So, to my mind, I did what was perfectly justified. At the same time, for some strange reason, it bothered me a lot that I had put the man down after he was empty. But, as we were able to show, there was no doubt he was going for more firepower.

"Later, through reasoning and counseling, I was told—and I also personally felt—that I'd done the right thing. But, immediately after the shooting I was really bothered and the people in charge didn't help the situation." This, he feels, is all too common in police-involved shootings.

"If you lose, you die. If you win . . . as Ricky Ricardo used to say to his wife Lucy, ". . . you got some 'splainin' to do!"

Officer Martin's wife, Cindy, had been aware from the start of both the shooting and what was happening to her husband. As a dispatcher at the Mena Police Department, though off-duty that day, she was able to follow developments at home on their scanner. She was horrified.

"Cindy knows my voice. She could follow my every move as I reported in. She'd heard me telling dispatch I'd been hit. Obviously that was terrifying because she had no way of knowing where the bullet had struck, or how bad it was. In her mind, I could have been bleeding to death.

"It was very traumatic. She broke down totally once it was all over."

Howard Massey's family arrived in Mena the next day and to the surprise of all, they were profusely, even embarrassingly, apologetic. Martin met them and it was clear from what was said that each of them regretted deeply what their dissolute relative had done.

They told him the dead man had been living in Houston and that he'd actually been separated from the family for a while, once he'd been told he had cancer. They know he might have contemplated suicide.

As Officer Martin recalls, Massey had told them he was going to Fayetteville, Arkansas, to die. He didn't mention anything about a mass murder.

Afterward, Officer Jim Martin spent many hours with the state police investigator going over the case. He was compelled to draw diagrams and write a report, and the higher-ups in Little Rock wanted both oral and written testimony. Psychological counseling followed, not that Martin felt he needed it.

During this entire time the prosecuting attorney couldn't make up his mind whether to press charges against Martin or not. He finally decided the shooting was justified, although that decision took three weeks in coming.

"That was painful for me. The man shot first. He hit me. It could easily have been cut and dried. It shouldn't have taken almost a month to get a ruling back from the prosecuting attorney that cleared me.

"There was this cloud hanging over my family and me because I had expended so much ammo. I was suspended from duty for two weeks with pay. This was the decision of the chief of police at the time, since we had no written policy on officer-involved shootings.

"What people failed to realize was that I was using a 9mm. We'd been issued with 147grain PMC bullets that were copper-jacketed hollow-points and were supposed to expand on impact. But they didn't because when the coroner recovered those bullets, they hadn't expanded at all. They'd just gone straight through.

"I got cleared eventually but that business left a bad taste and I eventually moved to Game & Fish. At least there we carry a .40 caliber Glock but even that's sometimes inadequate. I've had to shoot several deer with it and I'm not happy with its stopping power."

The Mena Police Department moved on to .45 ACP for its officers, which Jim Martin thought made much better sense.

These days, while working in the Arkansas Game & Fish Commission, Jim Martin operates from home. But he is still on call around the clock, seven days a week, holidays included. As with Greg Lovett, a couple of hours' drive to the north, his biggest single problem is drugs, primarily methamphetamines, which, he'll submit, are just about everywhere in Arkansas.

"It's not unusual to drive up to somebody in a recreational area, and they'll be on the tailgate cooking meth. And that in a public RV area, often with kids playing on the grass outside. Or you pull up to a camp out in the woods and they have a camper converted into a meth shack.

"We'll call for back-up if we have the time, which is why we work so closely with county deputies because they're usually the quickest to respond. Normally I'm out there by myself. It's kind of like the sheriff says, 'You catch 'em, you clean 'em.'

"As a consequence I have drawn my firearm more with the Arkansas Game & Fish Commission than I ever did with the city police. And we're not talking about only kids doing it. There's the occasional seventy-year-old in the business and some people in their sixties . . . lots of people my age, and I'm fifty-two. So it's not unusual to catch a sixty-year-old with his meth lab."

"And aggressive?" I asked.

"It depends on the individual. And of course on his or her personality. Some people get violent. Some are just 99 percent paranoid. Others see monkeys and quite a few see the federal government coming after them. It changes everything.

"You get a few that are laid back . . . They don't give a hoot one way or the other. But most of the time you're gonna have a fight on your hands."

The next question involved money. It was Jim Martin's view that most of the people that he and others encountered doing this stuff were what are called *user-sellers.*

"They're making just enough for themselves, with some over to sell and finance the next the batch. That's how they make their living. They perpetuate the situation and it can grow. We've impounded motor homes where the walls would be bright yellow from iodine fumes, which is a precursor for methamphetamine.

Of course the kids are in there breathing all these noxious gases and you can only imagine the long-term implications, healthwise."

"Been shot at again?" Silly question. "Of course," Jim Martin replied readily. Immediately after he came back off suspension—after the drama with Massey—he made a DWI stop, also somebody from Texas driving a big black pickup.

"It was a similar situation, only this time I had Cindy with me. It was dark, I was in uniform, and I went over to his rig. He then made a dive for the back of the truck. So a struggle ensued but I got him out onto the road in the end and found a handgun on the back seat.

"You handle it any differently this time?" I asked.

"I would say sort of, because the circumstances weren't the same. Certainly, I was more cautious. Once I'd taken him into custody we found that he was a convicted felon. Cindy wasn't amused. As soon as the fracas started she got on the radio requesting help, which this time arrived pretty soon."

In another shooting incident, Jim Martin was called to a night hunting complaint in Montgomery County. Somebody phoned in to say that shots had been fired at his house and he responded. Again he had Cindy in the cruiser.

"Once I got there, I'm shining a light to try to follow some tracks down to the man's residence. Then I hear a rifle being fired with bullets coming through the trees all around me, breaking tree limbs. It's the landowner shooting at the game warden—me—who is only trying to help.

"After a while he got tired of that, so he called the Sheriff's Office and said that he was trying to chase violators off his property.

"I then called the sheriff and told him to tell that SOB to quit shooting. We finally got him on the phone, and calmed him down enough to be able to talk some sense into his head.

"He was a real strange one, that man. A recluse, which is another of the problems you run into in these mountains, folks living in total isolation. There are people here who are very protective of what they own, some of them powerfully anti-government. Hotbed of right-wing stuff as well.

"They hate anything to do with authority, and then they have the balls to call us for government assistance . . ."

That is not dissimilar to something that happened to Black Deputy Rogal Rogers of Will County, Illinois, a short while afterward. Having responded to a possible suicide call, along with other units, Rogers entered a driveway when a man and a woman came out on a front porch. The man began firing at the police.

As Deputy Rogers retreated behind his vehicle, he was struck in the hip and in the back by .38 Special slugs fired from a six-inch revolver. While the hip wound was serious, his vest stopped the bullet from entering his back. The man was obviously a crack shot since he was firing his gun from fifty yards away.

The officers immediately retaliated and killed their assailant. We have no word as to what happened to the woman.

So too with Gregory Overstreet, on foot patrol in a wooded part of Ann Arundel County, Maryland, when he came upon a drug deal in progress. The druggies dropped their goods and took off running. Tough and fleet-of-foot, Overstreet followed and soon caught one of them. A scuffle followed.

At this point the suspect pulled out a revolver and shot the policeman in the chest, his vest preventing injury. The assailant then tried to shoot Overstreet in the face, but the cop managed to deflect that bullet into his right shoulder. Overstreet is listed as Save #525.

After being a cop for so many years, and now working for Arkansas Game & Fish Commission, Martin feels, as he puts it, "come home."

Much of his work is still law enforcement. He has full arrest powers and runs into all sorts of violations during the course of a regular patrol.

Since 9/11, his duties have ranged from protecting the President and Vice President of the United States when they come to Little Rock, to ensuring the security of major Arkansas dams and other large bodies of water from acts of terrorism.

"With the infusion of criminal gangs into the states from South and Central America—criminal groups like MS-13—we're on our toes.

"But there are other aspects that demand careful attention. People out here are accustomed to carrying firearms. There are hunters everywhere. In fact, almost everybody I come in contact with is armed. So we have to deal with them in a very different manner compared to the regular cop on the street . . . You just can't get paranoid when you see a gun, because the people around here have grown up with them.

"You just hope that person is not someone who has a warrant out on him or is wanted in some jurisdiction, or possibly hyped up on meth.

"That said, this is doing something I really love. The Game & Fish Commission is my life . . . I wouldn't trade places with *anybody*!"

---

[1] In the nineteenth century this might have been remotely possible, but since 1911 (or 1898, for that matter) many guns, even "six gun" revolvers, hold more than six shots. Plus how can you be sure that the criminal didn't reload or pull a second gun?

CHAPTER 18

Knife Attack: An Easy Way to Die

As a police officer you often find yourself in a position where knife attacks are likely to occur, perhaps within an arm's length of an unknown individual with dubious intent. It's a worst-case scenario, but it can happen at any time.

—Ernest Emerson

Richard Davis tells the story of a Michigan prison guard, an extremely lucky fellow, because he was wearing his vest while off-duty. The incident is so amazingly stupid that if it hadn't actually happened, it could be considered an urban legend.

The off-duty guard was walking in a shopping area when someone crept up behind him and stabbed him powerfully in the back with a large folding knife. The impact of the blow almost drove him to the ground. The attacker clearly intended to kill, as was confirmed later, under interrogation.

When the corrections officer turned around he was astonished to find his attacker lying on the ground. The man was screaming and in extreme pain. He held his right hand which spurted blood, not only over himself, but across the sidewalk. A large closed and bloodied lock-blade knife and a severed thumb nearby told the rest of the story.

The criminal had been paroled from jail a short while before and clearly had reasons of his own to get even. But he didn't do a good job of it, because a lock-blade is exactly that. You lock the blade back just before you use it. Instead of a successful hit, the blade closed on his hand as he struck. As cleanly as if it had been removed in surgery, it lopped off the top-half of his thumb.

* * *

Though rarely in the news for it, body armor has played a remarkably successful role in saving the lives of many law enforcement officers from knife or other sharp instrument attack, most notably in corrections facilities.

A casual search through the Second Chance Saves Club list reveals more than thirty incidents involving blades or sharp objects. That includes a triple save (#522, #523, and #524) of Veteran Affairs Dr. Robert Scherer and his two associates, Richard A. Davis and John Rixham, Jr. All three were stabbed and slashed trying to restrain a mental patient on a psychiatric ward. Fortunately, they all wore protective vests. The attack was so violent they would probably have been killed if their body armor had not absorbed a succession of repeated and vicious stabs by a lunatic who was not only out of control but was extremely powerful—as these people can sometimes prove to be.

The same sort of thing happened to Jay Harris of Baltimore (Save #776). He was stabbed in the back by a mental patient with a butcher's knife.

At the same time, not all knifings are random and senseless. Many are planned. Others are executed with remarkable precision.

Richard Kennedy of Port Chester, New York, survived two of the earliest Saves (#27 and #52): the latter being a shooting with a .32 auto that hit him in the middle of his chest, the first a powerful hit in the stomach from a broken beer bottle. He'd stepped between a man and woman arguing. Before he could react, his attacker had lunged at him several times. He would have been killed without his vest, he told Richard Davis afterward.

Save #33 was equally improbable. William Fisher of St. Joseph, Missouri, was stabbed in the chest with a metal Afro comb. The very next save, #34, was Thomas Ternerry of South Bend, Indiana, who took a blow from an eight-inch carving knife during a family-trouble call.

The knife that stabbed Richard Weldon of Maywood, California—Save #89—was only an inch shorter. There are no details about the knifings of Ronald Smigelski of Oak Park, Michigan (#88), and Verleen Hanes of Colorado Springs (#90), both of whom were stabbed in the chest.

More recently, Deputy Sheriff Carl Woods of Linden, Texas, was making an incident report on a female subject standing in a yard waving a knife. Having spent a while trying to persuade her to give up the blade, Woods then moved forward in an attempt to disarm her. She slashed at the deputy three times, each time hitting him about an inch above the waist. Protected from serious injury by his body armor, he maced and then cuffed the woman.

Another time two separate units arrived at an Ocala, Florida, motel in answer to a disturbance call. In trying to arrest the suspect, Officer James R.

Deas was stabbed in the chest but his vest prevented injury. That became Save #827.

St. Patrick's Day is not always a time of celebration for America's police. It wasn't for Officer Grant Strahle of Savannah, Georgia, when he was sent to a bar to break up a fight. The girlfriend of the fellow he was attempting to detain pulled out a four-inch lock-blade and pounded it repeatedly into the back panel of Strahle's Model Y2 concealable armor. There was no penetration.

There was a determined effort to murder Jeffrey J. "Triple J" Jones at the Pontiac Correctional Center in Illinois (Save #678). While Jones was dispensing chipped ice to celled inmates, one of the prisoners grabbed Jones by the shoulder and pulled him toward the bars, momentarily immobilizing him. Jones was stabbed hard enough in the chest with a two-inch sharp metal object with a cloth handle to leave him with some pretty impressive bruising. The shank was stopped by Jones' body armor.

Another unusual stabbing involved Earl Dosser of West, Texas. He took a hit in the chest with a screwdriver (Save #223). A few days before that a straight razor (Save #222) was used to try to split open the chest of Steve Napolitano of New York.

What one learns from a close examination of Davis' documented saves is that of the thousand-odd close encounters, those involving knives, blades, and sharp objects make up an astonishing number. Apart from the ones listed here, there are dozens more about which details are sparse.

It is also clear, as knife fighting guru Ernest Emerson points out below, it is just as easy to die from a sharp stab as it is from a bullet, particularly if the attacker wielding a blade knows what he's doing. People used iron and steel to kill others for thousands of years before firearms became a reality—and in some quarters, that trend persists.

A few more standout stabbings include Save #825 of John Burdick in Dearborn Heights, a particularly nasty Detroit suburb. It was never clear why the subject attacked the officer. Burdick had routinely stopped him for questioning at three in the morning.

The man got out of his car and struck at Burdick with a lethal blade that would almost certainly have killed him if he had not been wearing his body armor. The cop and a back-up officer retaliated with seven shots, killing the attacker.

Roberta Vargas, a Chicago woman police officer, may hold a record for surviving the highest number of stabbing attempts during one attack. Her vest, in Save #751, stopped fourteen stab penetrations.

Officer Donald Pierce of Pullman, Washington, had been called to a domestic violence situation. Pierce found a man assaulting his girlfriend. The man then lunged at the policeman and tried to slash his way into the cop's stomach. Pierce's vest prevented that.

Before that, Bill Delaney of Wareham, Massachusetts, whose vest prevented a ten-inch hunting knife from entering his torso, made Save #304.

Ernest Emerson has a lot of comments about knife attacks. As one of the leading international authorities on the subject, he teaches people how and why they happen and what countermeasures should be applied. The founder of Emerson Combat Systems, Ernest has written articles and produced videos on knife defense. He even gave this author one of his latest production blades for self-protection on a recent visit to Africa. It is one of the most impressive lock blades I've handled, and in an environment where it would be stupid to carry a firearm, it did provide a good bit of comfort.

Emerson's first survival rule is simple. *Until proven otherwise*, presume that all subjects are armed. He stresses that it is essential to be conscious of the fact that every subject has the ability to take your life.

There are many types of perps, Emerson warns, the first being what he terms "the stone-cold killer." This individual just knows that he is going to kill any cop he encounters. He will kill without hesitation to avoid arrest or possible incarceration.

There is the "opportunity attacker" who attacks spontaneously during a routine stop, say where a drug shipment might be uncovered. In such circumstances, the perp might decide to attack rather than be caught. He has no plan to attack, but when he sees an opportunity, he acts without hesitation.

Emerson's third category is the criminal caught in the act of a robbery or break-in. "If he has a knife, you can be pretty sure he'll use it." While he doesn't set out to harm or kill anybody, in such a situation, he believes he has been forced to react with violence.

"The mentally disturbed attacker is most likely a homeless man or woman, usually armed with a knife for reasons of paranoia or protection. Such perpetrators will attack if they feel threatened." Emerson warns that officers should be aware of the fact that their presence alone could pose enough of a threat to trigger an attack.

Others are people under the influence of alcohol or drugs, or somebody brandishing a blade during a domestic call. It should be noted that while the above saves all ended without loss of life or serious injury, there are many cases of police officers having been murdered by knife wielders.

In a most informative article on the knife threat, Ernest Emerson goes on to give valuable advice about confronting an attacker who has intent to kill with his or her knife. Originally published in the June 2004 issue of *Police: The Law Enforcement Magazine* (policemag.com), it could be worth a life saved to check it out.

The ploy to avoid being killed by someone with a blade that I found the most interesting involves what Emerson refers to as "introducing the unexpected."

For example, he says, "if a knife attack is overwhelming me, I can move backward and drop to the ground. By doing this, I have taken away the target. Thus I present something far less vulnerable (my feet) and in so doing, I minimize potential lethal injury. In a word, I *control* the situation. This allows me that fraction of a second that I need to access my weapon."

He has not heard of a single time when a knife-wielding opponent has leapt upon an officer who has used this technique.

All that notwithstanding, police departments increasingly stress the dangers of attack by a criminal wielding a sharp object—especially since it happens with a regularity that surprises the people who keep these statistics.

It is almost worse in Britain. In Glasgow, Scotland, sharp-edged weapons are the choice instrument of combat among some of the urban gangs the police now have to cope with. Sadly, the same situation holds for all the other big cities in England, Ireland, and Wales—and that for a country where you very rarely see a policeman with a gun on his belt. Part of the reason is that the general population has for decades been deprived of owning firearms following years of conflict with the Irish Republican Army. But even that is changing: not a day goes by without gunfights being reported in British cities.

In the United States there are increasing numbers of cases where felons wield sharp instruments like ice picks. In the case of Sheriff Deputy Ethan Smith of Jackson, Michigan, he was called to a domestic disturbance and was set upon by a very agitated subject who hurled everything in his workshop at him, except the forge. For a fourteen-year veteran, it was something that could have ended very badly for Smith. Certainly, as he recounted afterward, it was an experience like no other. Had he not been wearing body armor, he would almost certainly be dead.

Like his colleague Timothy Gonzales, also of Jackson, Michigan, most of the call-outs that he and forty-five other sworn deputies handle are pretty mundane. Many involve suspect traffic. For this, the Sheriff's Department has only one dog for sniffing contraband, though the city has two more hounds—which is not much when you consider that the east–west arterial Interstate-94 is one of the busiest highways in the nation.

The father of six children, Deputy Ethan Smith is among the fittest and strongest in his team. Though still in his early forties, he could easily pass muster for someone a decade younger, which was just as well considering the events surrounding a call he got one mid-morning.

"That wasn't the first time that I'd heard of Jeffrey Hammond. One of his neighbors called in to say that he was on the rampage, breaking fences and destroying things. The way it was relayed to me was that Hammond was acting psychotic and quoting Bible verses. I'd had dealings with him before, but he'd never been a real problem. Anyway, at about five feet six, skinny and with dark hair, he wasn't your archetypal tough guy. Also, he comes from a good family that has a nice business in town here.

"But things immediately went wrong as soon as my cruiser pulled into his yard. He started throwing things at me, including a pretty good-sized twelve-inch U-shaped bolt that must have weighed a few pounds. When it hit my windscreen, it just seemed to explode, though it didn't penetrate the safety glass. Suddenly I'm faced with a patrol car that is quite badly damaged, and naturally things begin to take on a totally different perspective.

"A couple of moments later Hammond came at me again, this time shattering the window on my driver's side. He was using a pretty hefty claw hammer and I had to duck smartly to avoid being hit. That was followed immediately afterward by a bundle of metal objects.

"Now I'm starting to think that this is bullshit. If he hits me with any one of those projectiles, some of which are pretty heavy, I'm going to go down." At that point Hammond had moved into a position alongside the patrol car, "which is when I kicked open the door and knocked him backward. I also drew my gun and ordered him to the ground.

"But the man was demented, clearly so. He heard none of my instructions because he was still throwing tools.

"I'm backing up toward the rear of my cruiser and I've got a serious problem because things are not getting any better. In fact, the onslaught has gone up a notch or two. I'm aware that I can stop him in a moment, but shooting him is not an option because my life is not in danger. On the other hand, I'm no longer so sure."

Using one of the oldest tricks in the book, Deputy Smith pulled out his pepper spray and unloaded the vial into his attacker's face. It had no effect whatsoever. As he recalled afterward, "I might have sprayed him with talcum powder . . . He lapped it up like a dog with a hose. And I'm thinking, What the hell do I do with a guy that hasn't got all his marbles?"

Dodging between his own cruiser and another vehicle that he had originally pulled up alongside, Smith suddenly tripped and fell, and that might have been the opportunity that Hammond was waiting for. His hands had barely touched the ground when his attacker jumped onto his back and started to pummel it with what he later discovered was a nine- or ten-inch screw driver. As he recalls, it was big and it was sharp.

"Now I'm on my hands and knees. As I'm scrambling to get up, I feel something hit me hard in the shoulder blade. I didn't yet know what it was but it was a tough, hard thud. Also, being a forceful blow, it hurt. Then I saw him standing over me with this screwdriver thing in his right hand and he's preparing to hit me once more, which was when I used my left foot and let rip outward, like a donkey kick. I planted him one square in his stomach. That had the effect of hurling him backward.

"I had just enough time to spin around on one knee when he came at me once more, so I did the only thing left to me: I shot him dead center in the chest."

The impact of the bullet stopped Jeffrey Hammond right there. He looked at the policeman, turned his gaze toward his chest, and looked back at Deputy Smith before dropping the piece of metal in his hand. Then he made two fists and came in running.

"This time he had nothing in his hands. It was simple for me to step aside. That he could still muster that kind of energy was surprising because the bullet that had gone into the front of his chest was a .40 caliber slug, which is no lightweight. As we discovered afterward, it just nicked the vein leading into his heart, went on through his chest, and emerged from his right shoulder blade. The man should have been dead, but he wasn't."

What had happened was that Hammond was bleeding out internally. As he again approached Deputy Smith, the officer grabbed him and put him into a choke hold. At the same time he shouted several times for him to stop.

As Deputy Sheriff Smith today recalls, "From the moment I had him locked in my grip I could actually feel his strength sapping away. It was quite strange: one moment he would be as tense as a rod of steel, and then he gradually relaxed and went limp, at which point I sat up and handcuffed him."

They got an ambulance to Hammond's place in time to save his life. "The medics came in, scooped him up, and by some miracle they managed to keep him alive until they got him to the ER. So he's still around today."

Jeffrey Hammond was finally made to stand trial and was found guilty. "The judge ordered him committed to an insane asylum in Ypsilanti with a sentence, quaintly, of one day to life, depending on whether the man could get himself fit for society again," recounted Smith.

He eventually served something like two months, moved out of town, but finally returned to Jackson. He was actually living in the same house where it all had all gone down when I visited Deputy Sheriff Ethan Smith in Jackson during the summer of 2005.

Strange world we live in . . .

CHAPTER 19

Michael Francis: The Save That Almost Didn't Happen

Richard Davis' Save #800 followed Murphy's Law. Everything that *could* go wrong did. Without telling his partner, Officer Michael Francis went into a low-rent, badly lit neighborhood in search of a drug suspect, who then turned around and shot him four times. A fifth bullet clipped his lapel radio, making it impossible to call for help. As he lay on the ground in the dark, the bone in his leg severed, Francis waited for the shooter to come back . . .

I'd heard of Patrolman Michael Francis, of Greensboro, North Carolina, long before I met him. As a cop, he'd been in numerous scrapes. He'd also been left for dead after being shot. His superiors at one stage believed he'd lost so much blood in the firefight that he wouldn't make it through the night.

"We thought we'd lost him," said Captain Mike Oates, of Greensboro Central Division. "He was cut off from help, couldn't reach us, and we didn't know where he was. But he's plucky, and he made that extra effort."

The man I met didn't look like a superhero.

Officer Francis was remarkable all right, but he was smaller than I'd anticipated. Also, he was so quiet-spoken that, with only one working ear from all my war work, I sometimes had difficulty catching what he said. He was one of the most self-effacing people I'd met; actually modest to distraction. Not yet thirty, Officer Francis is one of those dedicated individuals who consider life on the force the center of their existence. He cannot imagine being anything other than a cop.

Officer Francis considers his job as neither exacting nor unduly stressful. Rather, he thinks of it as a means of "providing a service to the community where I live." If he lost sight of that ideal, then he'd clear his desk and go home, he added.

"Sounds corny, I know, but I get a kick out of being useful. I'm doing something I like when I'm helping, and perhaps I put a smile on the face of someone to whom, moments before, everything looked hopeless. That's what life is about, don't you think?" The question was rhetorical and in his view there was only one possible answer.

"Call it dedication—though some people regard that kind of thinking as simplistic, or even stupid—but what I do is exactly what I *want* to do." Officer Francis obviously wasn't doing it for the money. Taking home about $2,200 a month, he'll never get rich. "Though I'm not flush, I manage, as we all have to do . . ."

A native of Long Island, New York, Francis achieved grades at school that were distinguished enough to have been awarded a scholarship. But he never considered an academic career. Francis holds a Bachelor of Science degree from Greensboro's Guilford College, achieved while working days and studying nights. Working forty-hour weeks, he managed a B-plus average, with honors in electronics and mathematics.

Originally he wanted to be a lawyer. But his airline mechanic father got injured in Francis' sophomore year and was retired from his job. That meant hard times. It also resulted in the young man having to pay his own tuition.

"So I gave up my plans for law school and it was a real wrench, believe me. My heart was set on it. It was actually the blackest day of my life when I finally made the decision. But, because I loved jurisprudence, I decided that I'd become a cop instead. That way I'd remain in the mainstream of law enforcement."

On being accepted for training, Officer Francis began his career at the Greensboro Police Department's (GPD) in-house academy, with twenty-seven other hopefuls of whom all but three went the distance. He was then put on the road as a uniformed patrolman.

His first serious confrontation came soon afterward when he and his zone partner, Greg Gardner, tackled one of the biggest felons, literally, in town. What should have been a routine arrest became a test of strength with a whacked-out, three-hundred-pound crack addict. This powerful hulk who regarded all white folk as fair game stood six feet three or four in his socks, which says Francis, "made my five feet seven and a hundred and seventy pounds look puny."

The man had a record of run-ins with the law that went back years. Recalled Francis, when the man was on dope, which was just about every other day, he'd go looking for trouble. Invariably he'd find it.

"He insulted us, spat on us, and before we arrived on the scene, he caused so much trouble that some of the shopkeepers in the area dialed 911.

"We ordered him to move on. He didn't listen. Told us to go fuck ourselves and then he walked away. After we'd warned him again to stop, and he ignored us, we had to act. He'd become a spectacle in a part of town where the law needed to be observed."

The altercation started in the middle of a busy Greensboro street, just before the evening rush hour. Two policemen, scuffling with a giant and not achieving anything tangible, caused a crowd to gather. Wisecracks flowed. Officer Francis decided that because nothing else had worked, he'd use Mace to blind the offender. He did, but unfortunately he sprayed his partner as well, and we've already seen how often that happens.

"Both Greg and the big guy went down like they'd been pole-axed. Then they got up, groped around blindly, with me dodging the perp.

"We were still in the middle of the road with cars passing, which really worried me." The scuffle, he felt, could easily result in an accident. "So, I told Greg to hang on to my belt and I shoved hard, forcing both of them toward the sidewalk."

Mace is an effective persuader, but instructions are clear. Stand to leeward and be sure that your partner is not in your line of fire.

Officer Francis had hit his partner because while he was spraying the Mace he was being twirled around like a rag doll by the big guy. That's why Gardner got a face-full, as well as the perp. Normally Mace will incapacitate a person for twenty, sometimes thirty minutes. In addition to blindness, most Mace victims can't breathe properly. The perp—sightless or not—was still getting the better of the two cops trying to cuff him.

The raggedy fight went on for another twenty minutes. Gardner held one arm and Francis the other, but it took a long time to restrain the man. That only happened after the older man began to tire. Finally they cuffed one arm and then, after another five minutes of slamming around, the other.

"We got him back to jail eventually, he did a bit of time and then went his way again. Big, bad hombre . . . hated the police, loved violence, and, in particular, made a specialty of brutally assaulting females who were usually too terrified to report it.

"Ended up dead not long afterward. Probably overdosed. They found his body in a condemned house after about a week, his face completely eaten away by maggots. That's the way it goes, because nobody goes looking for guys like that when they disappear. When people don't see them around, everybody just prays they're never coming back."

• • •

Francis: "There was another time we were called out on a domestic and that guy was very, very drunk! We didn't know if he had a knife or a gun. In fact, we didn't know anything.

"So three cars roll up and this is also a pretty hefty guy, more than six feet tall, very muscular and furious too. He had one of those half-gallon jugs of rotgut and took a long pull while we were trying to talk to him.

"We asked him what was going on but he was not answering. Just swearing and threatening. Then his wife came out of the house and she was really beat up: had a couple of shiners and a busted face. I mean she looked like she'd been through the wars. She tells us that he's drunk and that he's been hitting her, again and again.

"'Okay,' we say to him, 'That's it. You're under arrest.' It's like he doesn't hear us because he's still as aggressive as hell. By this time we'd called dispatch and they sent another car. So now there's four of us. We Mace him and tackle him but the chemical is having no effect.

"There was no flipping a coin about who would go in first. It just happened with all four of us going in together, as if we'd been ordered to do so, though I was fractionally behind the others and only managed to grab hold of a foot. And that didn't do that much good. Took a while, but we got him. Took him in."

The uncertainty of his career is probably why Officer Francis always wears body armor.

"When we started at the Academy, we had to wear vests, even when we attended classes. They made a big thing about it. I believe they still do—which is why, in a force of more than five hundred, there's no more than four or five officers who don't wear concealable body armor. That's about 1 percent.

"I finished training, joined the department, and got to see the real world out there." For patrol officers the city is divided into three districts—Alpha, Bravo, and Charlie—with six or seven cars out at any one time, each of them working a specific district.

On November 2, 1999, Officer Francis was working Bravo. The weather was unseasonably warm and he'd already made a couple of arrests, one for fighting in public. There was a warrant out on the other, which came up when they ran his name through the system.

"After that we found ourselves in a kind of open-air curb market. We call it the Quickie-Mart and we'd been told that there'd been problems with some winos and druggies. As part of the routine, my zone partner and I would come and go, brush the baddies away from the place. Once we'd gone on to the next job, they'd shuffle back and when we showed our faces again, we'd do it again.

"We knew these people and they knew us. The minute I'd hop out of my car they'd start moving along, 'cause that's the game we played. But that evening there were two new faces in the crowd, people we didn't recognize and I'm usually pretty good with faces.

"They had that kind of look on their dials. 'Oh no, a cop. What do we do?' So I wanted to talk with them. You get that feeling when you do this kind of thing long enough.

"I had the one guy sit on the curb and told the other, the younger of the two, who we found out afterward was twenty-four years old—same age as me, just then—that I wanted to pat him down. He was wearing a kind of puffy jacket that you can wear inside out, but it was black on the outside. It was formless and sort of hid his body features. He had on blue jeans and sneakers, and of course, the inevitable back-to-front baseball cap."

It is Officer Francis' view—and that of most officers who work center-city areas—that a search is warranted if there is a reasonable suspicion the suspect might be trying to hide something. "And that was exactly how I felt, especially since this was a high drug area." That and the nervous reaction of these two when the rest of the transients moved along.

"When I told the man to put his cigarette down, he acted like he was going to, but then lunged across the road. He rushed off, trying to get away. He knew I wouldn't shoot him, so I suppose he thought he had nothing to lose. Naturally I followed, leaving the older of the two behind, knowing full well that younger guys are more likely to get violent. My partner was on the far side of the block, so he saw none of this.

"I was starting to gain on the runaway—we later found that his name was Jimmy Ford—when I noticed he was fiddling with his right front pocket, digging in there, looking for something. It didn't worry me because when you're chasing someone with dope or a crack pipe, they'll sometimes throw the paraphernalia in one direction and try to escape in the other. Even if you catch them, the evidence is gone, because, sure as hell, somebody else will pick it up for themselves.

"We reached a fairly dark street where there were almost no street lights. By now I was eight or nine paces behind him when Ford fell. I stopped in my tracks, still not having drawn my gun, and told him to stay down. We were both breathing pretty heavily.

"At that point I hadn't thought of radioing in because I didn't believe I had a charge on him. I was thinking, Okay, he's just running. So he probably has something, but nothing that I can pin on him and make stick.

"Then Ford started to get up off the ground; he wasn't doing what I told him. So I take my big heavy flashlight, the Maglight, and I'm about to hit him behind the knees to force him to ground, when I hear *Blam!* There's a flash and I didn't have to be told what that was."

Typically, Officer Francis never saw the gun in Ford's hands. Nor could he see the expression on his face. All he knew was that he was a few paces from the corner of a house and he had to get there to take cover, exactly as he'd been trained. Countless times he and his colleagues at the Academy had been drilled: if you're in a gunfight, seek cover first, draw your weapon second, and only then react to the threat.

"So I turned and ran to the corner, but Ford just kept on shooting as fast as he could pull the trigger of the 9mm semi-auto that he'd pulled from his jacket.

"I'd just about got there and as I turned, I pivoted on my right foot to get around the corner when my leg collapsed and I went down. I didn't know it yet, but I'd already been hit four times. Two bullets were absorbed by my body armor, another hit me in my armpit in an area not protected by the vest, while the last bullet struck my leg about halfway between the knee and hip. It completely shattered the bone."

The way the doctors later described Francis' leg wound, when the bullet hit his femur, the bone shattered like a glass dropped on concrete.

"So, now I'm down and kind of feeling around. I know that I've got to try to work out what's going on and soon! At least I was behind the house, so for the first time I pull my gun and I wait for him in the dark to come and finish the job.

"I wasn't over-optimistic about anybody being curious enough to come and see what happened, because it hardly ever works like that. When there are shots exchanged in that kind of area, people take off in the opposite direction."

The wounded policeman waited a while and when nothing happened, he holstered his weapon and tried to stand, but couldn't. He looked at his legs and even in the bad light saw that his right foot was pointing one way, and the knee another.

"The whole leg just swiveled on me. Even more surprising: when the realization of what happened dawned on me, there was no real pain. Only when I tried to move and heard the bones grind together, then it hit me. It was like a bolt, and at that moment I also became conscious of the blood, which was all over me. I had spurts of it running down my side from the armpit wound, down my legs and where I could feel ragged bone sticking through the flesh.

"You get quite a shock when that sort of thing happens. One moment, everything is perfectly normal, or almost, because I'm chasing a criminal. The next you realize that this is the most *abnormal* situation in which you've ever found yourself.

Francis tried his radio. No reaction. He could pick up the normal early-evening radio traffic, but no Code-9, which would have signaled officer down. One of the bullets fired by his attacker had severed the transmit wire on Francis' lapel mike before hitting his vest.

"That frightened me. There was I, leg severed and bleeding like a pig and there's not a soul in the world that knows anything about it. I hadn't even been able to tell Greg that I'd gone after this felon and since he was busy with something else, there was no way he could have known."

So what to do? By now Francis had discovered that he was bleeding from wounds on his back. Though the vest stopped two bullets, their impact had perforated his skin and caused superficial lesions. But, right then, he believed they were serious wounds since there was a warm feeling also trickling down his back.

What he didn't yet know was that the shooter had missed his neck by half an inch. Had it been hit, he would already have been dead.

Michael Francis had seen enough of the ER in his brief career to know he couldn't stay where he was and wait for rescue. Nobody knew where he was or his predicament. The pain had quickly become acute and his wounds were causing him to feel lightheaded, which was an additional worry because he feared he might pass out and bleed to death. Also, there was no way to tell whether the shooter would return.

He used his good leg and the side of the building to push himself erect. The pain was excruciating, like nothing he'd ever experienced before. Each time he moved the shattered bones ground together and the wound started bleeding again. He made several steps toward a fence, which he used to support his weak side as he hobbled back toward his cruiser. But, he still had more than a hundred yards to cover, almost all of it in almost total darkness.

It was a slow, draining process that required constant stops. A couple of times he thought he might black out, but somehow, he managed to hold on.

While there was some traffic on the other side of the street, there was nobody out on foot. Scared off by the gunfire, everybody remained clear.

It took a while, but gradually Officer Francis reached a point where he could see his zone partner sitting in his car about a block away. The other officer had seen Francis' cruiser and pulled up alongside, thinking he had to come back sometime. Only Officer Gardner had rolled up his window and was concentrating on a bunch of papers in his hand.

"That wasn't like him at all, actually," Francis recounts. "He would always drive around with his windows open a crack, in case, he would quip, he heard somebody screaming for help or gun shots. Then he'd know where it was coming from and he could do something about it. But not that night . . .

"Also, in my effort to get mobile after the shooting, I'd concentrated on my balance and the leg, so I'd left my flashlight behind. Had I kept it, I could have flashed it and attracted his attention.

"The only thing left was my ASP, which, in a desperate effort I threw to try to hit his car. But the distance was across a darkened back yard as well as four lanes of traffic. Without adequate balance, there was no way I was going to reach that far. And anyway, I've never had much of a throwing arm. It fell well short—and so did I a minute later because I lost my balance and collapsed."

At that point, one of the winos that Officer Francis had brushed off earlier ambled up to Greg's car and told him that he'd seen his partner running after one of the suspects. Pointing in the general direction of where Francis now lay, he said he'd heard some shots coming from there.

"You might want to go back there and check on him," he suggested.

"I could see everything from where I lay and I watched Greg get out of his car and walk across the road toward me. I start shouting, but he can't see anything. So he moves even closer and I'm still calling him and he's looking everywhere but down.

"'Look down at your feet, Greg. *Down!*' Which he does, and says, 'Oh my God!' and I tell him I've been shot and he just goes bananas.

"It took a little while, but I had to do the calming down after I'd asked him to call an ambulance. He gets on the radio and tells them that I've been hit. The worst part is that I'm dating Jennifer who is working dispatch that night.

"But she's not taking the call. The other girl was. Though she's sitting in the room, she wasn't party to the calls except, when the dispatcher unplugged her headset; then everything could be heard on the loudspeaker.

"'Francis has been shot,' was the message Greg blurted out. After which she was back taking emergency calls. All she could think was that her boyfriend was dead.

"So again, everything that could go wrong went wrong. Finally the cars started to arrive and the ambulance too. They were able to tell her the good news, which wasn't all that good, because by then I was in a pretty bad way.

"As for Jimmy Ford, the man who tried to kill me, he used all this confusion to make an exit."

Officer Francis spent a week in the hospital. It took him another eight months to become fully active again, his bones mended by a steel plate and screws. For a lot of that time he walked with a cane, but with time he started to exercise again. He feels fitter and stronger today than before it all happened.

GPD found out later that Ford was originally from Virginia and had headed back up there. He also dumped his Greensboro girlfriend. But not before he told her he'd shot a cop. Ford was picked up and brought to Greensboro for interrogation.

"We scammed him. When the interrogating officer walked into the room, he threw a videotape on the table.

"'We know exactly what you did," he told Ford. "Surveillance cameras are everywhere in that part of town and you're on this one,' the officer lied, pointing to the tape. 'You're done,' he said, staring down the criminal. After that Ford confessed . . . came right out with it even though it was so dark that even if there had been cameras, they wouldn't have been able to record anything . . .

"I saw Ford in federal court in Winston-Salem when I was still walking with the cane. Caught his eye, but he showed no emotion . . . didn't react in any way, though he knew who I was.

"The judge gave James Ford life-plus-ten. He told him that he would die in prison. So his career is effectively over."

At last report, Officer Michael Francis and former dispatcher Jennifer Johnstone were about to tie the knot. He told me they were going out the next day to buy the ring.

I called him to clear a few details about the shooting and the subsequent trial, including the fact that an interrogator had lied to the criminal that he was on tape. That is perfectly legal, as long as no coercion is used.

Was he still helping people? I asked.

"Can't be otherwise," he said. "If I can turn one person's life around, it makes it all worth it. Same with taking a gun off the streets, a weapon that might be used to kill somebody. Just one illegal firearm out of harm's way, and it's a victory. Turn a single kid away from drugs, and that's the biggest achievement of all."

Since the shooting, Officer Francis has been in several mentor programs in the Greensboro elementary schools. The idea, he explains, is to try and help troubled kids make a place for themselves in the community. It's not easy, he says, because most times the problem is not the children but the parents.

"But still, you try. You do what you can. There are more minuses than pluses. But I really believe each of us has a chance to change somebody's life for the better . . . to have that tiny positive effect that might alter everything."

CHAPTER 20

Three Shots from a Crack House

When you meet Dave DeBiasi for the first time, you encounter a soft-spoken articulate professional whose existence revolves around his God, in whom he places all his trust, his family, and his work. Then you notice that he wears around his neck a .357 magnum bullet cast in gold. It's the same one that hit him square in the chest and which was later recovered from the vest. This one is inscribed with Dave's name. Every cop has a bullet with his name on it, he declares proudly, "though my wife can't come to terms with what it represents."

Dave DeBiasi doesn't paint a pretty picture when he talks about crime in his hometown. He feels that the situation in Detroit is grim.

A graduate of Michigan State University and a cop for half of his fifty years, DeBiasi—at present doing contract work for the Bureau of Alcohol, Tobacco and Firearms (ATF)—calculates that there were more than a thousand nonfatal shootings in Detroit in the past year. When we spoke, in the summer of 2006, there had already been close to two hundred and fifty murders. That statistic assumes a ratio of one-to-four. Most *countries* in the West don't have that many murders in a year, he stresses.

Some of these crimes are serious, like the party store owner chased down the middle of an intersection by a group of gunmen and indiscriminately shot. The killing took place in front of a crowd, "like a dog," as one cop termed it.

"It was just for fun," one of the perps told his interrogators afterward. There was no reason for murdering the man, he said, because he and his pals had robbed the place. They'd got what they wanted. Then they went after the owner. Their haul was something like two hundred bucks.

According to retired Executive Lieutenant DeBiasi, there are hundreds, even thousands of times a year where shots are fired within city limits that go unreported. "Usually there's no victim found, no calls to the police. When a patrol car shows up, they find the place deserted, with perhaps a few shell casings lying in the street. And when they ask who fired a gun or whether somebody got hurt, nobody saw a thing. It's ghetto culture: we're the enemy . . ."

The law enforcement ethic runs thick in DeBiasi's veins. Dave's father was a cop for most of his life. For a while, in the 1950s and 1960s, he worked undercover for the Federal Bureau of Narcotics. He stayed on the job until he got hurt and was forced to retire. Dave's grandparents originally came from Italy, some from the Venice area and others from Naples.

These days, Dave DeBiasi lives in a house in the suburbs with five females: his wife and four daughters. As he states nonchalantly, "They take priority in everything I do, which is why I went local."

While still with the Wayne County Sheriff's Department, Harold Stockton, one of Dave's investigators, stopped a bullet in the shoulder after making a forced entry in a Detroit suburb while working narcotics. It entered his vest in the epaulet of the shoulder of his body armor and is in the record books as Save #420.

"After receiving information and making a buy with an informant, we raided the place. Shots were fired and Harold was just ahead of me on some steps while heading to the second floor. He didn't even know he'd taken a hit until I found the slug lodged in his vest, right alongside his collarbone.

"He never told his wife. He's a sergeant now, working out at the sheriff's road patrol in Westland, and she still has no idea about it. She'll probably read about it in this book for the first time. I'll see he gets a copy to take home when the time comes. While he's Save #420 and I'm #455, not a lot of time elapsed between the two shootings.

"Another strange thing is that after Richard Davis replaced Harold Stockton's body armor, I was actually wearing his replacement vest when I got zapped. I was a sergeant in the narcotics unit, the commanding officer of a Metro Narcotics Task Force. So when I got my replacement vest from Richard about a month later, nobody was standing in line to inherit that vest. Probably didn't want to test the three-strikes-you're-out principle."

Cops are superstitious, DeBiasi admitted. Once an item or an individual is considered tainted, they give it a pass—apparently, and maybe *especially*, including body armor.

• • •

Narcotics work in those days covered a wide area. As the drug problem exploded, task forces became commonplace because they pooled both resources and personnel. "It was more efficient," says DeBiasi, "because they'd be a team of eight or ten of the more experienced people on the police departments involved. The Metro Narcotics Task Force included the Wayne County Sheriff's Department, Hamtramck Police, River Rouge Police, Royal Oak Township Police, and occasionally Southfield Police.

"It operated in an area sort of within the city limits of Detroit proper, and we had ATF working with us quite a lot too. That way we could move from one area to another, sometimes at very short notice. Also, we wouldn't be stuck within a single jurisdiction waiting for things to happen: we were both aggressive and proactive in our approach.

"For my work, I carried a Glock, but we were allowed to use whatever was approved by the department, as long as we were qualified with the weapon. Some of the guys liked Sig Sauer semi-autos and a few opted for good old-fashioned revolvers, usually 357s. There was an occasional .45 ACP pistol. Then for entries, we always took along a Remington 870, which was used for house clearing: very efficient. The shotgun was also pretty effective against the pit bulls these kinds of people like to have around for protection, not only against us, but to counter other drug people too. The dogs would often attack us when we went in, forced entry or not."

During this period DeBiasi ran a reverse undercover operation to make a deal with bad guys who wanted to buy fifteen kilos of cocaine. It happened at extremely short notice, which meant that the department had to quickly mobilize a team of about ten people, all with vehicles assembled and surveillance sites pre-checked.

That was what made the unit so efficient, he added. "We'd gotten word from an informant about some dealers wanting to make a buy and were in a position to get in on it, all of it within three or four hours, not days. One of the undercover guys was my old pal Harold Stockton. With ATF involved, we did some excellent work that day.

"The deal was that they would come to a Burger King on Grand River in Detroit where the exchange would be made to happen. The money in exchange for a duffel bag full of cocaine. We had outstanding surveillance officers; they watched the bad guys leave a house in Detroit in three different vehicles and saw the criminals load one of the cars with two long gun cases and another with a large duffel bag. Consequently, we knew beforehand that all three cars had guns in them.

"One of their cars had two men totally dedicated to counter-surveillance and I can tell you, these guys weren't amateurs. They knew exactly what they were getting into.

"The money car had a Benelli shotgun and a 9mm handgun. Their main counter-surveillance car had two fully automatic AR-15s, with ninety round magazines, the same kind of weapon the military uses. The caliber is .223, and let's face it, this is one powerful weapon considering that we were in a built-up area. The other surveillance car had a Mossberg 12-gauge shotgun with a pistol grip.

"We spotted their counter-surveillance cars fairly quickly and watched as they parked about a block from where the drug deal was supposed to go down. Our guys took up positions where they couldn't be seen, so in effect, we'd placed the counter-surveillance under surveillance.

"Before the bad guys reached the undercover operator's location, our people watched them load up heavy armament in a convoy of three vehicles. That worried us. If it came to a shoot-out, they'd be able to inflict much more damage with their carbines than we might have been able to do with our handguns and shotguns. Never mind the real possibility of collateral damage because the place was busy: lots of innocents around.

"In the end, the entire operation went down without a shot being fired. After a brief high-speed chase, we got their vehicles and everybody in them as well as their guns and the money. So there was somebody out there that took a bit of a financial knock on that one. Pleased us all . . ."

According to DeBiasi, there were ultimately much bigger fish. A follow-up search at their house netted another $53,000, in addition to the $337,500 they brought to the deal. Also found was the M-16 conversion manual they used to convert the AR-15s to full auto. He intimated that most of those felons were spending the rest of their lives in a federal prison.

"I've been with the DEA when they seized $5.4 million in cash. Another time, right out there on the street, we shook down a mule in a car carrying forty-five kilos of cocaine. They'd taken a lot of pains to hide it and we had to literally tear the vehicle apart to discover how the hidden electronic compartment worked. Got it all in the end; that haul too was worth millions."

But with time, the modus operandi has changed. With all of the heightened security at airports, drug gangs now prefer to use mules to move the merchandise, very much like the international traffickers do, he ventured.

"So you have a bunch of nondescript people hired for as little as $500 a trip, though usually it's a grand or two. That would include elderly people, youngsters in college, young families with two or three kids, and so on. They pay them the money to drive a car from A to B with no questions asked. And if they're caught, these people have to sit out ten years in prison and that's the end of the family. Or any kind of domestic life.

"Tough luck, but that's the law. It was our job to enforce it and I'm not being callous; the damage caused by drugs is horrendous. What's more, it's getting worse."

According to DeBiasi, the drug people would sometimes take a vehicle and cut and weld the gas tank. That would result in a container within a container. The gas will flow into the outer surrounding tank and an inner tank will be filled with cocaine or heroin, or whatever else needs to be transported, including weapons occasionally.

"But our guys are pretty good too. They've got the business down pat. They can tap on a tank and they will know by the sound whether it's been worked on. Just like US Customs, who run into the same thing. Especially since we're right here alongside the Canadian border. And let's not forget the dogs, because they tend to come up with a surprise or two now and again. It's difficult to fool the hounds."

David DeBiasi's own shooting is a good one to examine. For one, it had a significant personal element.

An investigator working for the unit had been linking up with a known drug house on the west side of Detroit, collaborating with an informant making buys. Eventually the department was able to identify the seller as a known criminal by the name of Rory Jones. Based on this piece of information, they were able to determine his associates.

Rory Jones, like so many of these criminals, had a long history of violence, DeBiasi discovered. More important, he was also a cousin and a close associate of the person who, almost a year before, had shot his ATF partner, Special Agent Roger Guthrie. Struck in the face at almost point-blank range, that was a hit that took place with a .45 Auto.

"Roger was wearing body armor, but, dope dealer luck being what it is, the bad guy shot Roger in the face. The bullet traversed his cheekbone, and exited just ahead of his ear, so it did minimal damage. Still serious though. By the grace of God, he had no damage to his eyes, ears, or teeth. Granted, his cheekbone was shattered, but that was probably the best part of the face to take a hit.

"He was rushed to Mt. Carmel Hospital where eventually one of the best oral maxillofacial surgeons in Michigan, Dr. Richard Scott—who just happens to be my brother-in-law—was able to pop the depressed cheekbone back into place, kind of like a dented fender. It took a while, but he manipulated the bone very carefully and all that was left to do afterward was suture it.

"Roger is fine. In fact, looking at him today, you'd never know he was almost killed in a shoot-out . . . He has minimal scarring to show for it."

Digging for details about the gang, DeBiasi established that the man who'd shot his partner was a cousin of the drug lord; they were very close, part of a crime family. A lot of legwork went into it after Guthrie was shot, with the result that the cousin was taken into custody. It was DeBiasi's objective to get the big man himself.

"We knew that Rory Jones was one seriously bad person. He had a reputation for violence. Also, he had been involved in shoot-outs with cops before but always had the money for expensive lawyers to get him off.

"The plan was to go in with a raid crew of eight to ten officers very early in the morning. It was on the west side near Outer Drive and 96, definitely not the best part of town but still a fun place to work if you're a cop.

"My job—as the man in charge of the operation—was to supervise the raid. Since I was the most experienced at it, I had to handle the haligan bar—the pry tool—to force open the bars in front of the hollow-core entry door. So obviously, I was right in front, the first one up there.

"Some of the guys had established a perimeter around the house, so everything was secure. All we had to do was get inside." Through intelligence information, the crew was aware that they'd find cocaine and almost certainly firearms. But there was no indication how many."

Once the team moved forward, things went bad almost immediately. Rory Jones had not only reinforced his front door, but he'd used actual jailhouse bars. That made the place inordinately difficult to breech . . . It takes an experienced haligan man to access it quickly.

"I'd barely applied the haligan when several shots went off. They came right through the door."

Three bullets were fired, two into Sergeant DeBiasi and the other wild. One went directly into DeBiasi's chest's x-ring and the other into his lower right rib cage area. The impact of both bullets was absorbed by his body armor, one of Richard Davis' models.

"So we backed off, followed procedures, and treated it as a barricaded gunman situation. I'd felt the bullets impact hard into my chest, and at first, because of the pain, I had visions of a vest failure. There was no letting up, though. Since I was still dealing with the situation and making sure that the perimeter was intact, I didn't have either the time or the inclination to check. I was still standing, I felt sore but fine, so I went on with the task in hand.

"My main concern just then was for the safety of my officers. I checked to make sure no one else had been shot. Then I directed them to hold the perimeter.

"We talked to Rory Jones through the closed front door. Once we assured him he wouldn't be harmed—even though he'd shot a cop—he actually opened it. He came into the light with a female and an infant in front of him for protection . . . brave man!

"We could see where he'd tried to hide the money. It was sticking out of the baby's diaper. Another five or six adults followed him out. We also discovered that Jones was wearing body armor, so if we'd had a shoot-out and I had hit him in the chest, which is where I would have aimed, he wouldn't have gone down.

"As it was, crack-head luck being what it is and without having me visual, he still managed to hit me in the heart. The grace of God . . . Thanks to the vest, I was still the first one to enter the house to secure it."

Though Jones had managed to destroy all the drugs in the house, it was clear that he wasn't expecting a raid. The police later recovered a fairly large supply of dope in the garage area together with numerous firearms in the house. They also found the Dan Wesson that Jones had used to fire through the front door: it had been hidden in a vent pipe and had his fingerprints all over it.

At that point, after handing over the scene to a Detroit police supervisor, DeBiasi began to feel the pain. "When I took the vest off, I found it intact: it had done its job. A few minutes later I was hauled off to the hospital in an ambulance.

"I remember the emergency room physician telling me that because of where the bullet impacted on my heart, that if there had been a vest failure I wouldn't have survived.

"Rory Jones was charged with shooting a cop, with an additional ATF rap of a felon in possession of a firearm. He got seven or eight years. Whereas, he should have been charged with attempted murder, he pled to felonious assault. Obviously I, and everybody associated with the operation, was furious. There was nothing any of us could do about it."

Since then, Jones has been released from prison and, according to DeBiasi, has surfaced again doing what he does best. He recently pled guilty to a federal drug trafficking and conspiracy charge and was sentenced to federal prison for a long time. He is also awaiting trial in state court on similar charges.

"After five hours in the hospital, I went straight back to the office and finished all my reports. Then I went home, did a phone interview with one of the local newscasters, and an hour or so later, at six in the evening, our doctor called to say that my wife was pregnant with our third daughter, which is the one I'm about to take to soccer in about twenty minutes."

Earlier, while still at the hospital, DeBiasi had called his wife to tell her that he was okay. He didn't want her to hear anything adverse over the radio or television, or have others tell her that her husband had taken a serious knock.

• • •

Dave DeBiasi talked about one aspect of a policeman's life that very few members of the public appreciate: the effect that a cop's lifestyle has on his family.

"When I got shot, it was extremely difficult, not only on my wife, but also on my entire family. By the time I opted out of the service and took the job with the ATF as a contractor—which meant I was no longer breaking down doors or making a target of myself and my men—I'd been a participant in more than three thousand five hundred raids. Almost all were drug related. Because of the nature of the work, many were not only risky, but extremely dangerous.

"There was a point where my wife became a total nervous wreck. That was because every time I went out, she could never be sure that I'd come home again. In one sense, it was like we were fighting a war . . . still fighting a war. You could never tell what would happen.

"And it's for real too. I've lost track on the fingers of two hands the number of friends and colleagues killed, injured, or maimed during the course of performing their duties.

"But with time, you learn to live with it. Our families in contrast, they never do! To them, they know you're going to get shot. It's just a question of when. It takes an incredible woman to deal with that sort of stress, and I can tell you, I've got the best."

Dave DeBiasi, who ended his police career with the rank of executive lieutenant, was candid when asked whether the police were winning the drug war in America. Or rather, whether they would ever win it.

"You know, I'm somewhat pessimistic about it. I've been involved with these drug issues for almost all of my professional life. I just don't see the end in sight. I was fighting the same battles my father fought. It seems to pass from one generation to the next. In fact, I've arrested someone my father did and the perp remembered him. How bizarre is that?

"In my opinion, there are many reasons for the problem, one of the most important being the breakdown—at a national level in all socioeconomic areas—of the basic family structure. The statistics are all there: single-parent families without fathers, and the consequent upbringing of offspring, or, more appropriately, a lack of upbringing of children of all ages. Obviously it is much worse in the inner city than in outlying areas, but they too have serious problems of their own.

"We all know that the educational process starts in infancy, when the kids are still toddlers and not in middle school or high school. So when a child with no hope, no opportunity, and no prospects gets the chance to make some good bucks on the side hustling drugs, there's nobody around to teach or show him otherwise. With $50 in your pocket you can go into the crack business and be successful . . .

"What I fear now is the 'meth bomb' in this country. I was around when the crack epidemic started in the 1980s and I see the same thing happening with meth. Back then, we observed heroin addicts switching to crack, with them believing they were choosing the lesser of two evils. They soon realized how much more effect on the body and brain crack has. I can't tell you how many children I've had to remove from neglectful, abusive homes as a consequence of drug abuse.

"Right now—as we talk—I suspect that the same is happening with meth. The children, ultimately, are the most vulnerable and that makes it a very sad state of affairs. Unfortunately, as long as there is a demand for the stuff and money is there to be made, supplies of that poison will be made available. As soon as we take one dealer down, others are standing in line to take over."

DeBiasi made the point that one of the measures instituted by the State of Michigan was what was termed the *Forfeiture Law*, where dealers, buyers, and users of drugs are specifically targeted. This measure, he said, was having something of an effect. "One of our strengths is our ability to find, seize, and forfeit assets that are then used to cover the department's costs of operating the drug enforcement unit.

"Under a program we initiated with the prosecutor's office, called Operation Pushoff, when people make a drug buy," he explained, "the police grab the vehicles of those charged under criminal law. The car is then seized under the Civil Forfeiture Law. We would take about two thousand cars a year.

"Here, you're not always talking about hoodlums that are buying or using. These are very often, under different circumstances, good solid citizens, but people who are hooked on substances. Their numbers include businessmen, housewives, lawyers, doctors, teachers, civil servants. The list goes on.

"What typically happens is that when the cops take a car, there will be a redemption fee that the prosecutor will assess. Those collared will have to pay $900 to get their car back. The fine doubles the second time, tripling the third time around. If it happens again, the car is forfeited unless the guilty party can work something out with the law, which is why smaller dealers use rental cars.

"The same thing happens with morality and vice, where another two thousand cars are seized from johns picking up prostitutes or perhaps propositioning our officers who act as decoys. It has been an extremely effective and successful program."

It is worth noting that during the course of a career not yet ended, Dave DeBiasi graduated from the FBI Academy at Quantico in Virginia. His specialty during that eleven-week course was an executive level management program for local law enforcement. He also attended another ten-month executive level course at the Police School of Staff and Command at Eastern Michigan University in Ypsilanti.

That time he was voted vice-president of his class and he received the class leadership award.

CHAPTER 21

"My Sixty Seconds of Insanity"

It took barely a minute for Joseph B. Lira—now serving three concurrent life sentences without the possibility of parole in Michigan's Muskegon Correctional Facility—to shoot two police officers in what he later called, in a letter to me, "my sixty seconds of insanity."

Paul Smith went through three wars—including almost two hundred missions as a radio operator on a C-47 in Vietnam, followed by hostilities in Bosnia and a stint in Iraq during Operation Desert Storm—only to come home and get shot.

Though not really proud of the wound he received at the hands of Joseph Bonacho Lira—a parolee from Oregon, also referred to in records of the 46th Judicial Circuit Court as "Gary Marrow"—he doesn't mind displaying it as a testament to the fact that his life was saved by body armor. Though his body armor took the brunt, the 9mm Para bullet hit Smith in the center of his chest, just over the breastbone. The welt is still there and when he gets angry, he'll tell you, it turns bright red.

"So I tasked my anti-drug class here in Grayling—the kids that I teach in DARE—to design a tattoo for me that would cover it, and they came up with this picture of a Viking with my save number on it. A week later I had a pro stick it to me." Paul Smith raised his shirt and with pride displayed epidermis artwork that would have gladdened the black heart of a Hells Angel chapter president. The Viking's face goes bright red whenever he's annoyed, he added, with a wicked smile.

"Would have been stone dead were it not for Richard Davis' vest. As it was, the shooting knocked me out cold for a minute or two. In those few moments we had this bastard running around shooting at the other cops who'd come out on the call . . . went right past me, gun-in-hand twice. Probably could have finished me off, but as I lay there he probably thought I was dead.

"So I'm alive. That man is never going to see another wide open space for the rest of his years, which," he confided, "couldn't be all that long, since he was HIV and is Hepatitis B positive."

Smith admitted that about once a month he would get on the Internet, log onto a secure connection on Michigan Corrections, go into DOC on their Web site, and check Lira's progress. Because Joseph Lira was considered terminal, he'd allowed himself to be a subject in experimental drug testing, which might prolong his life.

"But that's only going to last so long. When he dies, I'm going to whoop it up. I'll throw one heck of a party. It'll be one big event to celebrate because he's caused grief to a lot of people."

The Lira episode vies with a Vietnam experience for Paul Smith's narrowest escape from death. Apart from three crash landings during his year in Southeast Asia, this stocky, buffed martial arts specialist who stands about five-eight in his socks was operational in a sensitive area in the Vietnamese interior. They were flying low at the time, their job being to monitor things below where the war was at its worst.[1]

"I knew it was a hot area because there was lots of movement during the flight. Of course, there were also radio reports constantly coming in. At one point I dropped my pencil. The desk on a C-47 isn't very big and that happened from time to time, so I bent down to pick it up, sat back up with the strangest feeling. You know, it was like a fly had just touched the back of my neck. An eerie sensation because up there, there were no flies . . . no other insects either. Lots on the ground but certainly none in the air.

"Then I turned my head sideways and exactly level to where my head had been—had I not bent down—was a hole the size of a quarter in the fuselage. Probably a 20mm shell . . . went straight through . . . must have just missed my neck when I bent down."

The call that almost resulted in the death of Crawford County Deputy Sheriff Paul Smith was made just after five on a Thursday evening of a busy September week in 1995. It came from Grayling, a town of about two thousand people in north-central Michigan.

The manager of Gaylord's Upper Lakes Tire and Gas Station said that two vehicles had stopped, pumped $27 worth of gas into two vans, and then took off fast without paying. He'd followed them southbound on Interstate-75 in his own vehicle, got their plates, and called the dispatch lady at 911. Details were immediately relayed to the Michigan State Police who had a car patrolling the area.

Barely ten minutes later, State Trooper Ronald Croskey of the Houghton Lake post radioed that he'd spotted two vehicles matching the description at the Hartwick Pines Rest Area, but generally referred to as the Frederic stop. He'd pulled into the area, reported back, and requested back-up. Though he wasn't aware of it at the time, the suspects were in the process of changing the plates on their vehicles.

Deputies Conrad Niederhouse and Paul Smith were immediately dispatched to the area.

Initially, the officers intended to escort the filchers back to Grayling to ensure they paid what they owed. Apart from getting their names and addresses—and having to show their licenses—the matter would probably have rested there: too much hassle, too much paperwork for such a small amount otherwise. But unfortunately that's not the way it played out.

Sandy-haired Paul Smith, who, his friends say, looks like a younger, fitter Mickey Rooney, takes up the story.

"We arrived at the rest area and immediately spotted the two vehicles, a couple of brown and silver-gray vans parked alongside each other. They'd stopped just beyond the bathroom area with its Coke and candy machines and the usual display of area maps."

As he explained, Interstate-75 is a major arterial route linking Western Ontario with Detroit and beyond.

"Follow it through, and it'll take you all the way to Miami, Florida, so there was quite a bit of traffic that evening. We must have had five or six cars, together with a truck or two already parked there in addition to the two errant vehicles in which we were we were interested."

The two deputies found the state trooper's cruiser parked just behind the vans. "So he was kind of blocking them in," explained Smith.

"Since Conrad, my partner, was driving, I told him that I'd do the necessary and go and talk to these people. It all seemed pretty straightforward. I didn't think there would be a problem, but then we all know these things sometimes just take off. And when they do, it's usually mayhem.

"Still, during vacation times we tend to give travelers who slip up the benefit of the doubt, especially since there were two vehicles and the one driver might have thought the other was paying. Or vice versa. Normally we'd give them a chance to settle the bill and get them on their way again.

"So I got out, checked a few things with the trooper—including whether the vans had been stolen or not (we discovered afterward they were, the one with Californian plates filched from Washington state and the second from Arizona)—

and told the four suspects to sit themselves down on the curb between their two vans so we could talk. The woman and the two youngsters immediately complied, but not the man.

"At first he started to walk toward me. Then he kind of turned away and went back toward his vehicle, which was when I told him to stop.

"He wasn't a small guy, bigger than me, perhaps six feet, reasonably well built and about thirty years old. But I found him scruffy and unkempt. He had on some really baggy clothes, including one of those hooded sweatshirts with the pouches in front. What I thought really odd were his dark glasses. It was before six in the evening, but there were heavy shadows everywhere in the area, which was wooded right up to the perimeter of the rest stop. The last thing he needed in that kind of light was a pair of shades. Also, he had his hood up, so his face was in shadow . . . couldn't make out his features clearly.

"I was about five feet from him, in full uniform, and he knew exactly who I was. But instead of letting me talk about the stolen gas, he turned around and moved away. He was still walking away from me when I told him again to halt, but he just kept on going toward the rear of his van.

"So I thought to myself, hello, we've got a problem here. But I'm still not expecting anything to happen. In fact, though, I'd unsnapped my pistol, which I'd do if I was not happy with a situation.

"I called to him to stop a final time and when he still ignored me, I stepped forward and told him that he was under arrest. To be sure he understood me this time, I placed my left hand firmly on his right shoulder, pushed him against his van, and told him to assume the position."

That was the start of the "sixty seconds of insanity" that Joseph Lira wrote about in his letter to me from the Muskegon Correctional Facility. The moment he felt Smith's hand, he turned around with a pistol in his right hand and shot the deputy in the chest.

Asked about Lira's gun afterward, Smith said that everything happened so fast he had no idea whether the man pulled it from his belt or from his sweatshirt. "Suddenly the weapon was there. A split second later I was knocked to the ground by the blast."

Joseph Lira moved swiftly toward the state trooper's car parked ahead of Deputy Smith's and shot him through the open window in the left thigh area. He then moved to the other side and pumped two more shots in quick succession into the side of the officer's chest. Though Trooper Ronald Croskey was wearing body armor, the two last bullets entered his body just below his left armpit, incapacitating him.

As Smith recounted afterward, Lira had to run right past him to get to the trooper's cruiser. And then he had to hurry back again, his path taking him right alongside where he still lay on the pavement. Both times the criminal could have ended it, but he didn't. That became evident when others in Lira's party spoke to the police after they'd been arrested. He told them that he had absolutely no intention of going back to jail; he had done his time in an Oregon prison and that was that.

Also disclosed in subsequent interviews back at the station was that when State Trooper Croskey arrived at the rest stop, Lira had already decided to kill him. He told the others that when he'd finished, they'd flee. However, things changed radically once Smith and Niederhouse arrived. Lira told the others something to the effect that, "Now I'm going to have to kill three cops."

Lira's attempted murder of State Trooper Croskey spurred Smith's partner, Deputy Niederhouse, into action. Having succeeded in dropping Smith and then shooting the state trooper twice, Lira fired a volley at the only cop still standing. Meanwhile, Niederhouse took cover behind one of the vans.

While Lira's aim was good, his 9mm hollow-points couldn't penetrate the car door the deputy stood behind. Niederhouse didn't waste any time returning fire.

When Lira saw he was getting nowhere, he ran back to his van—once again past the prostrate Smith—and got into the driver's seat. His intention, he said after his arrest, was to escape. Deputy Niederhouse ran for his own cruiser and his service-issue 12-gauge shotgun.

Smith, meantime, having returned to the land of the living and hearing shots, quickly appraised the situation. He got to his feet, and ran to the side of the bathroom building, having pulled his pistol and firing at Lira's van as he did so.

In documents before the court, Smith said he was uncertain exactly how many rounds he fired that night. His .40 caliber Glock held fifteen rounds and he reloaded once during the shootout. Niederhouse, in contrast, told the court that that by the time it was over, he'd fired four pistol rounds and two from his shotgun.

Immediately afterward Lira jumped from his van and tried to escape into the forest. He was hit by a full charge of 00 buckshot. At first deputy Niederhouse thought he'd killed him.

While all this was taking place, there were several ancillary developments. The first was that the three other occupants of the two vans ran screaming into the nearby forest.

Concurrently, Jeff and Pat Snyder—the occupants of one of the cars already at the rest area, who were out walking their dog—had heard the first gunshot fired at Smith. From then on, curiosity aroused, Pat Snyder was all eyes. She saw Lira approach the trooper's cruiser and shoot him. With that the Snyders jumped into their car and headed back toward the highway entrance where they stopped the driver of a just-arrived large semi. He pulled his vehicle up in such a way that it would prevent anybody else from entering the area. They also called 911 and reported what they knew.

The Snyders subsequently told the court that while parked at the rest stop, Adam Jackson—the seventeen-year-old son of Lira's girlfriend, Linda Bertrand—had tried to sell them stereo equipment for $30, which they refused. Jackson was later indicted for carrying a concealed weapon.

"At this point," said Smith, "I knew I had to do something about the others, so I went after them. They'd stopped in the forest about a hundred and fifty yards from the rest area, with the two females sobbing and obviously very clearly distressed. The mother, Linda Bertrand, and two kids—one of them a sixteen-year-old minor girl who was the girlfriend of Adam Jackson—must have been aware by then that their leader had been shot. In going away with Joseph Lira, they hadn't banked on his trying to commit murder.

"Initially, once I'd reached them in the forest, I sort of blacked out again and went down on one knee. Linda Bertrand told one of the kids that I needed help. I didn't in fact, but I must have looked pretty bad for her to comment that way.

"What I found were three very scared individuals. They were terrified by the time I got to them. Obviously I didn't know whether they were armed so I had my pistol in my hand . . . [and] told them to get up and come with me. I covered them the whole time.

"I'd have been a lot more careful if I had known that a second .45 ACP was found in the van in which Adam Jackson was traveling."

By now the message had gone out and there were several high-speed police and sheriff's cars roaring in from all over. Several ambulances also pitched. It took two EMS crews a while to stabilize State Trooper Croskey before he was rushed off to the hospital. He was life-flighted the 150 miles to Ann Arbor the following morning.

A great deal of Joseph Lira's past history only came to light afterward. He had been in prison in Oregon, was paroled, and released. The police had been trying to follow his movements from the West Coast where he and others had been on a crime spree for months. Ballistics showed that his 9mm Para pistol was used in a murder in Arizona. But, as Lira was sentenced to life in Michigan, he is unlikely to answer those charges. Ever.

As Paul Smith said afterward, "We deal with a lot of people who have guns. Almost everybody around here has them. They use them for hunting or target shooting. Almost all these folks know how to handle firearms; it's part of the culture in these country areas. But it's people who come from outside, the Liras and others who bring their troubles with them, who are the ones we have to watch."

Both Lira and Trooper Croskey were in wheelchairs when they appeared in court. The state patrolman was retired with a physical disability not long afterward, having never properly recovered from his wounds—which is another reason Officer Smith remains so outspokenly acrimonious about the man who tried to kill him.

A lot of things came together that night in Grayling. When first reports of the shootings came through, every one of Grayling's surgeons was gathered for a meeting at a local doctor's house. One phone call and within minutes, they were all in the ER theater ready and waiting. That was fortuitous because Officer Croskey's condition was critical. It deteriorated further during the night and had that kind of specialist medical help not been available, he would almost certainly not have survived.

Once Paul Smith got back home—he was treated at the hospital and released—there were several other developments. Within a couple of hours he got a call from Fred Smith, his cousin in Jackson, who told him that the incident was all over the radio and TV in southern Michigan. Word was that he'd been killed in a shootout, he said.

About fifty family members then had to be called and told that, in fact, he had been in a shoot-out but *hadn't* been killed. Fate had been truly kind, he would often say afterward, in giving him his "second chance."

"It took awhile, though, because each time one of them phoned, and it went on for hours, I had to fill in all the details, go through the whole rigmarole again. That must have happened about a dozen times over.

"Then, well past midnight, our departmental psychologist arrived at the house. His first question was 'Paul, how does it feel to have somebody try to murder you?'

"I looked at him, and the reality of what had taken place set in. Until then I hadn't even given it a thought; I was alive . . . that was all that mattered. The question came as quite a shock and I suppose it was to be expected that we'd spend a couple of hours talking it through.

"By now it's about five in the morning and I still have to get some sleep. They'd planned a trauma session for everybody involved in the shooting, wives included, and even though it had been a hard night, I was a major player and expected to be there." Smith explained that the meeting was a sort of defense mechanism against post-traumatic stress disorder, and has since become standard in many police departments following a shooting.

"It was there that I realized that it wasn't just me, Paul Smith, who was involved in this drama. There was also my wife Bonnie and all the other members of my family, as well as our children, and so on. The same with Conrad Niederhouse and his family, and of course Croskey, whose family was going through some real misery. We weren't sure that he'd survive and it stayed that way for some days.

"What did come out of these group discussions," he related, "had the makings of a tremendous support system between all of us involved, which, when you examine the consequences, was vital. Of course some took it better than others, but then I suppose that's what being a cop is all about.

"Richard Davis was the next to arrive. He was just passing through Grayling on his way back to Central Lake, from Wisconsin, where, ironically, he had been given an award for saving two officers there. He was all smiles.

"I was immediately designated Save #639. Afterward he went straight to the factory to arrange for a new vest for me, which Bonnie and I watched them finish when we visited Central Lake two weeks later."

There was still more emotion when the kids in Paul Smith's DARE class were told the next morning that he had been shot. As he says, they went ballistic. "I was a pillar to most of them. As an instructor, I not only knew each one of them, but their families as well—Grayling being a relatively small place.

"The drama touched them all, to the extent that one of the parents got hold of me two or three days after and said, 'Paul, If you don't do anything else, you've got to go to the school and show yourself. You've got to let them physically touch you. They're devastated. They need the assurance that you're alive.'" One of the parents told him that their daughter had barely slept since the shooting. The mother of another child said her daughter had cried the whole night.

"So I went to the school. I spent a few hours there and it was one of those occasions I'll always remember. These children all came up to me and we talked and laughed and I suppose they were reassured. Some were actually touching me. It's a pretty heartfelt thing."

The shooting had other consequences. Paul and Bonnie—who he still calls "the most wonderful person in the world"—were going to renew their marriage vows on August 26, 1995; but Paul's mother passed away that morning so it was postponed. Several things—including Paul's bad knee, and his father's illness—prevented them from doing it then.

When Deputy Smith was shot, Bonnie was at home getting ready to go to church for choral rehearsal (both of them being part of a singing group that has performed at various venues in the United States and Europe) when she heard about the shooting on their scanner.

Says Paul: "Without being told, she knew I was involved and that I'd been shot. She then called Nikki, our daughter-in-law, and asked her to come to the house to fetch her and go to the hospital. When Bonnie was finally told that it was me, she accepted that I'd be okay.

"She looked Nikki straight in the eyes and said, 'Don't worry, he'll be fine. He's wearing his vest.'"

Paul Smith's career hasn't been easy. Apart from squeezing three military tours into his thirty-three-year career as a cop, he still does active duty as a policeman.

He and Bonnie married a month after they met. It had been on a blind date on her eighteenth birthday. He decided from the start that once the kids came, he'd prefer to have her raise them at home. There were two youngsters eventually, and today the Smiths are grandparents.

So apart from working as a cop and studying for his degree in police administration, Paul Smith had to take on two more jobs to help pay the way. Having been allocated the midnight shift for the Grayling Police Department, he additionally worked two part-time construction jobs when he wasn't going to lectures.

"It was a tough call," he maintains. "Basically neither Bonnie nor the kids saw very much of me, and here we're talking about several years. I was either working, studying, or, if I was really lucky, sleeping."

Because the shooting of Sheriff Deputy Paul Smith made such a compelling account, I asked Smith during our last interview, in the spring of 2005, whether he could use his office to make contact with the prison authorities holding Joseph Lira. I'd like to speak to the man face-to-face.

Lira's story, like that of most crooks on the run, had the dark mystique I would have liked to examine up close. Through Smith's contacts at the Muskegon Correctional Facility, I was able to make personal contact with Lira, and an exchange of letters followed over more than a year. Ultimately I'd hoped to interview him on tape.

I even arranged with my publisher to send him my last book, Iran's Nuclear Option: Tehran's Quest for the Atom Bomb, in part, to set his mind at ease that he was dealing with a published and, hopefully, reputable writer. But it was not to be.

I made a formal application to the correction facility—through his counselor, Mrs. Linda D. Schultz—to meet with Lira. But for reasons the system is not prepared to make public I was denied that access. My guess is that this decision had to do with pending charges in Arizona.

While my written exchange of confidences with Lira (by snail mail, since prisoners are not allowed access to the Internet) started hesitantly, our letters resulted in a fairly deep insight into the mind of this criminal. In his first letter, he intimated that he had additional information that he knew I would find interesting.

That letter, dated May 2, 2005, said that he had been approached by a Muskegon facility staff member and told about my request for access. "I understand that you are in the process of creating a manuscript concerning shooting survivors," he wrote. He went on:

> To say the least, I am surprised to know that you wanted me to consider adding my unfortunate experience toward your work. I have some questions of my own that I would like to know a little about before I consider doing so.

In a style that was both erudite and informed, Lira went on to ask where I had heard about his case, whether I had made contact with any of the officers and families in the incident, and, to conclude, he added:

> There was so much more that lead up to that moment, than just those sixty seconds of insanity. I was wondering whether you were at all concerned about what had led me to this unfortunate act, or just concerned about the incident and the survival of the officers involved.
>
> There are many more questions that I would like to ask you in order to see if sharing my "side" of the story is in my best interest, because there is so much more to the situation than just that one day. Some of which might place me in very unusual situations.
>
> What I can tell you, Mr. Venter, is that you have picked the right man for the story, but at the wrong time, so unless you can give me some measure of confidentiality when it comes to those I care for, then Sir, I must unfortunately decline your request.

My reply was forthright. I explained what kind of book I was writing and exactly where he fit in. I also wanted more of his background to possibly discover what led him into a life of crime. I would have liked to hear about his childhood, his social and family conditions, from him personally in a face-to-face meeting—but that wasn't allowed to happen.

A few weeks later I received an impersonal printed form with a single tick on it. My application to visit Joseph Bonacho Lira had been refused.

Muskegon Corrections also returned the dozen postage stamps I had included in my second letter to him. "Gifts," I was told on another printed form, were prohibited to inmates.

Lira's letters continued to arrive, as they still do. Gradually he was able to provide me with something of an insight to his life in prison, his family and childhood, together with a lot else besides, which set the scene for a life in crime. It was his early life that caught my particular interest. I quote from a subsequent letter of July 19, 2005:

> I should start at the beginning . . . I was born in Spain in August 1962 . . . my parents met in Casablanca and my father was in the military. I couldn't have asked for two more loving and caring parents. I was raised formal Catholic and even served as an altar boy. But from birth, my life was questionable . . . I was born a blue baby and at birth was pronounced dead. Go figure.
>
> I grew up in Germany the first eight years of my life in a small town called Birkenfield [sic] . . . it was a very good time in my life . . . as children [my brother and I] were taught from the beginning what was right and wrong. The family was always taken care of, no matter what. You see my father had a very hard childhood and never wanted to see his family want or need for anything. He was a very serious and firm man when it came to discipline.
>
> We were never beaten, nor abused, but when we were wrong, we often deserved the spankings that we received. Believe me, I especially received my share as I was the little devil.

Joseph Lira's early school life after arriving in California sets the scene for what was ultimately to become a lifestyle. I quote from the same letter:

> [On arrival in the United States] I was an outsider, a foreigner who spoke broken English as readily as I spoke Spanish, German and French. The children didn't know what to make of me and would often make fun of my brother and myself. I wanted to fit in so much . . .
>
> Shortly after arriving, I met a few kids who were "outcast" in the sense that they often sat in the rear of the schoolroom and shied away from all the other kids . . . But I was eight years old and for the first time in my life I was about to experiment with drugs, marijuana. Every morning, before school started, us kids would flock to Danny's house to sit and watch cartoons while smoking those little

rolled cigarettes that Danny's mom would roll from this tray. Everybody did it and I thought it was the thing to do. I had to fit in this new world I found myself in. From that moment forward, year after year, my drug use escalated beyond my control. To me I thought it was a normal way of life.

I don't know how I actually managed to graduate my school studies, but I soon found myself in Junior High School, 6th to 8th grade. Pretty much the same went on through those two years, with exception that I was now drinking on a regular basis and using cocaine along with all the other substances that we could lay our hands on.

You are probably asking yourself, Where were my parents and why did they not realize that something was amiss? Well . . . I was a great chameleon. I could hide the fact of my drug and alcohol use by avoiding my family as much as possible. I was always at my friend's house doing this or that. My family never really questioned my unusual absence (from home) because they knew that I was doing fine in school and was never in any trouble. That came later, the trouble, that is . . .

By the time I finally got into High School, I was a very accomplished manipulator. I could get what I needed each and every day by various means, even theft from those who loved me. I did not care how I managed to get what it was that I needed. I just did what I had to in order to get it. Drug money was a very helpful thing and I would often go out of my way in order to help the "older" crowd get what they needed. Us kids, knowing that we were juvenile had its perks. [We] would transport and deliver many things for various people. Even the police in our little town were making money hand over first with the commerce at hand. This is the reason why us kids really never did get into much trouble with the law . . .

By the time I was 16, I was still a citizen without an arrest record. Sure I got into trouble with the law for little things, but was never arrested for anything major . . .

In this and subsequent letters Joseph Lira admits to having assaulted a police officer the first time when he was twelve or thirteen.

We were behind the local bowling alley drinking from a half gallon of vodka that we had stolen and an officer appeared . . . I remember he was a rather large man who nobody really liked. He told us kids to gather and come to the patrol car. I hit him with the bottle and we kids all scattered like cockroaches.

Another time, we were sitting in Danny's mom's car behind an overpass smoking dope to our hearts' content when a car appeared behind us. We didn't know who it was until he turned on his lights.

* * *

Lira goes on to explain that there were seven youngsters in the car at the time and before they were obliged to open the doors, they'd swallowed all the evidence, adding, "Would you believe it that we [didn't have a driver's license between us] and actually got to drive the car back to Danny's house."

Clearly, there is a book in the life of Joseph Bonacho Lira. His letters provide an intense, vivid, and intimate insight to a developing life of crime and curiously, there is remorse aplenty, especially since he is well aware that he will eventually die in prison. He has also reached a point where he talks to some of the younger inmates about the alternatives awaiting them once they get out.

---

[1] Jim Morris, a Vietnam vet of repute who has a few books of his own under his belt, and who edited this book, wrote to me while working on Paul's chapter. He said: "I was interested in Smith's account of almost being shot in an aircraft in Vietnam. Something similar happened to me. I was standing in a C-123 taking off from Da Nang when a round went through the floor, pretty much between my feet, and about a foot in front. Not as close a call as Smith's, but close enough. That would have been in October 1964."

CHAPTER 22

A Child's Premonition of Doom

When your little girl senses danger, you need to take notice. Tulsa County Sheriff's Sergeant John "Randy" Pierce—then still a deputy—became Richard Davis' Save #903 when he was forced to heed the increasingly desperate pleas of his five-year-old daughter, Taylor. "Daddy," she cried passionately, "you *must* wear your protection. You can't go to work without putting it on," she told him between sobs. Asked later why she insisted, little Taylor replied that if he didn't put on his vest, "Daddy might get hurt . . ."

Randy Pierce—then with roughly five years' police work behind him—says his daughter's reaction to his not wearing body armor on a boiling hot day in May 1998 was nothing like it had ever been before.

"It was almost summer and I was on our farm out toward Bristow, about thirty-five miles from town. I'd been feeding the cattle and doing some agricultural work. Because I normally went on duty at four in the afternoon, I liked to time it so I'd get to the day-care center—just around the corner from my parents' house—about an hour before time to leave. After picking Taylor up, I'd spend some time with her, get into my uniform, and prepare to leave. Also, I'd change cars, because I wasn't allowed to take the cruiser home."

It was a strict routine. He'd deliver little Taylor to her mother just before he headed into the office.

"That afternoon Taylor and I had a little time together. I played with her, read my newspaper, but at the time I thought it was strange because she was clinging to me real hard that day. Shortly afterward I started to get dressed.

"I was in the room with the full-length mirror that I normally used to check that everything is in place. Having got myself tucked in and put on my gun belt and the rest of the stuff, suddenly there was Taylor coming in from another room dragging my body armor. Remember, she was only five at the time and the vest was almost as tall as she was."

Because it was one of the hottest days of the year, Pierce had already decided that it was too hot, too muggy for the vest. He might wear it later, he thought, but just then he'd decided against it. Department policy at the time left it to the officer's discretion whether to wear it or not, though today it's mandatory.

"In those days, if I thought I might pick up trouble, I'd stop the patrol car on the way to the call-out, strip down, and quickly put on my vest—if I had time, of course, which sometimes didn't happen.

"But Taylor got to the door with the vest and she said I should put it on. Small as she was, she insisted. It was cute. I told her it was too hot. I took the body armor and dropped it onto the bed. She threw a hissy-fit like none other! Taylor was sobbing. She begged me to put on my vest, like my life depended on it. That surprised me, because she'd never done anything like it before.

"I told her I didn't need it. All I'd be doing that evening was a lot of protective orders, paperwork that people file on each other, injunctions, court orders, that stuff—terms she'd often heard me use before, but at that age [it] probably meant nothing to a five-year-old.

"But now, my little Taylor is throwing a monumental fit and is definitely not taking no for an answer. So I thought, what the hell, for the sake of peace, I'd put it on. It worries me when she cries like that. I'm also running a bit late, so I grabbed her, put her in the cruiser, and drove to the day-care center where she would play for that last hour before Darla, her mother, arrived. There were more problems when I tried to hand her over to the staff there.

"She simply wouldn't let go of my neck. Taylor was having another serious tantrum, her tiny arms clutching me and screaming that she didn't want me to go. Once or twice I thought that, because she was so desperate, perhaps I should stay with her. But we were a bit short-handed. There was no way I could take off from work. I tried explaining that to her, but she didn't buy it.

"Then I reminded her that the next day, being Saturday, we were all going to the Silk Club. The Kentucky Derby would be on one of those big screens at the Remington Park Horse Track and we'd all watch the race together. My family, grandparents, cousins, uncles, everybody—including Taylor—would be there and she liked that. There'd be a big buffet with lots of good things to eat. She was still not buying it.

"Finally, with her still bawling, the day-care people had to pry her arms off my neck before I could leave. It was dramatic and obviously I was upset.

"I get to the office where the sergeant comes in and first-off tells me we've got a person who needs to be picked up on a mental health order. He gave me the court papers and they showed that I'd be dealing with an old man by the name of Darrell Manning Ford."

The mental health facility in Tulsa's Department of Human Services (they use the acronym COPES) had petitioned a judge for the Sheriff's Office to apprehend the man because he was barricaded in his house. According to testimony, not only was he acting weird but he was also regarded as a health threat. His water and electricity had been cut off, which had created a serious sanitation issue.

"My partner, Hastings Siegfried, and I agreed that it was all pretty straightforward. I'd pick up the old feller and meet him at Parkside Hospital, which is the local mental health facility and not that far from the house."

It wasn't so simple. On the final stretch to the Ford house, Deputy Pierce was flagged down by a group of women, including psychiatrists who had an interest in the case. Their spokesperson said they had tried everything to coax the old guy out of his house but he'd resisted. Simple as that: wouldn't budge. That was why they applied for an order for a forcible entry.

She told Deputy Pierce there was a lot wrong with the old man and that it was essential that Ford be given a mental health evaluation. She added that some detectives had been there earlier and tried, but nothing worked. Not even coercion. "Now we need people in uniform to do the necessary," she declared.

Just then, two other deputies, Garland Thompson and Kyle Hess, arrived, the former having been in the force since 1991, being the training officer for Hess. Together, the three men checked the papers to see that all was in order. Everything seemed fine, including the fact that the woman had spoken to Ford and told him that some officers would soon be visiting him.

Pierce asked the women whether there were any guns in the house. There weren't, they said assuredly. Also, Ford had no criminal record. He was seventy-three years old. Everything seemed fine. Most people brought in for an evaluation offered no resistance.

"We don't cuff them when we put them in the car, unless they cause trouble. But that's rare, hardly ever happens. We were looking to be like a taxi that day, taking someone really old from the house to the hospital."

The three officers entered the old man's yard. They could see he was a packrat because there was junk all over the place and Ford's property resembled a junkyard. The house, unpainted and ramshackle, wasn't much better.

Then something else caught their eye. There was a large sign pasted in one of the front windows that read "Help! They are poisoning my food." In another window he had put up a sign that called for the FBI, which was why the detectives had been there earlier. One of them had concluded that the old guy was a little crazy, so they'd handed the uniforms the job of extricating him.

Deputy Pierce: "I knocked on the front door to announce my presence. It took a little while before he opened it, and then only marginally. That was after I heard him moving stuff around behind it. In front of the heavy wooden main door was a screen door that I checked and found locked from inside.

"When he finally appeared, what immediately astonished me was that though temperatures outside hovered in the high nineties—plus the fact that he supposedly had no electricity or water—he was all buttoned up. He wore a heavy woolen overcoat topped by a stocking cap on his head, like it was midwinter. Didn't make sense. Now I'm thinking that maybe we're dealing with a screwball.

"Old man Ford asked me what I wanted. I told him I was from the Sheriff's Office. Then he closed the door and returned moments later with the two signs. One was about his having been poisoned and the other urged somebody to notify the FBI. I told him he really didn't need any kind of federal authority because we were there.

"'Mister Ford,' I said, 'nobody here is going to poison your food. What I have here is a court order. Please, come and talk to us.'

"He didn't listen . . . just slammed the door on us. By this time Garland Thompson had done a 360-degree check around the house and was back on the porch with me."

The three officers got their heads together. They decided there was probably no alternative to physically grabbing the old man. It was that or nothing if they were going to take him away. It certainly didn't look like he was going to cooperate. That was when Thompson suggested that the next time Ford opened the door, he'd get the screen door and the others could go in and snatch him.

They banged again and once more, after a short delay, the door was opened a few inches. Officer Pierce showed Ford the court order. Then they tried trickery. Pierce pointed at the signature of the judge and said that he'd like Mr. Ford to come out and sign it. He pulled out his new Cross pen from his pocket and suggested he use that. It was getting late, they told the man: the ladies were anxious to get home and be with their families. Again Ford slammed the door shut.

"Obviously, we had to do something but since we were dealing with a geriatric, I didn't think it necessary to send for the cavalry. At the same time, we had two obstacles, the first being the aluminum screen door. Behind that we faced what appeared to be a heavy wooden one. The first would be easy; the second presented a more serious problem."

After more deliberations the recluse suggested they slide the pen and document under his door. Said he'd sign it and return both the same way. But that wouldn't work, replied Pierce. The paper might get torn or dirty and that wasn't good for a court document.

Finally the three officers made their decision. They'd already moved the women away from the front of the house with the intention of rushing the door the next time Ford opened it. Garland would smash through the aluminum screen and Randy would shove his foot into the jamb and hopefully, they'd jointly prevent the old man from closing it.

That, basically, is what happened. Except that Deputy Pierce shoved his leg too deep into the opening, which was how Ford slammed the officer's ankle between the door and jamb. His scream of pain was both loud and involuntary.

"Now *that* hurt! I had to use all my strength to keep the door open. But all I managed that first time was to force it open about three inches and it wasn't that frail old man keeping it shut. There was obviously something big and heavy in place to cause an obstruction. We discovered afterward that what he'd moved there—old as he was—was one of those all-steel metal drill presses that probably weighed something like half a ton. Small wonder we weren't able to force the door."

With all three officers pushing, they managed to edge it open far enough for Deputy Pierce to squeeze into the darkened house. He was appalled at what he saw.

"The light was bad. In fact, coming in from the sunshine momentarily blinded me and for some reason I couldn't pull the flashlight from my belt. I should have known it would be dark because of all the barricaded windows. Then I was overcome by a nasty, overwhelming stench—like a wet cloth that has been left forever in a filthy laundry or toilet.

"Standing at the door—and blocking the others from coming inside—I was trying to adjust my eyes to the gloom when I saw that entire front room was a junkyard. I looked for the source of a most disgusting odor and spotted a row of five-gallon buckets. All were filled, almost to the brim, with crap, toilet paper, and urine.

"Ford had been using them as his toilet, apparently for months. He never bothered to throw out the mess. Probably couldn't if his toilet was blocked. And that was how he was living, like an animal. It was barbaric. By then Garland Thompson and Kyle Hess were inside as well.

"I then realized that almost involuntarily I'd been plunged into a very unusual situation: an old man dressed for the arctic, the filth, the stench, his intractability. All three of us had drawn our pistols by now. I held mine in the traditional two-handed Weaver grip in front of me, the barrel tilted upward.

That was standard procedure, like we're trained for building entries so as to not frighten residents."

The officers slowly made their way into the front room. Ahead they could just dimly make out what looked like a kitchen. A bedroom was somewhere toward the left.

"I scanned around, looking for the old codger. Then I spotted him near the kitchen door, about ten feet to the right. He stood in a darkened doorway, sort of silhouetted, which is why I didn't pick up immediately that he had a gun in his hand. It was a .45 ACP pistol and he even had the right two-handed stance for it. It took me a moment to register, but the last thing you expect from somebody so old and frail is violence. We were there to help him, my goodness!"

Deputy Pierce just managed to shout the warning "Gun!" to Thompson who was right behind him. He turned toward the old man to ask him to put the gun down when the first of four shots rang out.

"I got as far as the word, 'Put . . .' when the first bullet hit me square in my arm and blew out my bicep . . . and that was my gun hand as well. So I'm at a spectacular disadvantage. I remember the muzzle flash as it lit up the entire room and then everything went into slow motion . . ."

Talking about it afterward, Deputy Pierce said he could remember it clearly, almost like a movie. It was also weird, he said, since the flash couldn't have lasted more than a nanosecond. Yet his eyes were able to take in everything, like the event had been transposed to his brain as an image onto a negative. Even today, he says, those impressions remain incredibly vivid, almost luminously so.

He can still picture the disgusting buckets and their vile contents, looming piles of garbage—half a ton of it—the unpainted walls with pictures hanging at odd angles, that heavy piece of machinery to his side that held the door in place. Finally, there was the shooter himself.

"My first thought was that the son of a bitch had shot me. I was flabbergasted. If it had been the usual cop-versus-criminal type of situation, I'd probably have shot back, but it took me a second more to accept how really dangerous that old bastard was and what a really critical situation I was in.

"Shattered arm or not, I lowered my gun. I had to do something or I was a goner. I'd already tried to get my finger around the trigger but it remained straight. It was like, ouch, that really hurt bad!

"I looked toward Ford and in this peculiar slow motion, eyes adjusting to the bad light, I saw his finger tighten on the trigger. It was amazing. I actually watched the hammer of his gun falling, knowing that I was on the receiving end."

The second shot was a loud bang. Two more blasts followed and all three hit their target. Deputy Sheriff Pierce had been shot four times.

Pierce tried to shift his pistol from his right hand to his left but everything happened so quickly that there was no time. Because both his arms were still raised ahead of him—even after taking the first bullet in the one—two of the remaining shots were stopped by his body armor, one at kidney level and the other just below the heart. The last bullet hit his left elbow. The first bullet into his vest was like a mule kick. "It hit me really hard!"

Throughout, the first two deputies in the door were standing so close together at the entrance that Thompson could actually feel the impact each time his partner was hit.

Pierce: "Now my mind is really kicking in. I'm about to be killed by a lunatic with a gun and I realize that I've just got to get out of there. There wasn't any thinking about it, and I threw myself backward as Garland and I both decided to move."

Kyle Hess had already extricated himself. The other two officers stumbled out of the darkened house into bright sunlight a moment later, almost falling over each other in the process. Pierce collapsed in a heap on the porch while Hess sought cover behind Ford's red Honda in the driveway.

Garland Thompson asked Pierce whether he was okay. He didn't expect an answer because there was blood spurting from his open wounds in an arch that was five or six inches high over his prostrate body. Doesn't sound like much, but anyone who has seen these open wounds will tell you that the effect can be devastating. In minutes, half the porch and almost all of Deputy Pierce were covered in blood.

Randy Pierce was in serious pain. Also, he'd dropped his pistol inside the house. One of the women who had met the deputies earlier ran up the driveway. She looked at the fallen officer and, in shock, raised her hands to her mouth.

"You've got to get away from here, ma'am," the wounded man told her. She left, but managed to tell the officers that an ambulance was on the way. Then more of the women ran to the porch asking whether they could help.

The second deputy waved them away. "We're under fire . . . get the hell out of here, ladies!"

Two thoughts ran through Randy Pierce's mind about then. The first centered on his gun. He told Thompson that Ford might get it. He said so several times. Thompson placated him by saying that he'd recovered it.

For Pierce meantime, the pain had become excruciating. Until Thompson put pressure on the wound to partly stem the flow, he watched in utter bewilderment as it pulsed from his wounds in a series of low, slow arcs. At the same time, a part of his brain told him that he would miss the big day at the track tomorrow and somehow he kept focusing back to it.

"I remember thinking that in getting shot, I'd let the family down. What would my mother, my father, even my daughter think? Illogical as it was, these were real fears.

Garland Thompson improvised a few techniques to tend to Pierce. He grabbed his blue, First Responder bag and tried to dress the larger of the two wounds with compression bandages. The heavy flow of blood made this impossible. There were moments that followed when Thompson felt totally inadequate. If he couldn't stem the flow, Pierce would bleed to death.

Pierce: "I'm lying there and Garland is trying to do what he can, when I hear the front door slam again. It was like it was right next to me. Though I was a bit groggy by now, I thought that was peculiar. Then I heard another bang and I realized it wasn't the front door slamming, that old bastard was still firing at us.

"You got to get away from here, Garland," Pierce shouted. "Leave me . . . you find cover."

Thompson didn't even have to think about it when he grabbed Pierce by his belt and dragged the wounded man all the way down the porch to a more secure position behind one of the squad cars. He then retrieved his shotgun from his own car and gave it to Hess. His instructions were to keep them covered if the old man again showed his face.

Pierce reckons he must have lain there for ten seconds when he realized that there were people coming toward them. That included some of the women and also some local people.

"I imagined that with all this shooting and the blood, they were curious. But now I'm lying low on the ground and Garland and a neighbor are working on my wounds. But from that position under the cruiser, I could see the front of the house. Then I saw one of the old man's windows open and he poked a rifle out and started to shoot at us again. He was targeting all of us gathered there at the bottom of his garden.

"You couldn't miss the flash. But nobody else was taking any notice because they were all intent on me lying there on the ground."

Fortunately Ford was using a .22 rifle. He pushed the muzzle out through some heavy drapes and fired. It was random and inaccurate, and nobody retaliated. No one could get a clear shot at him. Pierce recalls hearing the sirens getting closer. Then more deputies arrived.

The officers were dismayed by what they found. Clay Davis, one of Pierce's old partners, a rough, tough, and fearless cop, took one look at his old friend, bent down and kissed him on his forehead. "You hold on there, Randy," Davis said as his voice broke. Then Deputy Eric Kitch, all of six feet five and three hundred pounds—strong like a mountain mule—arrives, and he's reduced to tears at the plight of his buddy lying there in his blood.

The first ambulance arrived. So did the Tulsa Police Department's SWAT (known locally as the Special Operations Team), together with roughly another hundred police officers.

While some attendants rushed forward to help Pierce, their drivers held back. They refused to take their vehicles forward until there was no risk. This didn't exactly endear them to the uniformed officers. Everybody involved had followed the firefight on the radio and they were aware of the danger but they wanted none of it which, under the circumstances, was almost culpable.

Randy Pierce was finally removed after a unit from the Berryhill Fire Department brought in a truck to block off the house. That provided a shield for an ambulance crew to come in, load up, and take him away.

It was later concluded that if Garland Thompson hadn't stopped the blood flow, Pierce would have suffered brain damage in another three or four minutes. He would have been dead shortly afterward. Also, Ford had used hardball ammo, which, as we now know, made a significant difference in the wounds. Had they been hollow-points, which tend to fragment, he could easily have lost both arms.

The stand-off with Ford lasted another two hours or more with the very professional Captain Tracy Crocker in charge of negotiations. During this time the old man was warned that having shot a police officer, the police would have no compunction in using adequate force if he didn't surrender. The implications weren't lost on the old man. He was doddering and crazy, but not stupid.

For his efforts, Deputy Thompson was awarded the Medal of Honor.

Prior to being rushed to the Tulsa Regional Medical Center, Deputy Pierce had trouble breathing. The area where the bullets impacted his chest actually hurt more than his arms did. Stopped by his body armor, the bullets never broke his skin, though his chest bruises were immense. He faced additional surgery to remove part of a bullet from his shoulder. It had split in two after hitting his arm, though the wound wasn't severe.

For all the delays in getting him into an ambulance and delivering him to the hospital, another couple of minor dramas followed. First, he told colleague and friend Randy Chapman that it was imperative to call his mother. He had to let her know before she picked up things on the radio—or perhaps saw a TV clip of him wounded—that he was fine, which Chapman did.

Then a chopper arrived to life-flight him to the hospital. But because of the stand-off with Ford, it couldn't land.

Kurt Franklin, another of Pierce's colleagues and also a good friend, then climbed into the ambulance to travel with his buddy and was summarily told to get out. Pierce insisted. He wanted Kurt there, he told the ambulance crew, and they didn't argue. They couldn't, actually. The man was in a critical condition and the moral support of having his friend there seemed to help.

In radio contact with doctors at the ER, eager to know what to expect in order to prepare for any eventuality, the medics were ordered to look everywhere for wounds. They started by cutting off his shirt and trousers and didn't finish until they'd taken his vest.

The first thing the medic felt for was broken ribs. There were none. They had already stemmed the blood flow in his arms. All the prodding and poking in the chest hurt like hell, and, as he recalls, he had still received no pain medication.

"The result was that, at each bump in the road, the reverberations went right through me. Obviously, taking every corner at speed, all four of us in the back were slammed around. Having both my arms incapacitated and not being able to brace, didn't help either. I don't know whether it was good or bad but I never passed out. I think I was on my last reserves of adrenaline, and that kept me lucid.

"Getting to the hospital was something else. I know the place well, because I've worked in the ER there part-time. I know the people and the layout. They'd completely sealed off the emergency room. Then, they wheeled me in and everybody is so dead serious . . . lots of long, grim faces . . . Now I'm starting to worry because it's all stat this and code that and I'm familiar with the lingo. Stat means fast. Code Blue means you're dead, and here are thirty medical people who are trying to avoid looking me in the eye.

"Which was when somebody senior, obviously one of the doctors, walked in, and said in a loud, authoritative but friendly voice, 'Welcome to the Tulsa Regional Medical Center . . . the emergency room is all yours, Randy.' She was kind of like, right, now let's get down to business . . ."

But not before he got into an altercation with one of the doctors who kept talking about his neck wound.

"I'd been shot in the neck, he was telling the others, in part because my entire upper half was just one great mass of blood. It might have been the medic in the ambulance that had put that word out, but I had to try to half sit up and tell all those medical people that I *did not* have a fucking neck wound." That was confirmed after they'd cleaned him up a bit.

Following that first intrusive examination, the last thing that Deputy Pierce heard was, "This thing's worse than we think . . . let's get him prepped for surgery, and *let's do it now*."

"Even then, I still hadn't been given my first shot of morphine. The next thing I knew was that I woke hours later in a bed in one of the wards and was covered in gauze and bandages."

The media had followed the entire drama on radio and TV. They were already there in droves when Pierce arrived at the hospital.

"I told one of the male nurses I was glad I'd put on new underwear that day. Mom always said to. He laughed as he scissored right through them. That's when I realized that though I had a pretty good tan, working in the open like I do—and also, I'm part Indian—my skin had actually turned white, almost like it was bleached.

"I asked another nurse why I was suddenly so white and she said something about me being in shock. But I knew that wasn't it. I'd lost more blood than anybody believed possible and that was the more likely reason. But she wasn't saying anything."

The media crush at the doors of the ER continued. The nurses tried to clear the passages but nobody was listening, with television camera and microphones being pushed into everybody's face. Until Captain Bill Thompson arrived. He and Major Lynn Jones, his sister-in-law and a major in the Tulsa Police Department, issued immediate instructions. Within minutes, the area was cleared.

Randy Chapman meanwhile, had got through to Deputy Pierce's mother. With four of her sons in law enforcement, she knew there was something up. Call it motherly instinct or whatever, she said afterward, but someone at the station would always call when there was an emergency. They'd unfailingly tell her that her kids were fine. Apart from Randy, her son Ed was a sergeant in the TPD. There was also Don, a canine patrol officer, and Chris, a deputy. They said nothing to her this time but, she admits, "I just knew."

"My folks are in their seventies, both of them seventy-two. They're strong people, but when they got to the hospital and I saw them after surgery, I'd never seen them that fragile. It was a real shock to me.

"Suddenly they both looked tired and old. Teaches you something when death stares you in the face; ask anybody who has been shot."

Deputy Pierce stayed in the hospital for eleven days, including seven in ICU. There were so many coming through the ward to visit him that they finally had to move him to home health care.

He had eleven operations over a period of months. For a long time his doctors and therapists reckoned there was zero chance he'd ever use his right arm again. Amputation was considered but Randy Pierce wouldn't hear of it. With all the medications, his liver and kidneys started to fail. That meant that they had to cut down on pain killers but that then became so intense, he ruminates, that he ground down all his teeth during therapy. Once it was over, he had to have seven of his teeth capped.

Tough and focused, Randy Pierce persevered. Though both arms were shattered and he got what he called *spaghetti arms*—with steel plates embedded in the bones—he began a routine of lifting weights to build them up again. It was extremely difficult, he recalls. Throughout, there was a lot of pain, and it was very intense at times.

But in the end, he didn't lose his arms. Nor did he retire from the force, even though he was offered a full disability pension.

"I felt very sorry for myself for quite a long time. There were phases of deep depression and though the family helped, it was awful. At one point they cut back on my pain pills even more."

Then something peculiar happened. Back in the hospital after more surgery, he found himself in a ward where a teenage boy was brought in and put in the bed beside him. The boy's parents had bought him a Jeep on his sixteenth birthday, an open-top Jeep. He had an accident and was paralyzed from the neck down, effectively a quadriplegic. The patient on the other side was also pretty far gone. A diabetic, he'd lost both his legs and an arm.

"These two guys are lying there with me between them and they're joking back and forth. It's almost like there's absolutely nothing wrong with them. From that day on I told myself that I wasn't going to be a cripple and that, come what may, I'd make this thing work. That meant learning to become left-handed, shoot left-handed, everything.

"These days I can outshoot everybody in the department with my so-called disability and I can tell you, it's a great feeling being able to do that.

"There's a lot of things I can't do now as well as before. I used to oil paint and I can't fasten certain buttons. But I came back to the office and went on light duty for a while, just kept training, working out, getting on with it. Then I returned to full duty.

"I became a detective, went undercover, and worked gangs here in Tulsa. I also worked motorcycle gangs, black gangs, Hispanic gangs. Then I returned to Human Resources for some hiring and training work and made sergeant. That was when I took over extradition, transportation, and, among other things, mental health court.

"That's why I know that the old man Ford, after spending time in a mental institution, was let out to go to an old age facility, where he is now. At least there are people looking after him and he doesn't have to shit in a bucket.

"Once the SWAT guys finally got into his house they found an armory of firearms. There was also a huge supply of ammo, a thousand rounds. In all, they found seven handguns, eleven rifles, and four shotguns. Being a veteran of World War II, Darrell Manning Ford knew pretty well how to use them as well.

The final touch to this saga came from little Taylor Pierce, Randy's five-year-old daughter, who'd just turned eleven when I interviewed him in Tulsa.

"Just about the time that I was shot, Darla—we were separated at the time—went to pick her up later the same day after a bit of delay. She'd already been told by the department that I'd been hurt, but there were no details. All they'd said was that I'd been admitted to the hospital. Nothing was mentioned about a shooting.

"She was strapping Taylor into the car when the little girl asked her mother whether her Daddy's arms were alright.

"Darla answered that she didn't know. But, she said, they were going to the hospital to find out about everything. Taylor looked at her mother and told her that my arms were bleeding. 'But they're going be alright again one day, Mommy,' she added smiling."

None of it made any sense to Darla Pierce. Or even Taylor's final comment about her father "being able to hold me again."

Prior to going to press, I again spoke with Sergeant Pierce. Crimewise, this usually affable and quiet-spoken sheriff's deputy conceded, things had gone bad for Oklahoman cities, and for Tulsa in particular. A third the way through 2006, forty murders had taken place, which he suggested was well above average for this usually placid conurbation. Robberies had also gone through the roof, he said.

Asked why this was happening, Randy Pierce was specific: "I put it down to the string of casinos that have opened up around these parts lately," he declared. "Since the doors of the first of these gambling joints opened, we've watched the graph climb. Also, it is not going to get better any time soon," he reckoned.

"Really keeps us on our toes." He added that things were hardly improved by the fact that local law enforcement offices were not able to increase staff levels to cope with this burgeoning level of crime.

Acknowledgments

There have been a host of individuals and organizations that played roles in bringing this work to fruition. A venture that was originally planned for twelve months turned into a three-year project that took me through great swatches of the United States and Canada. I ultimately clocked up about thirty thousand miles, most of it in a delightful RV that eventually became something of a "home away from home" and that in the end, I was loathe to leave.

One of the reasons for this extended time line was because while I had the names and, in theory, the addresses of most of Richard Davis' thousand "saves," some of these went back decades. People move on. Some of those involved have passed on, each one of them leaving a fine legacy for later generations, if not to emulate, then perhaps to take note of and avoid making the same mistakes.

One of the most interesting chapters deals with a Canadian police officer. Until recently Constable Jan Nickle served with the Ontario Provincial Police, or OPP, in a role that is the rough equivalent of state trooper in the United States. A trio of youthful but deadly criminals on a rampage—very much as Bonny and Clyde tried to evade law enforcement officials three quarters of a century before—led the authorities on a merry dance halfway across Canada. While this was going on, they shot Constable Nickle in the chest at very short range and almost killed him.

Jan gave me hours of his time. Without all that, Chapter 10 would almost certainly have been a non-starter. In fact, his story is compelling enough for me to make a book of it.

Many people were involved in bringing this work before you. The most notable of them is the man himself, the illustrious, quiet-spoken, self-effacing Richard Davis.

Davis was uncomplaining and always helpful, even during difficult times, and he was equally unstinting in offering the kind of material aid that made this book possible. This is also the same old friend whom I first met thirty years ago in Africa and who spent many hours giving me the background on how he put concealable body armor on the map. What a story that is: how many people do you know who have saved thirty—or even three—American lives, never mind three thousand?

Also involved in this book from the first was Pat Crawford, Richard's illustrious sister, who today makes stout efforts at keeping the new company, Armor Express, viable. Barely three years old by the time this book appeared in print, Armor Express has already had its tiny quota of saves.

On the production side, there were many people involved in *Cops: Cheating Death*. The book was originally to consist of fifty chapters, which was why it took so much time to research and write.

Looking at the project from the publisher's perspective, there is little doubt that a seven-hundred-page book was too unwieldy. So my editor Tom McCarthy split the manuscript in two. *Cops: Cheating Death 2* will soon appear as a companion volume.

For this reason there were two editors involved. Prior to making contact with Tom at Lyons Press, Jim Morris, another old buddy, took the manuscript in tow and set his mind to creating much of what you see before you. It was a mammoth task: he worked on all fifty chapters, and it took him months. Once the book had been scheduled, East Coast editor Andrea Gow was brought in to bring an element of cohesion to it. I am indebted to you both.

Throughout my travels, I always kept in touch with "home base" in Central Lake, Michigan, through the good offices of Diane Kucharek, who has worked with Richard ever since she left school more than thirty-five years ago. Karen McCraney, formerly Karen Davis, provided me with some of the early background, which is where Matt and Andrew, Richard and Karen's two sons, come in.

It is interesting that over the decades, Richard turned a gun on himself and took more than two hundred shots in the gut to prove that concealable body armor really does what it is supposed to do. Today, his son Matt, CEO of Armor Express, has carried on the tradition, having to date, shot himself twice.

Another individual who played a seminal role in the book was Mary Crawley, an impeccable repository of much historical information about saves. Through Mary I was able to initiate contact with individuals who, until I actually met them, represented little more than a series of numbers in a record book. It was notable that over time, she'd made personal contact with just about all those saves who were still around.

There are several more souls who helped, sometimes inadvertently. Joyce Otterson, one of my neighbors in Chinook, Washington, was an enthusiastic reader of my chapters from the start. More than once she returned a set of pages with enough questions attached to tell me that perhaps I had better start again. And when I got it right, Joyce was right up there, always enthusiastic and pushing me for another chapter to read.

Former U.S. Special Forces operative Floyd Holcom let me park my RV on Astoria's Pier 39 for almost six months. At one stage, he even provided an office for me from which to work. To you, Floyd, *muchas gracias*.

So, too, with fellow scribe Patrick Webb, managing editor of *The Daily Astorian*, who followed my antics with interest. It was always Patrick who pulled something relevant off the Web, as he has done with issues raised in my other books on more esoteric themes, like contemporary weapons of mass destruction threats. Thanks, Patrick, and here's to eventually getting to see a bunch of Scottish rugger buggers beat England at Murrayfield!

You cannot spend a couple of years on the road and not have visitors. Apart from my son Luke, among those who traveled with me was book editor Jim Mitchell, an American national living in Johannesburg. Jim and I covered a lot of ground from Detroit (where we inadvertently tangled with the Al Gore election entourage) through Pennsylvania, West Virginia, Maryland, Washington, D.C., New Jersey, and Connecticut.

Later I was joined by my nephew Robin Wentzel, and we took in much of Ontario. I also spent time with my brother's illustrious son, Dr. Etienne Venter. It is interesting that he has chosen a career that deals with many criminal issues that could easily be related to some of those found between these covers, and on a continent-wide basis. Etienne and Yvette have made a lovely home for themselves and their young family near Vancouver.

Peter Sachs, my old diving buddy—Cape Verde Islands, Lake Tanganyika, and the rest—took over when I moved into Vancouver for an extended stay. He and lovely Angie played host often enough that I'd need another incarnation to be able to reciprocate.

Closer to home at Sault Sainte Marie in Ontario, Canada, I have several individuals to thank for maintaining my links with the world outside. The most important must be Allan Bertolo, who was always ready to provide coverage when communications went down. And William and Ann, who run the best seafood emporium north of the border: the halibut, served at their Catch This Aquatic Eatery in "The Soo," is incomparable. Certainly that delightful couple kept Marilyn and me alive while my compilations went on. And Roberto Rivera, my Philippines barkeep friend who, while at 82 North—one of our favorite after-hours hangouts in Sault Sainte Marie—must rate as one of the best in the trade.

Finally I come to my beloved friend, compadre, and confidante, Susan Sizemore, who played a bigger role in my peripatetic life than even she can imagine. For some years "CuzSuz" has been an inspiration for much of what I do, especially in the spiritual sense. I will always be grateful for your input, my very dear friend. It's worth mentioning that a lot of Suzie's strength lies in her delightful turn of phrase and a sense of humor that can be as sly as it is sometimes wicked.

After having been jerked about by an individual for goodness knows how long, it was she who suggested very appropriately in a pretty forthright e-mail: *illegitimi non carborundum* . . .

To all these lovely people, I am deeply indebted. You all pulled together to make it happen, and let's face it, it wasn't easy.

Al J. Venter
Sault Sainte Marie, Canada
March 2007